Other Delta Books in Biography

EBAN
Robert St. John

T. S. ELIOT: A MEMOIR
Robert Sencourt

JEAN RENOIR
André Bazin

GO EAST, YOUNG MAN
William O. Douglas

PILGRIMS OF THE STARS
Dilip Kumar Roy and Indira Devi

MEN WHO HAVE WALKED WITH GOD
Sheldon Cheney

A LONG VIEW FROM THE LEFT:
Memoirs of an American Revolutionary
Al Richmond

The Life and Death
of YUKIO MISHIMA

by Henry Scott-Stokes

A DELTA BOOK

For Gilbert

A DELTA BOOK

Published by
Dell Publishing Co., Inc.
1 Dag Hammarskjold Plaza
New York, New York 10017

Grateful acknowledgment is extended to Alfred A. Knopf, Inc., for permission to quote from their copyrighted translations of the works of Yukio Mishima.

We are also grateful to New Directions Publishing Corporation for permission to quote from two works by Yukio Mishima: Yukio Mishima, *Death in Midsummer and Other Stories*, copyright © 1966 by New Directions Publishing Corporation; reprinted by permission of New Directions Publishing Corporation. Yukio Mishima, *Confessions of a Mask*, translated by Meredith Weatherby, copyright © 1958 by New Directions Publishing Corporation; reprinted by permission of New Directions Publishing Corporation.

Grateful acknowledgment is also extended to Kodansha International Ltd for permission to quote from their copyrighted translation by John Bester of Yukio Mishima's *Sun and Steel*, and from *Landscapes and Portraits* by Donald Keene.

Reprinted by arrangement with Farrar, Straus & Giroux, Inc.
Printed in the United States of America
First Delta printing—August 1975

CONTENTS

FOUR
The Four Rivers (1950–70)

FIVE
Post-mortem 300

Beauty, beautiful things, those are now my most deadly enemies.

Yukio Mishima, *The Temple of the Golden Pavilion*

The Life and Death
of YUKIO MISHIMA

PROLOGUE

A Personal Impression

I first saw Yukio Mishima, whose name is pronounced Mi-shi-ma with short vowels and equally stressed syllables, on April 18, 1966, when he made an after-dinner speech at the Foreign Correspondents' Club in Tokyo. He was spoken of as a future winner of the Nobel Prize for Literature, hence his invitation to the "press club." He came with his wife, Yoko, and after having drinks with members of the board, the Mishimas took their seats at the head table, flanking an Associated Press journalist, John Roderick, who was then president of the club. I was seated a little distance from the head table but I could see that Mishima had a remarkably mobile face for a Japanese, with heavy black eyebrows and a crew cut, and he conversed fluently in English. His wife seemed meek and retiring, but she was pretty, and had lips somewhat heavier than other Japanese women.

In his introduction that night, John Roderick described the career and achievements of Yukio Mishima. He was born Kimitake Hiraoka in 1925, the eldest son of an upper-middle-class family in Tokyo; he had a brilliant record in school and received an award from the Emperor when he graduated at the top of his class from the Gakushuin (Peers School) in 1944. The following year he was drafted but failed his army medical and did not serve with the Japanese Imperial Army. After the war he became famous with the publication of his first major work, *Confessions of a Mask*, in 1949; at twenty-four he was hailed as a genius. His important novels thereafter were *The Sound of Waves* (1954) and *The Temple of the Golden Pavilion* (1956), both of which were translated and published in America. But Mishima, said Roderick, was much more than a novelist. He was a playwright, a sportsman, and a film actor; he had just completed a film of his short story "Patriotism," in which he had directed himself in the part of an army lieutenant who commits hara-kiri. Mishima was a man of many and varied talents, the "Leonardo da Vinci of modern Japan."

In his speech, Mishima talked at length about his war experiences. He described the bombing of Tokyo in 1945: "It was the most beautiful firework display I have ever seen." His peroration, which followed a jocular reference to his wife ("Yoko," he said, "has no imagination whatsoever"), went as follows, in his forceful but often incorrect English:

But sometime, sometime during such a peaceful life [Mishima had spoken of his married life]—we got the two children—still the old memory comes to my mind.

It is the memory of during the war, and I remember one scene which happened during the war, when I was working at the airplane factory.

One motion picture was shown there for the entertainment of the working students, which was based on the novel of Mr. Yokomitsu. And it was maybe Maytime of 1945, the very last of the war, and all students—I was twenties—couldn't believe that we could be survived after the war. And I remember one scene of the film. There was a street, a street scene of Ginza, before the war, a lot of neon signs, beautiful neon signs; it was glittering and we believed we couldn't see all in my life, we can never see it all in my life. But, as you know, we *see* it actually right now, in the Ginza street, there are more and more neon signs on it. But sometimes, when the memory during the war comes back to my mind, some confusion happens in my mind. That neon sign on the screen during the war, and the *actual* neon sign on the Ginza street, I cannot distinguish which is illusion.

It might be our . . . my basic subject and my basic romantic idea of literature. It is death memory . . . and the problem of illusion.

Mishima spoke slowly, enunciating his words. His pronunciation was idiosyncratic; he said "urtist" instead of "artist." That he made mistakes in English did not seem to bother him: he was remarkably un-Japanese in this respect.

After the speech, foreign correspondents asked questions. I wanted to know what Mishima, who had spoken so freely about the war, thought about Japan's entry into World War II. He stated that he considered the turning point to have been the Ni Ni Roku Incident of February 26, 1936, the most spectacular of the many coup d'états which took place in Japan during the 1930's. Another journalist, Sam Jameson (*Chicago Tribune*), asked Mishima about the origin of the Japanese practice of seppuku, as hara-kiri is known to the Japanese—the word "hara-kiri" is almost never used in Japan. Mishima replied (I have polished his English a little):

> Once I was asked that question by the English cineast, Mr. Basil Wright, and I replied to him in a letter: "I cannot believe in Western sincerity because it is invisible, but in feudal times we believed that sincerity resided in our entrails, and if we needed to show our sincerity, we had to cut our bellies and take out our *visible* sincerity. And it was also the symbol of the will of the soldier, the samurai; everybody knew that this was the most painful way to die. And the reason they preferred to die in the most excruciating manner was that it proved the courage of the samurai. This method of suicide was a Japanese invention and foreigners could not copy it!"

As Mishima spoke, his words were punctuated by loud guffaws from the audience. He joined in the laughter with a peculiarly raucous "huh-huh-huh."

A year later I was sent back to Tokyo again as Bureau Chief for *The* (London) *Times* and I came to know Mishima

well, following a first meeting which I myself proposed in
the early part of 1968. I have reconstructed a picture of our
friendship from diaries and notes made between 1968 and
1970, the last three years of his life.

March 1968. Met Yukio Mishima for the first time this
week. We had a rendezvous at the Okura Hotel. I mixed up
the meeting place. He was waiting in the Oak Bar, I was
downstairs in the Orchid Bar. After half an hour I had a message via the waiter: "Mr. Mishima is waiting for you in the
Oak Bar." I went up there and spotted him at once, sitting in
an armchair facing the entrance. First impression: irritated
at having been kept waiting; he sprang to his feet at once,
though, and came forward to shake hands, with a broad
smile on his face. Mishima came up to my shoulder only; he
must be six inches shorter than I. Had his hair cut very
short. A charming and captivating man. Quite un-Japanese;
fluent in English; gestures and manner of speaking Western;
funny way of laughing, deep down in his throat, very hoarse
. . . went on and on, "huh-huh-huh"; embarrassing laugh.
Loved attention from others; very conscious of others looking at him (bar waiters knew him well, other customers
were aware of his presence). Wore Western suit, shirt, and
tie. Very formal in a way; didn't talk about himself. Intrigued by Japanese politics and international defense questions; not well informed. After a while we retired to my
room (at the Okura) and drank most of a bottle of brandy.
His face darkened and went red with the alcohol, at least
Japanese in that respect. Smoked Churchill cigar with much
gusto. Gave impression of titanic energy. He declined
brandy after eleven (has the habit of working at night) and
returned home, promising to keep in contact in future.
Could anyone be less Japanese? A forthright man, he looks
directly at his interlocutor. Seemingly very confident and
contented with his life.

May 1968. Invited by Mishima to his home for dinner.
Other guests were Takeshi Muramatsu, a literary critic and
expert on French literature (reminded me a bit of Action

Française types, same combination of right-wing views and intelligence one saw in the Action Française in the 1930's) and a senior man from the Jieitai [the Armed Forces, generally known as the Self-Defense Forces]. Surprised by luxury in which Mishima lives. Modern, three-story home set well back from road in quiet suburb of Tokyo—on the southwestern side of the city: quite a large garden for a house in Japan, in it a huge figure of Apollo on plinth, surrounded by some kind of mosaic (didn't inspect it). Everything spick-and-span and freshly painted; mostly black and white. Very solid house with solid walls, painted white. Maid at the door in cap and apron! Ushered into downstairs room full of furniture, with heavy curtains, and then up steep staircase on one side of reception room to little alcove above, where we had drinks and snacks; vast drinks trolley over which Mishima hovered. Aggressive conversation: never been subject to such a barrage in Japan. Mishima started off: "Why are you interested in us rightists?" Accompanied this by monstrous laughter, giving me no chance to reply. Muramatsu acid and clever: rarely met a more penetrating intelligence; not at ease with him physically—nervous creature with big brows. Dinner served at table downstairs by Yoko, who did not sit with us or speak to us. Mishima treating her like servant, in Japanese style. And after dinner, brandy and cigars. Don't know any other Japanese intellectual with this Western style of entertaining. Not sure whether I can take Mishima's self-confessed "rightism" seriously. More a joke than anything else? Nonetheless, enormous tension in the room about him; pent-up feeling.

July 26, 1968. Had not seen Mishima much this summer but letter arrived yesterday. Suggested that I come down to Shimoda to visit him during summer holidays; said he always stayed at Shimoda Tokyo Hotel for his holidays with his family (wife, two children). Strange letter. Mishima said Rintaro Hinuma [a critic and friend of his] had recently died; Hinuma, he said, had often remarked to him that suicide would be the only solution to his (Mishima's) literary career. Since Hinuma's death, he added, this remark about suicide had come to seem a serious comment. Am confused by this letter; do not know what he wants. Am not prepared to get into suicide scenario with Mishima, whom I scarcely know; not going down to Shimoda and will not answer letter. Cannot but detect self-pity in this odd letter to comparative stranger: a bit disgusted.

September 25, 1968. Mishima has published a strange article in *Chuo Koron* [the leading intellectual magazine] in which he states that the Emperor should once again present regimental colors. Cannot follow this article, entitled "Bunkaboeiron" ("On the Defense of Culture"). Have written piece for *The Times* in which I criticize the essay. Do not understand why a writer should involve himself in politics in this way. The most puzzling thing about the essay is that there is no connection between the body of it and the pragmatic conclusion (that the Emperor should present regimental colors, as he did before the war); a curiously muddy essay for such a well-known writer; poor arguments. Have reviewed politics of other leading writers (Abé, Oe), contrasting Mishima's right-wing attitudes with the leftist views of almost all other Japanese authors.

October 29, 1968. Nobel Prize has gone to Kawabata. Mishima rushed down to Kamakura to be the first to congratulate Kawabata. A picture has been published in the papers showing the two of them together, Mishima smiling his big smile and Kawabata looking shy as usual: huge forehead and melancholy eyes. There is an impression among my Japanese friends that Mishima is jealous of Kawabata; Mishima had been mentioned so many times in the press and in interviews as future winner of Nobel, first Japanese to win Nobel, etc. Not as simple as that, I suspect. Mishima not *just* jealous. Complex man.

November 1968. Have not seen Mishima but seems he's founded some kind of "private army." Report to this effect has been published in the *Sunday Mainichi* [a weekly magazine friendly to Mishima]. Cannot really believe this. What does he need a private army for? Sounds crazy. Is this some reaction to his failure to get the Nobel? Don't think so, because the timing doesn't work. He seems to have founded the little army, called the Tatenokai [Shield Society], before the Nobel news came through. Must call him and find out what the hell he's up to. Could be a good story for *The Times*. "Famous Writer Starts Private Army," etc. Sounds too silly, though.

December 1968. Met Mishima after phoning him last week. He said it's true that he has a "private army." He prattled on about the need for a civilian militia and how necessary it was to "restore the sword" to Japan; talked about *The Chrysanthemum and the Sword* by Ruth Benedict, saying there was too much emphasis on the former (the arts) and not enough on the latter (defense). Cannot understand what Mishima was driving at. Whole private-army game seems amazing and silly. Also very funny, if Mishima is right. He treated the whole thing as a joke. Said the uniforms were fantastic and roared with laughter. Stated that they had been designed by the only tailor (Tsukumo Igarashii) in Japan to have made a uniform for de Gaulle. Hard to know what this clowning by Mishima means. Extraordinarily attractive man: couldn't care less what others think.

February 1969. Mishima phoned and asked whether I want to see the Tatenokai in action, something about an all-night exercise on Mt. Fuji. Can't resist this. Sounds too good to be true. Bit of a strain running about at night, but nothing else going on in Japan right now. Seems that the student left [the Zengakuren] is losing out to the police. Riots getting more and more tame and police on top, using tear gas. Are we seeing a right-wing revival at this stage, following the excesses of the left? Or is Mishima just playing the buffoon? If so, attractive buffoon. Told him I would go up to Mt. Fuji and review his troops; he screamed with laughter. Huh-huh-huh. Went on and on. Other Japanese friends regard the Tatenokai as a joke. Not sure I do, 100 percent.

February 1969. Invited by Mishima to karate session. Promised to go before and dropped out at last moment (he came to the *Times* office and asked me where I'd been). Not my first experience of karate but first time with Mishima. I

was not all that fit and could not manage all the fairly simple
exercises that we did. I didn't greatly take to bowing down
in front of a Shinto shrine either, even if pro forma. Interesting to see Mishima himself doing karate. He put a stunning
amount of effort into the exercises; bent and cracked and
groaned. In fact, though, he was a bit stiff; don't think he'd
ever be very good at karate, which he took up only two years
ago. He's just not elastic enough at his age. Saw him up
against younger men and it was most obvious. Just next to us
in the gym two little boys exercised, thalidomide victims
with no arms, and hands on their shoulders; sad mothers escorted them. My eyes went from the children to Mishima
and back again. Strange atmosphere. Poor mothers. Don't
think I'll do karate again. Not soon anyway.

March 16, 1969. Returned from Mt. Fuji last weekend.
Cannot understand the Tatenokai. We paraded about the
slopes of Mt. Fuji like a crew of idiots. At least the weather
was lovely (had to abandon the all-night exercise because
the snow was deep). Creamy snow. Longed to go skiing or
to climb the big mountain. We marched for hours in the
snow. The Tatenokai has no fieldcraft and very little training. Have written piece for *The Times* but feel a bit bored
by the "private army" lark. Can't see where it leads. Fantastic uniforms, Mishima's kitsch taste, that's about all. Color is
sort of yellow-brown and rows of brass buttons down front
which give wasp waists to Mishima's young men. Is this a
homosexual club? No evidence of that. Can't really see anything in the Tatenokai exercise beyond the uniforms. Met
Morita, student leader of the "private army," and found him
to be a dull boy, about twenty-three, not very bright;
seemed devoted to Mishima and to confuse him with the
Emperor. What is this all about, for God's sake? Mishima
drove back to Tokyo with me in a hired car and went to
sleep in the car at least. Finally, some evidence that he's
human and needs sleep like the rest of us. Very tired by the
exercise. Had a photo taken which I will keep as a souvenir.
Sent on to me by someone at Camp Fuji: shows me with a
bulge in my cheek, sitting in the snow, having lunch with

Mishima (am trying to digest a fearful dish called sekihan, glutinous rice and red beans). Picture shows Mishima looking a bit criminal though, thuggish almost; he does sometimes look like that. Told me at the camp that his books are selling like wildfire now. *Spring Snow* already sold 200,000 copies in first two months, according to him. I wonder what this novel of his is going to be? The whole tetralogy, I mean. Seems that he's putting a lot of work into it. But what did that letter last year mean? Have never asked Mishima. In a way I don't want to know about his personal problems, the suicide thing and so on. It's his business, not mine.

April 1969. Had a telephone call from Philip Whitehead in London—he's now at Thames TV as a senior producer. Wants to send out a team to film Mishima, having read my article about the Tatenokai in *The Times*. We had a few laughs on the telephone. He is sending out a reporter called Peter Taylor.

April 1969. Went up to Mt. Fuji to introduce Taylor to Mishima. He wouldn't let us see the Tatenokai in training, though. It seems that my article has stirred up a hornet's nest in the Jieitai; there has been talk of firing a general for negligence. The problem, it seems, is *The Times* used the term "right-wing" in describing the Tatenokai in a headline. In fact, I used the same expression in my story; but it was the headline that caused the trouble really. This is the first time the Jieitai has come under attack for training the Tatenokai. But so they should be! The Jieitai is a bit cuckoo. Unless the Tatenokai is just Mishima's joke?

Mishima agreed to meet us back in Tokyo, to show the film *Patriotism* to Taylor and the rest of the TV team; and he will also give us dinner. A chance to see that strange house and its Victorian bric-a-brac again.

April 1969. Spent last night at Mishima's home with Taylor. We were there until midnight drinking brandy and smoking Churchill cigars. Mishima handed around cigars like the most generous of tycoons. There was a strange scene upstairs after dinner (served by Yoko, who did not sit with us—odd combination in Mishima of Western and Japa-

nese, at least his wife might be permitted to speak to us!).
Went upstairs and Mishima got out brandy and asked if we'd
like to see his swords. Said yes. He went downstairs and
came back with a bundle of weapons wrapped up in cloths;
he had a dozen knives, swords, and the rest. Mishima all excited about the blades, but I don't know anything about
sword pedigrees and couldn't respond to his enthusiasm
very much. All the swords were sharp and with some pretty
patterns on them: very subtle, tempered patterns. In the end
Mishima asked Taylor if he'd like to know how classical
hara-kiri carried out: made me kneel on floor and pretend to
cut open my stomach. Meanwhile, he made passes at my
neck with the sword. Seemed he wanted to cut off my head!
He laughed his raucous laugh and I scrambled to my feet,
the back of my neck tingling; I discovered Mishima, shouting with laughter still, holding three feet of razor-sharp steel
in his hands. A long sword with a double-handed hilt; beautiful inlay in black and white diamond shapes. An old
weapon, seventeenth century, I believe. And much too sharp.

April 1969. Does Mishima have a taste for swords! He
sent us yesterday to a hall in Shinjuku, where he had laid on
a showing of *Patriotism*. I couldn't watch the screen all the
way through this film. It was short, about twenty minutes
only. And it included an interminable scene of a hara-kiri,
performed by Mishima, who also directed the film. I did not
watch him sawing his stomach in half. Shut my eyes tight
and waited for the film to finish. Sound track: the dirge from
Wagner's *Tristan*. Horrible taste! Other people seemed capable of watching the film, but not I. And how did he get
the idea of using Wagner? Bet he didn't pay for the rights.
Suppose the blood in the film was sheep's guts or something. Much blood, I am told.

Arnold [the TV director from England] and others have
been filming Mishima on the roof of a building at Ichigaya,
the Ichigaya Hall, a place Mishima uses for the Tatenokai.
It's just next to a big Jieitai camp which stands on a hill. All
the Tatenokai paraded on the roof, Mishima with them.
Hope Thames TV is doing a good film but not sure how

representative Mishima is of Japan! Here is a TV team which has flown halfway round the world, traveling first class of course (there ought to be a union for us too!) and no one Japanese pays any attention to the Tatenokai. The truth of the matter must lie between the two extremes: the "private army" is not as awful as the Brits think but much more interesting than the Japanese themselves imagine. Safe, middle-of-the-road Scott-Stokes.

July 3, 1969. Invited by Mishima to the première of *Hitogiri*, a blood-and-guts samurai film. A vast amount of blood shed. The film started with a scene in which samurai dueled and an older man fell victim to a young blade; the older samurai had a sword cutting into his shoulder, and the blood started to fountain from his neck as his heart pumped; he still kept fighting and in the end the enemy sword practically cut his head off; only then was he still. Entire screen spattered with blood. A slow death. Mishima himself played the part of a samurai named Shinbei Tanaka, a famous nineteenth-century swordsman who committed hara-kiri in the house of an ancestor of Mishima's (Naonobu Nagai, a feudal dignitary), of all places. "It caused much embarrassment to my ancestor," Mishima said to me. Quite. Interesting to see Mishima in a full-length feature film (by Daiei). He's not at all a bad actor. However, he flunked one scene. At one point Shintaro Katsu [famous actor with Anthony Quinn style] sobbed and wept on the shoulders of his friend Tanaka; i.e., on Mishima's shoulder. Katsu was sweating profusely and sobbing fit to bust. Mishima leaned away and started to giggle. Suppose they didn't have time to retake that scene, or Mishima refused. "You didn't do too well in that scene with Katsu," I said to Mishima afterward. He just laughed again. I didn't watch his own hara-kiri scene. Couldn't face it. The crucifixion scene at the end of the film was bad enough. Blood!

July 1969. I have agreed with Mishima that he should write an article for a special supplement of *The Times*. My idea. Want to pin him down a little on what he actually thinks. He will base the article, in part, on our talks together

on defense questions. Have not seen him for a few weeks
and talked on the phone. Am going down to Shimoda to pick
up the article, and will take the opportunity to spend a couple of days on the beach—virtually my only holiday this hot
summer. How hot and sticky Tokyo is! Will meet the Mishima family this time, not just Yukio.

August 15, 1969. Have returned from Shimoda. I swam
in the hotel pool with the Mishimas. Teased Mishima about
his "masculinity," body building and the rest. He is small
but has well-developed shoulder and leg muscles and is
slim. Replied that he didn't like fat men; fat men were spiri-
tually lazy, etc. I approached close to him in the pool and
had him put his arms on my shoulders, saying: "Feel and
see, I have no muscles at all!" He did what I said and then
turned away, as if embarrassed. Shy. Didn't like touching
someone else, or being touched.

He and Yoko had two rooms in the hotel. Yukio had a
little room where he slept and worked during the night.
Madman still works at night while he's on holiday. His room
is tiny. We changed in there into our swimming trunks and
talked about A. E. Van Vogt. Both of us like him. "Ah, my favorite SF writer," he said.

I picked up Mishima's manuscript. The Japanese characters are written so clearly that I could read some of them
myself. He has the most amazing hand. So plain and
upright, easy for a foreigner to read. I wonder if any other
Japanese writes like this: clear, straight, and simple. My
other friends all use a kind of speed-writing. Mishima's
characters go marching on. The article itself was not too interesting. He seems to know nothing about politics in Japan;
and I am not interested in the Shinpuren Incident [an event
of the Meiji era: in 1877 a samurai force composed of men
who rejected the Western attitudes of the government attacked an army camp; most of them were killed and the survivors committed hara-kiri], samurai, etc. After all, samurai
disappeared from Japan almost a hundred years ago; they
went with the feudal system. Mishima seems to share the
Western illusion that Japan is still a nation of samurai; of

course, the samurai spirit survives—but not the forms (top-
knot, pair of swords, kimono, and the rest). No wonder he
gets on well with foreigners! In him they find a Japanese
who *is* a samurai. That's part of Mishima's fun.

We went out to dinner together one night at Shimoda.
Lobsters. A marvelous little place on the sea. We went over
there by taxi and had a little room perched over the waves.
The coast there looked just as Japan is supposed to look:
pine trees sticking out at odd angles; savage waves and a
brutal coastline; sun sank slowly in the West with oblique
rays striking the foam, etc. Got quite drunk on saké, which
takes some doing, and watched funemushi [insects, like
man-of-war] on the balcony by our feet. Disgusting creatures. Strange combination: staggering view and these horrible insects crawling about our ankles.

Ate a pair of kicking, raw lobsters, scooping out their insides with chopsticks: delicious. Plenty of rice. Mishima and
I went home by taxi. What a lot of trouble he takes with
guests! Full of fun, teased me about staying in the Kurofune
["kurofune" means "black ship"; hotel was named after
the "black ships" of Admiral Perry of the U.S. Navy, which
appeared off Tokyo in 1853 and constituted the first unde-
niable sign that Japan would have to open her doors to the
West after centuries of total isolation]. We didn't talk about
Mishima's literature. I don't know what to say. Probably my
fault but do not greatly like *The Temple of the Golden Pavilion*. Still appreciate only *Confessions of a Mask*. Asked Mishima about Sonoko [a female character in the book, with
whom the protagonist—Mishima in real life—has a rela-
tionship]; he said he'd "had an affair with her afterward" (in
the book they do not make love). He announced this in the
manner of one who hadn't enjoyed it. Why did he have to
tell me this? Sounded as if he had programmed himself to
have the affair. Wondered who she is exactly.

Hagiwara [a historian friend] says many Japanese believe Mishima to be homosexual. Asked me whether I
agreed. Said I didn't know. We have never discussed the
subject.

September 1969. Talked with Mishima about collaborating on a book on Byron. He wanted to know my opinion of Byron's poetry. I kept my peace but know little about Byron, in fact; do not like what I know. Have asked Mishima for pictures to go with his article for *The Times*.

September 1969. Incredible batch of pictures arrived from Mishima. Marvelous one of him in Western suit, standing behind a No actor—latter in kimono, wearing the mask used in the play *Hagoromo*. Love this picture because it shows Mishima minus the famous mask: he looks childlike, quiet, sad. Suppose that is what he is really like, why he is so charming; perhaps he carries on with his buffoonery but knows that others are not deceived because it *is* buffoonery. Prime example of his clowning in another picture he sent me: shows him stripped to the waist, chest bulging like mad and beaded with sweat, he's holding a sword, that long sword I saw in his home. Has a pathological expression on his face: brows knotted, eyes popping out. Quite spoilt my breakfast and steeled my resolve not to see Mishima for a while. Can't have this kind of stuff landing on my breakfast table. He has a hachimaki [headband] on, in the picture, on which is written a medieval samurai slogan: *Shichisho Hokoku* ("Serve the Nation for Seven Lives"). Thank goodness this is not the real Mishima. Or is it?

November 3, 1969. Just came back from Tatenokai first-anniversary parade. All manner of important guests at the parade, held on the roof of the National Theater, just opposite the palace, facing the palace across the moat. Not good weather. A light drizzle most of the time. Gray Tokyo. Among the guests were Kazuko Aso [daughter of Japan's best-known postwar Prime Minister, Shigeru Yoshida] and the young Konoe [adopted grandson of the wartime Prime Minister]; also, actresses—particularly liked Mitsuko Baisho, hefty girl, should be more of them. Parade was most embarrassing; students marched back and forth in their silly uniforms while Mishima stood at one side. Felt embarrassed for Mishima. Prayed all the time that students would not bungle their marching and tumble off the roof or something; just wanted parade to end. (Why should it matter to me?)

Parade ended with Tatenokai students saluting the Emperor across the moat, a retired Jieitai general inspecting the "troops," and Mitsuko Baisho and Eiko Muramatsu [another actress] presenting Mishima with bouquets of flowers. Wonder what Emperor thinks of the Tatenokai and its salute? Doubtless not informed officially but this circus must be known about somewhere in the Kunaicho [Imperial household]. No doubt they're also embarrassed in their different way. Mishima was rather constrained, uncharacteristically quiet, throughout the parade. Don't wonder. Afterward he made a speech about *The Chrysanthemum and the Sword* again; his usual line. Everyone nibbled sandwiches or sushi [raw fish and rice] and drank tea, looking at their feet while Mishima spoke. Not inappropriate that these activities staged within (and on top of) a theater.

November 1969. Invited by Mishima to his Kabuki play *Chinsetsu Yumiharizuki* (totally untranslatable title) at National Theater. Took Akiko [girlfriend]. Play as long as the title. A monumental play with monumental staging. Boat came out on stage and split in two on a mighty rock; also a white horse on stage at one point—a real horse; and there was a hara-kiri scene with a seven-year-old child disemboweling himself. It was a typical Kabuki blood-and-thunder play, only more so; more blood. There was one Mishima scene. Snow: the mountains; a lodge, presided over by a stunningly beautiful princess (in kimono, naturally). An enemy of the princess stumbles into the lodge by accident and is duly taken prisoner; she tortures the man to death, using awls, with which her maids drill tiny holes in the body of their captive, who rolls in the snow, scattering blood all over the place. Only Mishima, who directed the play as well as wrote it, could have thought up a scene like this. The production was curiously amateur, though: lots of technical hitches; heavy objects crashed to the earth backstage; cast not knowing where to stand. Worthy of a high school. Has Mishima got too much on his plate now?

January 1970. Yukio came for dinner. He's been over to Korea and urged me to go there too, to have a look at the east-coast anti-guerrilla exercises. He was there with Ivan

Morris [British scholar and friend of Mishima's]. Wish I'd been with them. No doubt had a splendid time. Wonder what the Koreans made of Mishima. Now the Japanese are really trooping over there again—mainly the businessmen. Must try and arrange another Korean trip, preferably with Mishima: to see how the Koreans treat a Japanese rightist. We talked at dinner about the left-wing students but the subject soon petered out. Neither of us very interested in the World's Fair (which opened at Osaka in March) either. Played rock music on the gramophone, including the Cream's "Badge" and "White Room" (rock numbers). Mishima not interested; he's not musical, or doesn't like rock. Not his taste. Too many people to dinner, though. Mishima is better in very small gatherings or alone. He doesn't like lion shows; nor do I.

February 1970. Rare contretemps with Mishima. The other morning two Japanese in dark suits came to the door of my house. Heard them knocking and went out. Two little men in suits sang out in chorus: "We are from the D——— Bank. We represent Yukio Mishima." Knew what it was, and could have murdered the pair of them on the spot; I'd held up a remittance to Mishima from a London newspaper; this was intended to pay for a contribution he'd made to a special supplement on Japan published by this newspaper. I'd solicited the article from Mishima and it had duly been turned down in London.

I hadn't had the nerve to tell Mishima that his work had not met with approval at home. Must have been a very rare case of his writing being rejected and wondered whether my translation had been the cause of this. Anyway, the pair of bankers had evidently come to collect the money; they had presumably phoned Mishima for instructions and been told to go ahead and get it at once (he is very precise about money). Admitted the bankers to my sitting room and having confirmed the nature of their mission asked them to leave without further ado; did not spare their feelings. "We represent Yukio Mishima," indeed! They were so full of self-importance. It was a pleasure to see their faces as I hustled them out of the house: dumfounded; probably never been thrown out in their lives. "We represent Yukio Mishima!" They had treated themselves as if they were Imperial messengers. At once sent remittance to Mishima, though. We were all square on the day: drawn match.

August 5, 1970. Have seen little of Mishima this year but had invitation to go down to Shimoda again. Donald Keene [American scholar and friend of Mishima's] is going at the same time. Yukio wanted us both there simultaneously; expect he has train of guests as usual. Am going with Akiko.

August 15, 1970. Back from Shimoda again. Same scene as last year. Only more people around. There was a regular troupe about Mishima, including handsome young man from the National Theater. A whole party of family friends, too; don't know who they were exactly. Saw something of Yoko this time. A pretty woman. She seems to run the family. Makes all the decisions about daily life, when the family is going to the beach and so on. When and where. Mishima played role of henpecked husband. Liked that. Loaded himself up with nets and balls for the children and trooped off to the beach. Yoko drove the big, bright blue American car. Typical of Mishima to have large foreign car (hard to park) rather than less showy, common Japanese one. He doesn't drive at all, though. Interesting how Yukio chooses to take his holidays always at Shimoda and not with the rest of the bourgeois rich at Karuizawa. He makes a thing of being different.

Spent a lovely day on the beach with the Mishimas: white sand, strong sun. Yukio lying among cheap magazines scattered on the beach, listening to Japanese pop music on radio. He wore a funny pair of swimming trunks, minuscule black cotton ones with big brass buckles on the thighs: kitsch again. He didn't swim much. Yoko confided that he's scared of the sea. Two children with us: Noriko, the girl, beautiful and quiet, very feminine at eleven; Ichiro, a barbaric little boy with white teeth and very sunburned—two years younger. Only Yoko can control him. Children teased

Mishima about his trunks: "Won't you do a strip-tease, Dad," etc. Mishima rolled on his back in sand, narcissism exposed yet again. What a funny man! Went out swimming with Ichiro but he would only take his son out a few yards into the surf, though the waves were not big; they had a rubber mattress with them. All the same, he *must* be frightened of the sea. Funny: when there are so many descriptions of the sea in his books. You'd never have known it.

There was an embarrassing scene at the beginning of my visit to Shimoda. Went up to Mishima's hotel for lunch, having booked into a minshuku [lodging house] on the beach with Akiko. Thought to amuse Yukio with a description of my recent visit to Korea. I'd been up to the front lines, inspected an American military base, noting the village of whores just outside the base limits, and had gone on to visit a Korean base close by, the other side of the road. The Korean base had been full of virile, healthy young men; and they had no women—the Americans had them instead. The Korean colonel in command of regiment had put Bernie Krisher [*Newsweek* Bureau Chief in Tokyo] and me on a rostrum in the middle of the parade ground; and the Korean soldiers then did karate exercises for us. Broke bricks in half. Told Mishima all this and he listened with interest. Then I came, laboriously, to the point of the story. After the karate exercises the Korean soldiers had danced for us. In Western style. Tall men danced as men and the short men were the women; they had clutched one another and rotated slowly on the parade ground before our eyes, while others sang and clapped their hands in time. Some of the men blushed deeply. I myself had not known which way to look, but Bernie had taken pictures with great sang-froid. As I finished this story I saw that Yukio did not think it funny. Not at all amused. Stony-faced, in fact.

One night at Shimoda, Mishima suggested we go to a yakuza [gangster] movie. I agreed; there wasn't much to do. I waited for him outside a dirty little cinema in Shimoda, having walked over from the inn a mile away. After a while the Mishimas arrived, Yoko driving the big car. We all trooped in, Mishima acting as host as usual; he walked ahead with Yoko, into the cinema. It was a grimy hall and almost totally empty, just a few fishermen and lay-abouts. That was O.K. The problem was the air-conditioning. With so few people in the hall the place was a bit chilly, as there was a vast air-conditioning machine shooting cold air into the hall from the left-hand side at about 90 mph. I placed myself as far as possible from the machine. Was shattered to see Mishima seat himself exactly in front of air-conditioner. Icy gale played on his body; and he wore only a black shirt (with a stringed front). Yoko sat there for a moment, a shawl about her shoulders, and then moved forward, out of the path of the typhoon.

The movie itself was odd. I'd never seen a yakuza movie before. Got the hang of the genre first time, though. Bit like a Western. The "hero" acted reluctantly when provoked by the "bad guys"; finally, went roaring into action— his weapon: A SWORD! That is kinky part of yakuza movie tradition: the use of swords. At denouement we got a mighty spattering of the villains' blood. Mysteriously, swords in the hands of the heroes proved far more effective than pistols of the villains. But a pistol wound doesn't make enough blood flow. Therefore swords. Mishima was absolutely engrossed; he was still sitting in front of the giant air-conditioning machine two hours later. At the end of the film he didn't stir either. Wondered if he'd got lumbago sitting there. In the end he got up and came walking back to us, very slowly, shrugging his shoulders, as if getting himself out of a great dream. How seriously he takes the yakuza movie!

In the car Yukio told me he was planning to call the last volume of *The Sea of Fertility* by the title *Five Signs of a God's Decay*, in English. He said this was the idea of Seidensticker [American scholar who subsequently translated the book after Mishima's death with a final title of *The Decay of the Angel*]. Seemed that he had finished the book, or almost so. Wonder what he plans next. Yukio also invited Donald and me to a dinner at same restaurant where I had eaten lobsters with him the year before; to make sure we had enough to eat, he ordered lobsters and shellfish for five people; when that didn't seem adequate, he increased the order to seven portions—for three people.

September 3, 1970. Yukio came to dinner. He looked healthy and tanned, strong as usual. Sat on the floor on the cushions and drank Scotch brought to him by Akiko. Drank quite a lot of whisky but in his usual way: measured and slow. He never gets even faintly tipsy. It's control, control, control. You couldn't imagine him drunk.

He was in a curious mood. Talked in melancholy fashion about heroes in the Japanese tradition. He insisted that "all our heroes have failed, they have all been miserable failures." I can't imagine what he was trying to say. What are heroes to him or to me? Usually he is so cheerful but today he was really depressed. I was critical about his remarks on heroes but he ignored my hostility and plunged on with a story about Heihachiro Oshio [nineteenth-century Japanese hero], saying what a great man he had been. I attempted to tease Yukio. He just went on, concluding his remarks: "The body is a vase full of empty space. Oshio touched emptiness and died." I really could not follow him. I then cooked a meal for us. The steaks I made were grossly underdone. I had been put off by something in Yukio. The meat had to go into the pan again, bleeding red. After dinner he struck up in his pessimistic vein again. There were all manner of curses in Japan, he said; curses had played a great part in Japanese history. One family, the Konoe family, had been blighted by a curse that the eldest son die young—it had lasted for nine generations.

Normally, when he comes to my home, Mishima is cheerful and happy throughout the evening. Not so tonight. He went on and on about curses. The whole of Japan, according to him, was under a curse. Everyone ran after money; the old spiritual tradition had vanished; materialism was the order of the day. Modern Japan was ugly. Then he used a curious image. Japan, he said, "is under the curse of . . . a green snake." He paused for a few moments before he found the image; or so it seemed. Then he repeated himself: "There is a green snake in the bosom of Japan . . . and

that is the curse on us which we will not be able to escape."
He was drinking brandy but he was surely not drunk. I
didn't know what to make of his remarks. After he left, four
of us remained; Reiko [a friend] said he'd just been in his
pessimistic mood. We laughed. But I joined in the laughter
halfheartedly. Green snake, indeed!

At the end of the evening Yukio dodged out of my
house after making a quick phone call. He spoke to someone
in a hard, commanding fashion. Akiko thought it must have
been a Tatenokai member he spoke to, judging by his tone.
But we don't hear anything about the Tatenokai these days.
Subject is dead. The initial sensation is over. No one is writing about it at all in the foreign or the Japanese press—with
exception of one article in *The New York Times* [in August
1970, written by Philip Shabecoff—but it had been completed early in the year].

September 1970. Went to *Boris Godunov*, Bolshoi is in
town. Got the tickets from Hagiwara, accompanied by
Keene. Had quite good seats, though expensive. During the
first intermission we went outside to the foyer, to stretch our
legs. Suddenly Donald scampered across the foyer. He'd
spotted Mishima in the crowd. M. was with Yoko. Chatted
for a while and he introduced me to Yoshie Fujiwara [the
doyen of Japanese opera]. Secretly guessed that scene in
Boris which Yukio would like best would be the lavish, rococo scene in the Polish court. Bolshoi gives the Polish
scene everything. Very kitsch, in comparison with the rest of
the opera: slushy. Tackled M. afterward and accused him of
enjoying the Polish scene; he confessed at once, laughing
his big laugh. He rocked on his heels: "Oh, yes . . . oh,
yes!" Glad to find him more cheerful.

October 4, 1970. Letter from Yukio. Writes that he's finally coming to the end of *The Sea of Fertility*. Sounds most
depressed. Says that it is "like the end of the world," finishing this book. Am reminded of the letter in 1968 in which he
hinted at suicide. Depressed. Wrote to him asking him to
phone.

November 12, 1970. Dinner with Mishima. He was in a
most aggressive mood. Charming as usual but flashes of

great aggression. Implied that I might as well pack my bags
and go home, as "no foreigner can ever understand Japan."
Think he went a little far. In a sense, no Japanese can ever
"understand" the West. So what? Man's a perfectionist.
Took Janie [an Irish friend] to meet him, and Mishima
seemed attracted to her; complimented her lavishly on her
looks—white skin, red hair—and encouraged her with her
writing. Also had strange conversation with her about prosti-
tution in Japan. He claimed that it cost two million yen
($8,000) to sleep with a virgin geisha. Yukio laid much em-
phasis on this detail. He was also strangely critical of the
Western scholars in the field of Japanese studies; insisted,
looking me straight in the eyes, that the scholars ignore the
"dark" side of the Japanese tradition and concentrate upon
the "soft" aspects of Japanese culture. Why is he being rude
these days? And where has his sense of humor gone to? I
tried to cheer Mishima by telling him tales of travels in the
Philippines; also dredged up a few bloodthirsty details
about the Manila jail, in which a dozen men have been murdered by fellow prisoners recently. Told him about the local
warlord system in the country: how the local bosses put up
road barriers against one another. He asked me about my
forthcoming trip to Manila (to witness the first visit of the
Pope) and prophesied that there would be violence. [In fact
there *was* an attempt to assassinate the Pope at Manila airport.]

Yukio gave me an invitation to visit an exhibition devoted to Mishimalia at a department store (Tobu, at Ikebukuro). Don't think that I'll have time to go before I leave for
Manila. He seemed in a terrific hurry at the end of the evening and went shooting out of the restaurant (the Fon-
tainebleau, at the Imperial Hotel), bowed at on all sides by
white-coated waiters. He crushed a note into the hands of
the elevator man as he left; wondered what on earth he was
doing (tipping is very much the exception in Japan).

This was my last sight of Yukio Mishima—tipping an elevator operator, looking flustered. Normally he would have

waited to accompany us down in the elevator, but he seemed in a great hurry—to keep another appointment, or perhaps not to have a lingering goodbye.

If my trip had gone according to plan, I would have been abroad on November 25, 1970, but a typhoon made me cancel my booking for Manila, and so I was still in Tokyo when the first news came.

It was a lovely, sunny day typical of autumn in Tokyo, when a north wind blows the polluted air of the Japanese capital south over the bay. I worked at home during the morning and was at my desk shortly before noon when I received a telephone call from Sam Jameson, my friend at the *Chicago Tribune*. I heard from him the news which was just being announced on the radio: that Yukio Mishima had taken an army general hostage at the Jieitai military base at Ichigaya and that he was threatening to kill himself. When I heard this, I broke down. I was sure that Mishima would act on his threat; he was not one to leave an action uncompleted. If he had announced that he might kill himself, then he would do so, willy-nilly. I had completely ignored Mishima's warnings of his intentions. Regardless of whether this was a "rightist" action or not—and I had doubts about Mishima's interest in politics—I was appalled by my neglect of a friend.

I took a taxi outside my home and twenty-five minutes later I was at the gates of the base at Ichigaya. There was a small crowd gathered outside and I shouldered my way through it; I showed my press pass to the guards and ran up the steep drive in front of me. This led to the top of a hill. In front of me stood a long, utilitarian building—a structure built after the Great Earthquake of 1923, to judge by its ugly lines; it was yellow-gray and was badly in need of fresh paint. In the center of the building was a balcony; a pair of white streamers dangled from it and waved in the breeze. A steady November sun warmed the parade ground on which I stood.

It was almost deserted, but at the entrance to the head-quarters building—this was the headquarters of the Eastern

Army of the Jieitai—I found some soldiers. They were standing about in the portico underneath the balcony. From one of these bystanders I learned that Mishima had died minutes earlier; no one knew exactly what had happened. Five minutes later, just after 12:30 p.m., I heard that Mishima and Morita, the student leader of the Tatenokai, had both committed hara-kiri in the office of the commanding general of the Eastern Army, a General Mashita; this office was on the second floor of the headquarters building, just above us. We were not allowed to see the bodies.

What vast, immoral courage had enabled Mishima to kill himself in this manner? In 1960 he had written a short story, "Patriotism," in which he had glorified hara-kiri; and five years later he had made a film of "Patriotism," and had taken the part of the hero of the story, an army lieutenant who disembowels himself. In 1968 he had completed *Runaway Horses* (the second volume of his tetralogy, *The Sea of Fertility*), in which the protagonist, a right-wing terrorist, also commits hara-kiri. And in the following year he had taken the role of a samurai in a feature film, *Hitogiri;* once again he had played the part of a man who rips open his stomach. Thus Mishima endlessly rehearsed his own death.

ONE

The Last Day

1
Off to the Parade

Yukio Mishima rose early on the morning of November 25, 1970. He shaved slowly and carefully.

This was to be his death face. There must be no unsightly blemishes.

He took a shower, and put on a fresh, white cotton fundoshi, a loincloth. Then he dressed in his Tatenokai uniform.

His wife, Yoko, had gone out with the children, taking them to school. He had the house—a large, Western-style home in the southwest suburbs of Tokyo—to himself.

Mishima checked the items he was taking with him that day. He had a brown attaché case containing daggers, papers, and other things; he also had a long samurai sword and scabbard.

On a table in the hall he placed a fat envelope. It contained the final installment of his long novel, *The Sea of Fertility,* on which he had spent six years. The envelope was addressed to his publishers, Shinchosha, who would send someone for it later that morning.

At ten o'clock he made a couple of short phone calls. He spoke to reporter friends whom he wanted to be on hand to witness the events of the day. But he did not explain exactly what was to happen.

Shortly after ten he saw a Tatenokai student walk up the path through the garden from the front gate. This was Chibi-Koga, a short youth with a pointed nose. Mishima went out of the house to greet him.

He gave three envelopes to the student. They were addressed to Chibi-Koga, to Furu-Koga, a second student in their small group, and to Ogawa, the tall, pallid boy who was the standard-bearer of the Tatenokai.

"Take these out to the car," Mishima said to Chibi-Koga. "I will be out in a moment. Read the letters now!"

The student went back down the path.

Mishima gathered his belongings—the attaché case and the sword. He fixed the sword to his belt on the left side. Then he left the house.

An elderly man with silver hair—Azusa Hiraoka, Mishima's father—looked out of his house, next door to that of his son.

"Ah! So he's off to another Tatenokai parade," thought the father disapprovingly.

Mishima went down the steps into the quiet suburban street.

The Tatenokai party had come in a white Toyota Corona, a medium-size car. It was parked down the street.

Mishima climbed into the front seat, next to the driver, Chibi-Koga. He turned to face the others—Furu-Koga and Ogawa. With them was a third student, a stolid, thickset youth with heavy jowls—Masakatsu Morita, the leader of the Tatenokai under Mishima, and a close friend.

"Have you read the letters?" Mishima asked. "You follow? *You* are not to kill yourselves. That's clear? Just take care of the general. See that he doesn't commit suicide. That's all."

Mishima and Morita were to commit hara-kiri. The three younger members of the party were to stay alive. At their trial, according to Mishima's letters, they were to expound the principles of the Tatenokai; they were to follow the slogan *Hokoku Nippon* ("The Imperial Reconstruction of Japan"), a wartime, imperialist slogan.

Mishima had put into each of the envelopes a sum of about $120, three 10,000-yen notes for each of the students, to cover initial expenses.

"All right, let's go," said Mishima. "Start up!"

2
The Fight in
the General's Office

The car with Mishima and his four students arrived at the Ichigaya base of the Jieitai, in the heart of Tokyo, just before 11 a.m.

The guards at the gate saw Mishima in the front and waved Chibi-Koga through. They telephoned the HQ of the Eastern Army at Ichigaya to let the staff know that Mishima and his group had arrived.

Chibi-Koga drove up the steep road leading from the front gate to the top of the little hill on which the HQ stood. He parked at the edge of a big parade ground in front of Eastern Army HQ.

The men got out of the car. Mishima led the way toward the building, carrying his attaché case. His sword swung at his side.

The army HQ building was yellow-gray in color and three stories high. In the center of the boxlike building was the main entrance, which had a large, squat portico. Atop the portico was a spacious balcony; it faced the parade ground across which Mishima and his men walked.

An aide-de-camp to General Kanetoshi Mashita, the commander of the Eastern Army, came out of the main entrance. He was a major, dressed in the blue-gray uniform of the Jieitai.

"Do come in," he said to Mishima. "General Mashita is waiting for you."

The officer, Major Sawamoto, led the way. The Ta-

tenokai party followed him into the dark entrance hall. They
went up a circular flight of stairs to the first floor.

"I won't keep you a moment," said the major to Mishima. He disappeared into room 201, the general's office,
just at the top of the stairs.

The Tatenokai group stood outside.

To left and right there were long, dark corridors with
high ceilings. Senior officers of the Eastern Army, the command responsible for Tokyo and the surrounding Kanto plain,
worked on this floor.

On either side of the door of room 201 were opaque
glass windows. Glass alone separated the corridor from the
general's office beyond.

Major Sawamoto reappeared at the door. "Do come inside," he said. "The general is ready."

Mishima went through the door, followed by his men.

The major pointed to four chairs lined up close to the
door. "You sit here," he said to the students. Major Sawamoto then withdrew from the room, shutting the door behind him.

Mishima went forward to greet General Mashita. The
general was a dignified officer with gray hair. He was fifty-
seven and had served through the Pacific War; he had a
quiet, unpretentious manner.

"How nice to see you again," he said to Mishima.

The office was not large, no more than twenty by
twenty-five feet. It had a high ceiling and tall windows facing south over the balcony outside. Bright sun streamed
through the windows.

Access to the office was from all four sides: from the entrance door, from the balcony, and from two tall doors set in
the paneling on either side of the room. One door led to the
chief of staff, the other to the office of his deputy, a vice
chief of staff.

"Please come and sit over here," the general said to
Mishima. He gestured toward a low table around which
were armchairs.

Mishima took a seat next to the general.

"Please sit down," Mashita said to the students. At Mishima's suggestion they had brought their chairs up to the middle of the room; they sat in a row in their yellow-brown uniforms.

"I brought these Tatenokai members to meet you, General," Mishima said. He introduced them one by one.

Mashita nodded.

"We have just finished an exercise at Mt. Fuji. During the exercise some of our men were injured. These four with me today distinguished themselves by carrying down the wounded men from the mountain."

"Ah, is that so?"

"I wanted them to have the honor of meeting you," Mishima continued. "That's why I asked for today's meeting. Later today we will have a regular Tatenokai meeting at which these four will receive a commendation."

"Mm, I follow."

"The reason why we are in uniform today is that we are holding our monthly meeting."

"I see."

Mishima had taken off his sword before he sat down. The weapon was propped up against one of the chairs where Mashita could see it. An orange tassel hung from the hilt.

"Tell me," said Mashita, who had been eyeing the weapon, "what is this sword that you have with you? Did anyone ask you about it on the way in? I am not very clear about the rules on swords, as we don't carry them any more ourselves."

"It's all right to carry this sword," replied Mishima. "It is a military sword. An antique. I carry an expert's authentication." Mishima produced a piece of paper. "The sword was made by Seki no Magoroku, according to this. It's a genuine seventeenth-century blade. The Seki school."

The general glanced across at the sword. The hilt had diamond-shaped panels with mother-of-pearl inlay. It was an exceptional piece.

"Would you like to see it?" asked Mishima.

"Yes," replied the general. "It has sambon sugi, hasn't

it?" He referred to the smoky, wavy pattern of the temper-
ing of a sword of the Seki school.

"Let me get it out," said Mishima. He stood and picked
up the sword and drew the blade from the scabbard with a
practiced motion. He held the glittering weapon upright.

He and Mashita studied the blade for a moment. Its surface was obscured by grease.

"Koga," said Mishima to Chibi-Koga, "a handkerchief!"
The words were a cue for Chibi-Koga.

The student got up from his chair and came toward the
two men by the table. In his hand he carried a tennugui, a
thin, strong towel.

This was the "handkerchief." Chibi-Koga was to use it
to gag General Mashita. His instructions were to slip the
tennugui over the general's face, from behind.

At that moment, however, the general walked away. He
went to his desk to fetch some tissue to wipe the sword.

The student was in a quandary. He could not wait
where he was; that was not in the plan. And he was incapable of improvisation.

Chibi-Koga handed the towel to Mishima and went
back to his seat.

Mishima methodically wiped the blade. He held it up,
admiring its razor-sharp edge. It was in flawless condition.

The general, who had returned to the table, stood with
Mishima, who handed the weapon to him. He pointed the
sword upright and caught the light in it.

"Yes, I see them," he said to Mishima, as he glimpsed
the semicircular, smoky shadows which ran along the blade.

"It's superb," said Mashita. "I've never seen anything
like it in private hands before."

He handed the sword back to Mishima and sat down. It
was 11:05 a.m.

Mishima glanced at the row of students sitting on their
chairs close by. Chibi-Koga came forward for the second
time. Mishima gave him a look of silent command.

The youth stepped one pace forward, going behind Mashita, and thrust his hands suddenly, clumsily around the general's neck, throttling him.

Chibi-Koga's action was the cue for the others to move.

Furu-Koga and the lanky Ogawa came forward to help him. From their pockets they took two lengths of rope; with this they bound Mashita's arms and legs and tied him to the chair.

Mishima moved to the center of the room, holding the sword in his hands, high in the air.

Morita's task was to fasten the doors. Using wire and pincers, he worked quietly, securing the door handles. There was nothing solid to fix the wire to, and he did not make a good job of it. With the help of the other students he moved up Mashita's heavy desk to block one of the doors; the second door they barricaded with table and chairs, adding a potted palm as well.

Mashita, gagged and bound, observed all this. At first he had thought that this was a commando exercise of Mishima's. When he looked him in the eyes, however, he realized that Mishima was not rehearsing.

Mishima stood in the middle of the office, eyes blazing, sword aloft.

Unknown to him, there was a peephole into the room. The peephole was close to the entrance door, in the opaque glass window on the left-hand side. It consisted of a piece of transparent tape stuck onto the glass on the corridor side; with this it was possible to see through into Mashita's office, dimly.

Shortly after Mishima's group had struck, their action had been discovered. Major Sawamoto had come out from an adjoining office and had looked through the peephole, to see whether the men were sitting down, ready to take ocha (green tea). At first he thought a Tatenokai student was giving General Mashita a shoulder massage. But he looked again, realized that something was up—seeing the rope and the gag—and dashed off to fetch his immediate superior, Colonel Hara.

The two men, having tried the main door into the office and found it blocked, had informed General Yamazaki, the chief of staff, who had been in conference with a dozen officers in the room next to Mashita's. One by one the officers had peeped through the hole and had seen Mashita. Then they assembled in Yamazaki's office again.

From there they could hear furniture being moved about next door, while they decided what to do.

"What kind of game is this?" one officer asked.

"We will go in and find out," the general said.

By this time the Tatenokai party had done their best with the barricades. Mishima was about to move to the next stage of his plan: to compel the general to order his men to summon the garrison at Eastern Army Headquarters, about a thousand men. He wanted the soldiers to assemble on the parade ground in front of the HQ building; he would make a patriotic speech to them from the balcony.

His plan was already beginning to go wrong.

At 11:20 a party of men beat on the door leading into Mashita's room from the office of the chief of staff. "Open up!" they shouted. "Open up!"

Mishima gestured to the students to stand behind him and moved toward the door, sword held high. Chibi-Koga stood by Mashita with a dagger, taken from the attaché case. His orders were to remain by the general being held hostage.

The army officers beat on the door with their fists. "Open up! What's going on? Open up!"

One turned the handle and pushed. The weak barrier collapsed and five army men, three colonels and a pair of master sergeants, rushed into the room. Colonel Hara was in the lead.

Mishima barred their way. "Out!" he screamed at them.

The men were quite close to Mishima. They hesitated, facing him. None had weapons. Colonel Hara had an old wooden sword, which he had snatched up before going in.

"Out!" screamed Mishima once again.

The men facing him made no move.

Mishima swung the sword at them, swishing over their heads. Some moved, others flinched. The sergeants edged toward him, with a colonel leading the way.

"Out! Out! Out!"

Suddenly Mishima attacked. He aimed glancing blows at the men. A colonel ducked away. Mishima slashed him in the back. The man raised an arm in self-defense and Mishima hit him again.

A sergeant came at Mishima, who struck him on the wrist, almost severing his hand.

"Out!" screamed Mishima.

He stared wildly at the men.

He slashed at a second colonel, three blows in succession on the arms and the back, as Colonel Hara sought to parry the blows with his wooden sword.

The two uninjured men in the party helped the others out of the room. The door slammed to behind them. The wounded men were bleeding profusely.

Orderlies were summoned and a second conference ensued. The officers were excited and unable to think clearly; the sudden emergency was too much for them. Their main concern was for the safety of General Mashita, but they were also worried about their careers. A major scandal was in the making. Who would take responsibility for the fracas? What did Mishima want out of it? Failure to appreciate the importance of the last question led General Yamazaki to act unwisely; he decided to lead a second party into Mashita's office without having a plan of action and without arms, not even staves. He chose six officers and men to accompany him.

The men forced the door leading into Mashita's room from the vice chief of staff's office. Yamazaki was at the head of the party and entered the room first. Mishima was immediately in front of him, holding his bloodstained sword in the air. The general hesitated. Behind Mishima was the general's commanding officer, tied up in a chair; Chibi-Koga held a knife to his right side.

At Mishima's elbow stood three students. The pallid

Ogawa had drawn a black truncheon. Furu-Koga was behind him, a heavy ashtray in his hand. Close to Mishima stood Morita; he had a dagger.

Yamazaki had expected a situation like this. Still, he could not believe his eyes.

Mishima saw the half-dozen men behind Yamazaki. How many more would there be? With his sword he kept them bunched in the corner of the room, not allowing them to deploy to either side of him. His own men were not strong.

"Well!" Mishima shouted. "Now you've seen! Take a good look! If you do not leave, I will kill the general."

Yamazaki looked past Mishima at his commanding officer. He wanted guidance.

"I repeat," Mishima screamed, "get out or else!"

"Stop this fooling," Yamazaki said loudly. "Calm yourself."

"Out!" screamed Mishima once more. He took a step toward Yamazaki, holding the sword at the general's neck.

"Stop this play-acting," said Yamazaki.

"If you don't leave," Mishima repeated, "I will kill the commanding general."

The army officers edged forward. The men in the lead had climbed over the barrier of furniture, with the others behind them. Then there was a crash and a tinkling of glass. Other Jieitai men had smashed the opaque glass window between Mashita's office and the corridor. They looked in.

Suddenly Mishima backed off. He needed room to use his sword.

Yamazaki spoke again. "We do not understand what you want. Tell us." It was a parley.

Mishima suspected a trick. There were seven army officers altogether, including Yamazaki. Mishima had only three men; Chibi-Koga had to stay by the general.

Mishima swung his blade at Yamazaki, deliberately missing: "Out!"

The officers behind Yamazaki moved forward. One jumped toward Morita.

Mishima had taken up a posture with the sword held back over his shoulders again. He took a step to the rear and aimed a blow at Yamazaki. The general ducked, Mishima slashing him in the back. It was a light wound, but Yamazaki staggered. An officer caught him from behind and held him for a moment.

One officer grappled with Morita, trying to wrench the knife from his hands.

Three men came at Mishima simultaneously.

Striking back and forth, chopping down, right, left, right, left, he beat the men about their arms, shoulders, and backs with the open blade.

Blood stained the uniforms of three colonels.

Morita had lost his knife to his opponent.

"Out!" Mishima screamed at the officers. "Out!" He swung the sword over their heads. "Out! Or I will kill the general."

Yamazaki and his men had no time to think whether Mishima was bluffing or not.

"Out!" he shouted again, slashing at a colonel who had come too close, and hitting him on the arm.

The Jieitai men could not understand what Mishima was after. Had he gone mad?

Mishima gave them no more time. Prodding the men with his sword and administering broad strokes to their buttocks, he herded them out of the office.

The seven men tumbled back into the vice chief of staff's room as the door crashed shut behind them. They heard Mishima's men setting up the barricades again.

Yamazaki, though not badly injured, was in a state of collapse. The deputy, Colonel Yoshimatsu, vice chief of staff, took over command. He called for orderlies and conferred with his officers.

Then Colonel Hara, watching from the corridor, took the initiative. "What are your demands?" he shouted, staring through the broken window at Mishima, who stood a few feet away from him.

The two men began to shout at each other. Mishima in-

sisted that the Jieitai officers summon a parade in front of
Eastern Army HQ, and Hara said he would do nothing of
the kind. Finally Mishima passed a handwritten note to
Hara, giving his demands in detail. The colonel went to
confer with his senior officer, Colonel Yoshimatsu, in a staff
room close by. The men phoned the Jieitai main headquarters in the Defense Agency a mile away, asking for instructions; they were told to handle the situation as they saw
fit.

In Mashita's office, Mishima forced the pace. He was
behind schedule as a result of the two Jieitai attacks. He had
intended to start his speech at 11:30, after compelling Mashita and his men to summon the garrison to parade in front
of the Eastern Army HQ.

It was already 11:30. Mishima felt a danger that control
of the situation would slip from his hands.

He wiped the sword. Then he walked toward Mashita,
raising the weapon in the air. He held the sword over the
general.

"Take the gag off," he said to one of the students.

"Now listen, General," Mishima began. "I have some
demands to make. If you accept them, I guarantee your
safety. If you do not, I shall kill you and then commit hara-
kiri."

"What is this folly?" Mashita said.

"Read the demands to the general," Mishima ordered.
One of the students took a piece of paper from the attaché
case. It contained a short list of conditions on which Mishima would spare Mashita's life.

"Read!"

All soldiers at the Ichigaya garrison—a thousand men of
the 32nd Infantry Regiment, a signals unit, and the HQ
staff—were to gather in front of the HQ building by midday.

Mishima would make a speech to them from the balcony outside the general's office.

There must be no interruption of the speech. He must
be heard in complete silence.

The Jieitai must summon the forty Tatenokai members

who were waiting at Ichigaya Hall, a Jieitai center just outside the gates of the base. They must be present to hear Mishima's speech.

There would be a period of truce, lasting ninety minutes. During this time the Jieitai must guarantee not to attack Mishima and his group.

At the end of the truce Mishima would hand Mashita over to his own men. If, however, the truce were broken, or it looked as if it might be, Mishima would kill the general and commit suicide.

He wanted instant action.

"This is foolish," Mashita said. "What is there to gain?"

Mishima ignored him. "I will give these demands to your officers. You will order them to obey me," he said.

He wasted no more time on the general. It was late.

Mishima walked over to the broken windows looking out into the corridor beyond.

"Who is in command?" he shouted. "Bring him here."

A soldier rushed off to inform Yoshimatsu. The officer appeared a moment later. "I have taken over, as Yamazaki is injured. What is it?"

The two men faced each other through the broken window. Yoshimatsu saw the sword in Mishima's hand.

"I have made my demands," replied Mishima. "If you do not comply, I will kill the general and commit suicide."

The officer looked through the broken window. On the far side of the room was Mashita, tied to the chair.

"The general orders you to carry out my orders," said Mishima.

Mashita nodded.

"When?" asked Yoshimatsu.

"Now. And hurry!"

It was 11:35.

Yoshimatsu went back to his office. It was decided to call in outside help.

The Eastern Army staff telephoned a police station near the gates of the Ichigaya base. They asked for ambulances as well. They also communicated their decision to the Jieitai headquarters at Roppongi, two miles away. And they decided who should make the announcement to the garrison, summoning the soldiers to parade; they would do this after the police arrived.

Mishima, meanwhile, was relaxing quietly with his men. He had no notion that the police were being summoned.

The students took out a set of hachimaki from the attaché case. The headbands were dyed with red circles—the Rising Sun—and emblazoned in black Chinese ink: *Shichisho Hokoku* ("Serve the Nation for Seven Lives"), a medieval samurai battle slogan.

"Loosen your collars and tie on the hachimaki," Mishima said to the students.

The movements of the men were watched by soldiers posted outside, by the broken window. Mishima did not care. He took a cigarette from a pack he had brought in his case and puffed away cheerfully.

The loudspeaker announcement summoning the garrison to parade would be made at any moment. In the meantime, Mishima and his group had nothing to do but wait.

At 11:38 there was the sound of police sirens. At first it was faint, coming from the main road which ran below the hill at the top of which stood the Eastern Army HQ. The sirens came closer; the cars must be coming up the hill, inside the base.

A cavalcade of vehicles came to a halt in front of the HQ building on the parade ground. Helmeted men in white jumped out of ambulances and ran into the building, under the portico. Armed police accompanied them.

"What a lot of people for the party!" Mishima said.

A moment later an announcement was made on the camp loudspeakers. All troops were to assemble in front of Eastern Army HQ. Men ran to the parade ground from all over the base. In a short time, nearly the whole garrison had assembled.

Within the building, the police were taking charge. Men in dark blue uniforms appeared at the broken window and peered in at Mishima.

"What weapons do they have?" the police wanted to know.

"A sword. Mishima has it. And a dagger—the student next to Mashita has it."

The police calmly accepted the truce.

They posted men on the stairs, in the corridor, and at the doors leading into Mashita's office. They had no thought of using their weapons. Mishima was trapped.

Police cameramen were posted at the broken window; their photos would be useful in court. Mishima and Morita were both in full view.

Reports were made to the Jieitai headquarters at Roppongi and to Metropolitan Police Headquarters at Sakuradamon near the Imperial Palace, also two miles away.

At 11:45 the first helicopters arrived. They flew northward from the direction of the palace. Some were police helicopters and landed on a pad at the back of Eastern Army HQ. Others were newspaper and TV helicopters and circled above the building; they began to film the crowd of soldiers standing around on the parade ground. They filmed the HQ building and the large balcony in front of it and also the ambulances into which injured men were being carried on stretchers.

The Tatenokai party of forty students, however, was not in sight. Their leaders had refused to obey Jieitai orders to assemble on the parade ground at Ichigaya; they had not understood that the orders came from their leader.

Shortly before midday, Morita, a squat figure, appeared on the balcony, followed by Ogawa. The two students came out of one of the windows of Mashita's office and walked toward the front of the balcony carrying papers and cloths in their hands.

The balcony was large. It was thirty feet from the windows of the general's office to the front of the balcony.

The students, with the ends of their hachimaki trailing over their yellow-brown uniforms, came up to the parapet. Leaning over the edge of the balcony, they threw out long cotton streamers, facing the crowd. They fastened the banners to the parapet so that they dangled over the parade ground; on them were written conditions under which General Mashita's safety was guaranteed.

One of the conditions was that Mishima's speech would be heard in silence. However, the noise at that moment was tremendous. Soldiers shouted excitedly at one another. Police bikes, cars, and ambulances were all running their engines on the parade ground. And more cars were arriving all the time, including press vehicles flying company pennants. The helicopters made the most noise as they came in close to film the scene.

The two Tatenokai students were dropping papers over the edge of the balcony on the crowd below. Some of the papers were caught by the light breeze and drifted out over the parade ground.

The papers were copies of Mishima's gekibun, his last manifesto, a document modeled on statements made by rebel army officers in the numerous abortive coup d'états of the 1930's in Japan.

The gekibun read (as I have condensed it from two thousand words):

We, members of the Tatenokai, have been handsomely treated by the Jieitai. Why are we biting the hand that fed us?

It is simply because we revere the Jieitai. The Armed Forces are the soul of Nippon.

We have seen the Jieitai treated like a toy by the nation's leaders. And thus the Jieitai protects the very instrument which denies its right to exist: the Peace Constitution [the Constitution of 1947, drafted by the Allied Powers].

Opportunities to rectify this dreadful error have been missed. On October 21, 1969, the Jieitai should have been mobilized and thrown into the battle against anti-war demonstrators. The Jieitai should then have taken power and demanded revision of the Constitution.

The chance was missed. The honor of the nation is

at stake. The Jieitai is unconstitutional; and no steps are being taken to save it. [Mishima was referring to Article 9 of the Constitution, according to which Japan will "never maintain" Armed Forces.]

Our fundamental values, as Japanese, are threatened. The Emperor is not being given his rightful place in Japan.

We have waited in vain for the Jieitai to rebel. If no action is taken, the Western powers will control Japan for the next century!

The manifesto ended with this appeal:

Let us restore Nippon to its true state and let us die. Will you value only life and let the spirit die? . . . We will show you a value which is greater than respect for life. Not liberty, not democracy. It is Nippon! Nippon, the land of history and tradition. The Japan we love.

The soldiers on the parade ground picked up copies of the gekibun. Some read the document. Others stuffed the papers into their pockets. The men were puzzled. Most of them were young and had had no experience of the war. For twenty-five years Japan had been at peace, and the alliance with America, the cornerstone of Japanese foreign policy, had been challenged only by the left. Nothing in the experience of these young men had prepared them for this assault from the right. Many of them knew of the existence of the Tatenokai, but they had no notion of its purpose. Nor did they understand why Mishima—a famous novelist—had involved himself in this enterprise. Adding to their bafflement was the spectacle of wounded men being carried from the building. Why had Mishima attacked and injured their officers?

At midday precisely, Mishima himself appeared on the balcony. He strode forward to the front of the balcony, a small figure in the yellow-brown uniform of the Tatenokai. The men below saw only his head, with a hachimaki bound around it, the symbol of the Rising Sun in the center of the forehead.

He leapt up onto the parapet. His small, wiry frame came entirely into view. The buttons of his uniform shone brightly in the November sun. He wore white gloves on which bloodstains were visible.

He braced himself, shoulders back, his hands on his hips.

3

Tenno Heika Banzai!

"It is a wretched affair," Mishima began, "to have to speak to Jieitai men in circumstances like these."

The helicopters were making a great noise. Many in the crowd could not hear Mishima's words.

"I thought," Mishima continued, "that the Jieitai was the last hope of Nippon, the last stronghold of the Japanese soul."

His words were blotted out by the helicopters.

"But ... ... Japanese people today think of money, just money. Where is our national spirit today? The politicians care nothing for Japan. They are greedy for power.

"The Jieitai," Mishima continued, "must be the soul of Nippon. The soldiers! The army!

"But ... ... we were betrayed by the Jieitai!"

There were shouts from the crowd.

"Cut it out now!"

"Bakayaro!" (An untranslatable swear word.)

"Arse-hole!"

Mishima grew excited. "Listen! Listen! Hear me out! Listen! Listen! Listen to me!"

He resumed. "We thought that the Jieitai was the soul of national honor!"

There were shouts.

"Come down from there!"

"We don't agree with you!"

Mishima went on. "The nation has no spiritual foundation. That is why you don't agree with me! You don't understand Japan. The Jieitai must put things right!"

There was violent hooting.

"Listen!" shouted Mishima. "Be quiet, will you! Listen!"

"Bakayaro!"

Mishima tried to go on.

"Kiss your arse," shouted a soldier below.

"Don't you hear!" Mishima shouted back. "I ask you to be quiet! Listen! Hear me out!"

"Stop playing the hero!" another heckler shouted.

"Just listen to me!" Mishima hurled back. "What happened last year? On October 21? There was a demonstration, an anti-war demonstration. On October 21 last year. In Shinjuku. And the police put it down. The police! After that there was, and there will be, no chance to amend the Constitution."

"So what?"

"So the Jiminto [the Liberal Democratic Party], the politicians, decided that they could just use the police. The police would deal with the demonstrations. Don't you see?"

"Hooray. Call the police. Dial 110, somebody!"

Mishima fought on. "Look! The government did not use the Jieitai. The Armed Forces stayed in their barracks. The Constitution is fixed forever. There will be no chance to amend it. Do you understand?"

"No, no. Absolutely not!"

"No, we don't follow you."

"No!"

"All right," Mishima said. "Listen! Since last October 21, since that time, it is you who protect the Constitution. The Jieitai defends the Constitution. There will be no chance to amend it. Not for twenty years! The Jieitai waited for that chance, with tears in their eyes. Too late!"

"Japan is at peace!"

Mishima looked at his watch. He had been speaking for less than five minutes.

"Why don't you understand? Think about October 21 last year! Since that time I have waited for the Jieitai to act! When would the Jieitai come to its senses? I waited. There will be no further chance to revise the Constitution! The Jieitai will never become an army! It has no foundation, no center!

"The Jieitai must rise. Why?" he went on.

"Come down! Come down!"

"To protect Japan! You must protect Japan! To protect Japan! Yes, to protect Japan! Japanese tradition! Our history! Our culture! The Emperor!"

His audience exploded with shouts and jeers.

"Listen! Listen! Listen! Listen!

"A man appeals to you! A man! I am staking my life on this! Do you hear? Do you follow me? If you do not rise with me, if the Jieitai will not rise, the Constitution will never be amended!" He paused. "You will be just American mercenaries. American troops!"

"Bakayaro!"

"Stop talking!"

"Come down!"

Mishima could scarcely make himself heard above the din.

"I have waited for four years! Yes, four years! I wanted the Jieitai to rise! Four years!

"I have come to the last thirty minutes," he said. "Yes, the last thirty minutes. I am waiting. I want . . ."

His words were lost in the noise of helicopter engines.

"Are you bushi? Are you men? You *are* soldiers! Then why do you stand by the Constitution? You back the Constitution that denies your very existence!"

There were mock cries of alarm from the crowd.

"Then you have no future!" roared Mishima. "You will never be saved! It is the end. The Constitution will remain forever. You are finished!"

He hammered the point. "You are unconstitutional! Listen! You are unconstitutional! The Jieitai is unconstitutional! You are all unconstitutional!"

There was no reaction from the crowd.

"Don't you understand? Don't you see what is happening? Don't you understand that it is you who defend the Constitution? Why not? Why don't you understand? I have been waiting for you. Why don't you wake up? There you are in your tiny world. You do nothing for Nippon!"

"Is that why you injured our men?"

"They put up a resistance."

"Don't be stupid! What do you mean, 'resistance'?"

Once more Mishima appealed to the men. "Will any of you rise with me?" He waited ten seconds.

"Bakayaro!"

"Who would rise with *you*?"

"Madman!"

"No one?" Mishima asked.

"Are *you* a man?"

"You say that! Have you studied Bu [the warrior ethic]? Do you understand the way of the sword? What does the sword mean to a Japanese? . . . I ask you. Are *you* men? Are you bushi?"

Mishima's voice grew calmer. "I see that you are not. You will not rise. You will do nothing. The Constitution means nothing to you. You are not interested.

"I have lost my dream of the Jieitai!" he added.

"Come down!"

"Drag him down from there!"

"Why does no one stop him?"

"Bakayaro!"

Most of the crowd looked on in silence as the sporadic heckling continued.

"I salute the Emperor!" cried Mishima.

"Tenno Heika Banzai! Tenno Heika Banzai! Tenno Heika Banzai!"

As he shouted this traditional salute ("Long live the Emperor! Long live the Emperor! Long live the Emperor!"), Morita, who had been standing behind him—only

his head visible to the men below—joined in. The two Tatenokai leaders raised their hands thrice as they shouted.

"Shoot him!"

"SHOOT HIM!"

Mishima jumped down from the parapet onto the balcony behind it. With Morita at his heels, he retraced his
steps to the general's office. He stooped at the low window
and went down into the room beyond, out of sight of the TV
cameras. Then Morita, too, disappeared. The window was
closed.

4

Hara-kiri

Mishima came down a little flight of red-carpeted stairs that
led back into the general's office.

"They did not hear me very well," he remarked to the
students.

Morita followed him into the room.

Mishima started to undo the buttons of his jacket. He
was in a part of the room, close to the door into the chief of
staff's office, from which he could not be seen through the
broken window by the men in the corridor.

The general's gag had been removed. He watched as
Mishima stripped off his jacket. Mishima was naked to the
waist; he wore no undershirt.

"Stop!" cried Mashita. "This serves no purpose."

"I was bound to do this," Mishima replied. "You must
not follow my example. You are not to take responsibility for
this."

"Stop!" ordered Mashita.

Mishima paid no heed. He unlaced his boots, throwing
them to one side. Morita came forward and picked up the
sword.

"Stop!"

Mishima slipped his wristwatch from his hand and passed it to a student. He knelt on the red carpet, six feet from Mashita's chair. He loosened his trousers, slipping them down his legs. The white fundoshi (loincloth) underneath was visible. Mishima was almost naked. His small, powerful chest heaved.

Morita took up a position behind him with the sword.

Mishima took a yoroidoshi, a foot-long, straight-blade dagger with a sharp point, in his right hand.

Ogawa came forward with a mohitsu (brush) and a piece of paper. Mishima had planned to write a last message in his own blood.

"No, I don't need that," Mishima said. He rubbed a spot on his lower left abdomen with his left hand. Then he pricked the knife in his right hand against the spot.

Morita raised the sword high in the air, staring down at Mishima's neck. The student's forehead was beaded with perspiration. The end of the sword waggled, his hands shook.

Mishima shouted a last salute to the Emperor. *"Tenno Heika Banzai! Tenno Heika Banzai! Tenno Heika Banzai!"*

He hunched his shoulders and expelled the air from his chest. His back muscles bunched. Then he breathed in once more, deeply.

"Haa . . . ow!" Mishima drove all the air from his body with a last, wild shout.

He forced the dagger into his body with all his strength. Following the blow, his face went white and his right hand started to tremble. Mishima hunched his back, beginning to make a horizontal cut across his stomach. As he pulled at the knife, his body sought to drive the blade outward; the hand holding the dagger shook violently. He brought his left hand across, pressing down mightily on his right. The knife remained in the wound, and he continued cutting crosswise. Blood spurted from the cut and ran down his stomach into his lap, staining the fundoshi a bright red.

With a final effort Mishima completed the crosscut, his head down, his neck exposed.

Morita was ready to strike with the sword and cut off the head of his leader. "Do not leave me in agony too long," Mishima had said to him.

Morita clenched his wrists on the hilt of the sword. As he watched, Mishima toppled forward on his face onto the red carpet.

Morita brought the sword crashing down. Too late. The force of the blow was great, but the sword smacked into the red carpet on the far side of Mishima. He received a deep cut in the back and shoulders.

"Again!" the other students called out.

Mishima lay groaning on the carpet, smothered in his own blood and twisting from side to side. Intestines slid from his belly.

Morita struck once again. Once more his aim failed. He hit Mishima's body, not the neck. The wound was a terrible one.

"Once more!"

Morita had little strength left in his hands. He lifted the glittering sword for the third time and struck with all his might at Mishima's head and neck. The blow almost severed the neck. Mishima's head cocked at an angle to his body; blood fountained from his neck.

Furu-Koga came forward. He had experience in kendo, in Japanese fencing.

"Give me the sword!" he said to Morita.

With a single chop he separated body and head.

The students knelt.

"Pray for him," Mashita said, leaning forward as best he could, to bow his head.

The students silently said a Buddhist prayer.

The only sound in the room was the sobbing of the young men. Tears ran down their cheeks. There was a bubbling from the corpse; blood pumped from the neck, covering the red carpet.

A raw stench filled the room. Mishima's entrails had spilled onto the carpet.

Mashita lifted his head. The students had not finished. Morita was ripping off his jacket. Another student took from the hand of Mishima, which still twitched in a pool of blood, the yoroidoshi dagger with which he had disemboweled himself. He passed the weapon to Morita.

Morita knelt, loosened his trousers, and shouted a final salute, as Mishima had done: *"Tenno Heika Banzai! Tenno Heika Banzai! Tenno Heika Banzai!"*

Morita tried without success to drive the dagger into his stomach. He was not strong enough. He made a shallow scratch across his belly.

Furu-Koga stood behind him, holding the sword high in the air.

"Right!" said Morita.

With a sweep of the sword Furu-Koga severed Morita's head, which rolled across the carpet. Blood spurted rhythmically from the severed neck, where the body had slumped forward.

The students prayed, sobbing.

Mashita watched. "This is the end!" he exclaimed.

"Don't worry," one of the students said. "He told us not to kill ourselves. We have to hand you over safely. Those were his orders."

"You must stop," Mashita cried. "You must stop."

The students unbound Mashita. He rose to his feet, massaging his wrists. On one hand he had a deep cut. Otherwise, he had been uninjured in the scuffle.

"Make the bodies decent," he ordered the students.

They took up the men's jackets and spread them over the bodies, covering the torsos. They lined up the two corpses on the floor, feet pointing toward the main door of the office.

Then they took up the heads and placed them, neck down, on the blood-soaked carpet. The headbands were still in place.

The students prayed for a third time, before the two heads.

Then they rose to their feet and walked toward the main entrance. They dismantled the barrier and pulled open the door.

The students stood there, looking out. The police looked back. The yellow uniforms of the youths were lightly spotted with blood, their cheeks tear-stained.

No one moved.

An officer rushed to Mashita. "Are you all right, sir?"

The general nodded. But he was on the verge of collapse.

The police still did not move.

"Well," an inspector cried out finally, "arrest them!"

The police doctors went into the room. At 12:23 they confirmed that Mishima and Morita had died by hara-kiri and beheading.

An announcement was made downstairs to the press. A crowd of about fifty reporters and TV cameramen were standing together in a small room; I was the only foreigner among them.

A Jieitai officer stood on a low rostrum at the front of the room. "They are dead, Mishima and one other," he announced.

"What do you mean, 'dead'?"

"Their heads are off, yes, off, their heads are off, off, I tell you, off."

5

"Out of His Mind"

The first reaction to Mishima's action was complete incredulity. There had been no case of ritual hara-kiri in Japan since immediately after the war; most Japanese had assumed, if they ever thought about it, that the practice was extinct. And Mishima had been one of the best-known men in the country.

The police were very confused. Officers at the Metropolitan Police Headquarters in Tokyo did not believe the first reports. A senior officer was dispatched with the orders "If the body is still warm, do your utmost to save his life."

The Japanese press were also at a loss. A reporter for the *Mainichi Shimbun*, a leading daily paper, phoned in his story from Ichigaya, just in time for a late afternoon edition. "Go back and check your facts," the desk editor who took the call instructed him; and he drafted the headline INJURED MISHIMA RUSHED TO HOSPITAL.

At his home in the suburbs Azusa Hiraoka, Mishima's father, had been having a quiet smoke and watching television when the first report of the "Mishima Incident" flashed on the screen.

"Yukio Mishima . . . made an attack on the Jieitai camp at Ichigaya."

Azusa's thought was: "Now I will have to go and apologize to the police and everyone else involved. What a bother!"

The next line read: "Kappuku" (cut his stomach). Azusa worried that his son's right hand might have been injured too. Modern surgery would take care of him otherwise.

The next announcement was: "Kaishaku" (beheaded).

"I was not particularly surprised," Azusa said later. "My brain rejected the information."

The first official comment on the affair was made by Prime Minister Eisaku Sato.

Sato, a stocky, handsome figure in a morning coat, emerged from the Diet, the parliament. He had been making a speech at the opening of the autumn session, in the presence of the Emperor. Sato had known Mishima personally and had helped him, indirectly, to have his Tatenokai trained by the Jieitai.

Reporters gathered round the Prime Minister. "Would you comment on the Mishima Incident, Prime Minister?"

"He must have been kichigai, out of his mind," Sato

said. And he got into his big, black President car and was driven away to his office.

Shortly afterward the police announced the results of the autopsies on the bodies of Mishima and Morita. Mishima had a cut five inches long in his lower abdomen; in places, the wound was as deep as two inches. Morita had only a light scratch across his stomach; he had not had the great strength required to drive a dagger into his body.

What had led the two men to commit hara-kiri? The answer was not as simple as the Prime Minister had suggested.

TWO

Early Life

(1925–39)

But my heart's leaning was for Death and Night and Blood.
Yukio Mishima, *Confessions of a Mask*

1
The Chrysanthemum and the Sword

One of the last remarks made to me by Mishima was that it was virtually impossible for a non-Japanese person to understand Japan. We in the West, he went on, consistently underrated the importance of the "dark" side of Japanese culture and chose instead to concentrate on the "soft" element in the Japanese tradition. This was a theme which we had discussed from the beginning of our friendship; Mishima had illustrated his point then by saying that there was too much emphasis in Japan itself on "the chrysanthemum" (the arts) and an insufficient understanding of "the sword" (the martial tradition). And in this context he had referred approvingly to the work of the American sociologist Ruth Benedict, *The Chrysanthemum and the Sword*, a book known to all non-Japanese interested in the culture of Japan. Many times he would insist on the duality of the Japanese tradition, and he praised Benedict for having understood the nature of this duality.

I accept Mishima's point. Before and during the Second World War, Western commentary on Japan was almost exclusively preoccupied with the martial aspect of the Japanese tradition; it was said that the Japanese were soldiers at heart—ruthless, barbaric men who would not hesitate to commit the gravest atrocity as at the "rape of Nanking" in 1937. After the war, Western scholars changed their thinking, and most writing about Japan since 1950 has dwelt upon the Japanese aesthetic. Writers on a variety of subjects—the classical literature of Japan, Zen Buddhism, the tea ceremony—have delineated the Japanese sense of beauty. Neither school of thought gives a complete picture of Japan, however; the Japanese, as Mishima insisted, have a dual tradition of the literary and the martial arts.

Nonetheless, I see Mishima as a writer and not as a soldier. If one wants to understand the man, one must study his aesthetic; his exploits in the field of military endeavor are intriguing and reveal that he had *something* of the soldier in him; but he devoted almost all his adult life to writing, not to the Jieitai and the Tatenokai. My purpose here is to explain Mishima's idea of beauty, which he developed during his adolescence.

My study of Mishima's early life relies heavily on a single source, his autobiographical masterpiece, *Confessions of a Mask* (published by New Directions in 1958 in a translation by Meredith Weatherby). This novel is, I think, the best of Mishima's many works. It also reveals more of his character and of his upbringing than anything else he wrote: it gives a crystalline account of his aesthetic. *Confessions of a Mask* describes the genesis of a romantic idea which impinges directly on his eventual decision to commit suicide: the notion that violent death is ultimate beauty, provided that he who dies is young. This is a particularly Japanese idea and recurs often in the classical literature; for example, in the ancient chronicles, the eighth-century *Nihonshoki* and *Kojiki,* and in the monumental eleventh-century novel *The Tale of Genji.* Mishima, however, gave a romantic twist to the classical tradition; he had as much in common with contemporary culture in the West—for example, the cult of violence in Western rock songs and in films—as with classical Japan. One of the most striking features of his early life was the influence upon him of Western literature, from the fairy tales of Hans Christian Andersen to the novels of Raymond Radiguet and the plays of Oscar Wilde. Mishima knew a great deal more about Western culture than his contemporaries in Japan; that is one reason he could make friends with foreigners so easily.

2
Birth

Yukio Mishima was born Kimitake Hiraoka on January 14, 1925, in the Tokyo home of his grandparents, Jotaro and Natsuko Hiraoka, with whom his parents lived. The Hiraokas were an upper-middle-class family—Jotaro had been a senior civil servant, and his only child, Azusa, Mishima's father, was also a government official; and in Japan, which has a Confucian tradition, government service is considered the most honorable employment. The high social standing of the Hiraokas had been underwritten by Jotaro's marriage to Natsuko, who came from an old family; Kimitake's grandfather was the son of a farmer, but his humble origin had not counted against him in the late nineteenth century, when there had been great social mobility following the Meiji Restoration of 1868. The Meiji Restoration, in which Japan opened her doors to the West (as the cliché has it), had ushered in a period of social instability and great commercial and industrial progress. In this new era, men of ability had been promoted regardless of birth, and Jotaro had attained a high rank, serving as a provincial governor in Japan and as the first civilian governor of Karafuto (Sakhalin), the island to the north of Japan which has since reverted to the Soviet Union.

THE HIRAOKA FAMILY

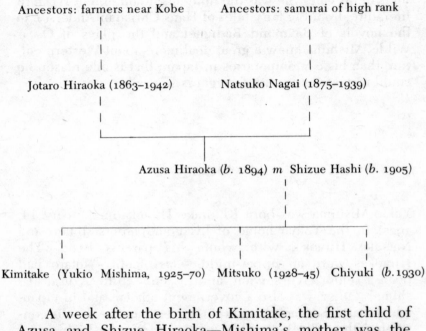

Ancestors: farmers near Kobe   Ancestors: samurai of high rank

Jotaro Hiraoka (1863–1942)   Natsuko Nagai (1875–1939)

Azusa Hiraoka (*b.* 1894) *m* Shizue Hashi (*b.* 1905)

Kimitake (Yukio Mishima, 1925–70)   Mitsuko (1928–45)   Chiyuki (*b.*1930)

A week after the birth of Kimitake, the first child of
Azusa and Shizue Hiraoka—Mishima's mother was the
twenty-year-old daughter of a Tokyo school principal—the
family held the traditional naming ceremony, the Oshichiya.
"On the evening of the seventh day," Mishima recorded in
Confessions of a Mask, "the infant was clothed in undergar-
ments of flannel and cream-colored silk and a kimono of silk
crepe with a splashed pattern. In the presence of the assembled household my grandfather drew my name on a
strip of ceremonial paper and placed it on an offertory stand
in the tokonoma." (The tokonoma is the alcove in the traditional Japanese room and is reserved for precious objects.)
Almost all of Mishima's childhood memories, however,
were unhappy. He did not like the house where he was
born, which was in the Yotsuya district of Tokyo: "There
were two stories on the upper slope and three on the lower,

numerous gloomy rooms and six housemaids." He blamed his grandfather. Jotaro had resigned from his post as governor of Karafuto, taking responsibility for a scandal in the administration, and "thereafter my family had begun sliding down an incline with a speed so happy-go-lucky that I could almost say that they hummed merrily as they went—huge debts, foreclosure, sale of the family estate, and then, as financial difficulties multiplied, a morbid vanity blazing higher and higher like some evil impulse."

Mishima's grandfather attempted to be a businessman after his return to Japan, but he was not successful; he was obliged to sell his ancestral estates at Shikata, near Kobe, where his forefathers had farmed since the seventeenth century. By the time of Mishima's birth in 1925, the Hiraokas had been reduced to living "in not too good a part of Tokyo, in an old rented house." Mishima described this residence, which no longer stands, as "a pretentious house on a corner, with a rather jumbled appearance and a dingy, charred feeling. It had an imposing iron gate, an entry garden, and a Western-style reception room as large as the interior of a suburban church."

Mishima was undoubtedly gloomy about his childhood. The causes of his unhappiness were not limited to Jotaro's failures and the decline in the Hiraoka fortunes. The fundamental problem was the tension in the family home, which is to be attributed to Natsuko, Mishima's grandmother; she "hated and scorned my grandfather. Hers was a narrow-minded, indomitable and rather wildly poetic spirit." Natsuko was much the strongest personality in the Hiraoka family and she overrode not only Jotaro but her son Azusa. Her hate of her husband was generated by scorn for his lack of pride; he lacked the samurai spirit of her ancestors; he was a jolly man with a frivolous streak, which Mishima inherited. Natsuko had a second reason for detesting Mishima's grandfather: "A chronic case of cranial neuralgia was indirectly but steadily gnawing away her nerves and at the same time adding an unavailing sharpness to her intellect. Who knows but what those fits of depression she

continued having until her death were a memento of vices
in which my grandfather had indulged in his prime?" Natsuko, according to Takeo Okuno, a Japanese biographer of
Mishima, had contracted syphilis from Jotaro; her brain was
affected by the disease. The unfortunate woman also had a
gouty hip and had to use a stick to walk.

The birth of Kimitake galvanized Natsuko. Disappointed by the commonplace success of her son—Mishima's
father had obtained a post in the Ministry of Agriculture and
Forestry and was nothing more than a highly competent
civil servant—she pinned all her hopes on her first grandson. She resolved to take personal responsibility for his upbringing and virtually kidnapped the little boy from his
mother: "My parents lived on the second floor of the house.
On the pretext that it was dangerous to bring up a child on
an upper floor, my grandmother snatched me from my
mother's arms on my forty-ninth day." In a traditional Japanese family, a mother-in-law had powers of life and death
over her son's wife; and Shizue, only twenty years of age
and frail in health, could not rescue the baby, whose bed
was placed in his grandmother's sickroom, "perpetually
closed and stifling with odors of sickness and old age, and I
was reared there beside her sickbed." A nursemaid changed
his linen and saw to his needs during the night.

Shizue's position had not been entirely usurped. She
still fed the child, but Natsuko kept her in her place, as
Mishima's mother recalled after his death (in *Segare Mishima Yukio*, "My Son Yukio Mishima," a memoir by his
parents published in *Shokun* magazine in 1972). "We lived
upstairs, while Mother [Natsuko] kept Kimitake with her all
the time, ringing an alarm every four hours, loud enough for
me to hear upstairs. Kimitake's feeding times had to be precisely every four hours; and the duration of the feeding sessions was exactly fixed in advance." Then Shizue was sent
upstairs again. This situation existed for a year and her
hopes of winning back the child were dashed when an accident of precisely the kind her mother-in-law had predicted
actually happened.

"One day," according to Shizue, "Mother was out at the Kabuki and Kimitake fell down the stairs, banging his head and losing a good deal of blood. We took him to the hospital and called Mother on the telephone. When she returned home, she shouted out: 'Is he past help?' Still to this day I cannot forget the terrifying look on her face." Mishima describes the scene only a little differently in *Confessions of a Mask:*

"When she arrived my grandfather went out to meet her. She stood in the hallway without taking her shoes off, leaning on the cane she carried in her right hand, and stared fixedly at my grandfather. When she spoke it was in a strangely calm tone of voice, as though carving out each word:

" 'Is he dead?'

" 'No.'

"Then, taking off her shoes and stepping up from the hallway, she walked down the corridor with steps as confident as those of a priestess . . ."

Natsuko had occult powers and thereafter she frustrated all Shizue's plans for regaining possession of her child. Curiously, she brought up Kimitake as a little girl, not as a boy. He was always attended by a nursemaid, although this annoyed him greatly; he was not allowed to run about in the house, but he was forbidden to go out; and he must stay on the ground floor all the time, usually with his grandmother or the maid. He was not permitted to play as he wanted. "Kimitake liked to brandish rulers and other long things [as we read in his mother's account], but Mother always confiscated these on the grounds that they were dangerous. Kimitake would obey her meekly. I felt so sorry for him."

These restrictions were imposed for Natsuko's sake: "Mother's hip made her very nervous of sounds, especially when the pain started. Toys like cars, guns which clicked metallically, and so on, were all banned." But she countered with hostility any threat to her control of the child: "When it was bright outside, I would try to take him out. But it was always in vain. Mother would wake up like a bolt and forbid it. So Kimitake was kept inside in her dark, gloomy room, full of sickness and ill health."

In February 1928, Mishima's mother had a second child, a girl whom they named Mitsuko. Natsuko made no attempt to take over the girl and it was nonsensical that one child should be confined to the ground floor and the other to the second floor; that, however, is what happened.

If Shizue had hopes of recovering Kimitake, they were destroyed by the onset of a grave illness. On New Year's Day 1929 the little boy had a sudden collapse. According to his mother, "Kimitake became ill with 'auto-intoxication' [jikachudoku] . . . The illness was critical and all our relatives gathered at the house. I put together his toys and clothing, ready to go into the coffin. My brother, a doctor at Chiba Medical University, came in at that moment; and he suddenly exclaimed: 'Look! He's urinating; maybe he'll be all right.' And after a while he urinated a lot more and my brother said: 'He will live now.' " "Auto-intoxication" is not a Western term, only a direct translation of "jikachudoku." Kimitake's symptoms and treatment were these: "I vomited something the color of coffee. The family doctor was called. After examining me he said that he was not sure I would recover. I was given injections of camphor and glucose until I was like a pincushion. The pulses of both my wrist and my upper arm became imperceptible." According to a Japanese pediatrician, Dr. Kiyoshi Nakamura, "the illness is usually found in children who are sensitive, intelligent, and over-protected, who have been trained by their mothers to be 'good' boys or girls." The cause of Kimitake's illness is unknown, but my guess is that Natsuko, who had a violent temper, was responsible for the attacks, which the child suffered thereafter at regular intervals.

He grew into an unusually delicate child, as one may see from a photograph of him in the summer of 1929. Kimitake has been taken for a rare treat, an outing to a park. He is seated on a donkey and appears strangely absent, and collapsed, like a balloon running out of air; he lolls forward, dressed in a sailor suit, his chin on his chest. The child looks as if he will topple off his perch any second.

3

Fairy Tales and Fantasies

Mishima described how his illness "struck about once a month, now lightly, now seriously." There were many crises. "By the sound of the disease's footsteps as it drew near I came to be able to sense whether an attack was likely to approach death or not." Natsuko rarely allowed him out of the house; and his brief encounters with the world beyond the iron gates of the Hiraoka home assumed great importance. The tiny, pale boy was preternaturally sensitive and he endowed anyone he met, however briefly, with significance. "My earliest memory, an unquestionable one, haunting me with a strangely vivid image, dates from about that time [when he was four] . . . It was a young man who was coming down toward us, with handsome, ruddy cheeks and shining eyes, wearing a dirty roll of cloth around his head for a sweatband. He came down the slope carrying a yoke of night-soil buckets over one shoulder . . . He was a night-soil man, a ladler of excrement. He was dressed as a laborer, wearing split-toed shoes with rubber soles and black canvas tops, and dark-blue cotton trousers of the close-fitting kind called 'thigh-pullers' . . . The close-fitting jeans plainly outlined the lower half of his body, which moved lithely and seemed to be walking directly toward me. An inexpressible adoration for those trousers was born in me . . . His occupation gave me the feeling of 'tragedy' in the most sensuous meaning of the word."

The tragedy was Kimitake's. He was eternally excluded from the lives of ordinary men and women—for example, the drivers of hanadensha (trams decorated with flowers) and the ticket collectors with rows of gold buttons on their tunics, whom he saw on his rare excursions. His grief for the night-soil man was, in reality, profound concern about himself. "The so-called 'tragic things' of which I was becoming aware were probably only shadows cast by a flashing presentiment of grief still greater in the future, of a lonelier exclusion still to come." Later in life, Mishima was to struggle against his alienation; he would identify with ordinary Japanese men—taxi drivers, bartenders, soldiers. But he could not escape his upbringing; as a Japanese proverb has it: "A man's character is determined by the age of three." Mishima was brought up with a false impression of Japanese society; being much influenced by Natsuko's talk of her "old family" and by the snobbishness of other members of the household, he did not know how egalitarian Japan was. He had a picture of Japanese society in which families such as the Matsudairas, from which Natsuko's mother was descended, and the Tokugawas, who had ruled Japan for 250 years, were pinnacles surrounding the Emperor, the highest being.

Another of Mishima's early memories was of a picture book: "I had several picture books about that time, but my fancy was captured, completely and exclusively, only by this one—and only by one riveting picture in it." This was an illustration which he gazed on for hours and which he felt he ought not to adore. "The picture showed a knight mounted on a white horse, holding a sword aloft . . . There was a beautiful coat of arms on the silver armor the knight was wearing. The knight's beautiful face peeped through the visor, and he brandished his drawn sword awesomely in the blue sky, confronting either Death or, at the very least, some hurtling object full of evil power. I believed he would be killed the next instant." The thought of the imminent death of the beautiful knight captivated the child. Great was his disillusionment when the nursemaid told him the knight was a woman—Joan of Arc. "I felt as though I had been knocked flat. The person I had thought was a *he* was a *she*. If this beautiful knight was a woman and not a man, what was there left?" He had to be a man or his death could not be moving; he quoted Oscar Wilde to make his point:

> Fair is the knight who lieth slain
> Amid the rush and reed . . .

Mishima was fascinated by death. "Yet another memory: it is the odor of sweat, an odor that drove me onward, awakened my longings, overpowered me . . . It was the troops passing our gate as they returned from drill . . . The soldiers' odor of sweat—that odor like a sea breeze, like the air, burned to gold, above the seashore—struck my nostrils and intoxicated me." He was not at an age when the odor of sweat had a sexual quality. "But it did gradually and tenaciously arouse within me a sensuous craving for such things as the destiny of soldiers, the tragic nature of their calling . . . the ways they would die . . ." Mishima attached great importance to his odd images that stood before him from the beginning "in truly masterful completeness." There was not a single thing lacking. "In later years I sought in them for the wellsprings of my own feelings and action."

The beauty of the violent or excruciatingly painful death of a handsome youth was to be a theme of many of his novels, from *Chusei* ("The Middle Ages," 1946) to *Spring Snow* (1969). Mishima thought the more violent, the more agonizing a death, the more beautiful it was; he made a cult of a Christian martyr, St. Sebastian, and he invested the ancient samurai rite of disembowelment, hara-kiri, with supreme beauty. A plain youth, Isao, the protagonist of *Runaway Horses* (1969), qualified as a hero by committing hara-kiri.

As a child, Mishima felt the desire to play-act. The period of childhood was for him "a stage on which time and space become entangled . . . I could not believe that the world was any more complicated than a structure of building blocks, nor that the so-called 'social community,' which I must presently enter, could be more dazzling than the world of fairy tales . . . Thus, without my being aware of it, one of the determinants of my life had come into operation.

And because of my struggles against it, from the beginning my every fantasy was tinged with despair." He had a fantasy of Night in which he saw "a shining city floating upon the darkness that surrounded me . . . I could plainly see a mystic brand that had been impressed upon the faces of the people in that city . . . If I could but touch their faces, I might discover the color of the pigments with which the city of night had painted them." Then a female magician, whom Mishima had seen on the stage, appeared before his eyes: "Presently Night raised a curtain directly before my eyes, revealing the stage on which Shokyokusai Tenkatsu performed her magic feats." He was fascinated by this woman who "lounged indolently about the stage, her opulent body veiled in garments like those of the Great Harlot of the Apocalypse."

The little boy decided to dress up as Tenkatsu. "From among my mother's kimonos I dragged out the most gorgeous one, the one with the strongest colors. For a sash I chose an obi on which scarlet roses were painted in oil, and wrapped it round and round my waist . . . I stuck a hand mirror in my sash and powdered my face lightly." Thus attired, the child rushed into his grandmother's sickroom; she was receiving a visitor, and his mother was also there. Running about the room, he shouted at the top of his voice: "I'm Tenkatsu." "My frenzy," Mishima said, "was focused upon the consciousness that, through my impersonation, Tenkatsu was being revealed to many eyes. In short, I could see nothing but myself." For a moment the child's eyes met those of his mother; she had lowered her head and was pale. Tears blurred the little boy's eyes. "Was the moment teaching me how grotesque my isolation would appear to the eyes of love, and at the same time was I learning, conversely, my own incapacity for accepting love?" Mishima's passion for dressing up continued until he was about nine. Once, with his younger brother and sister as accomplices (Chiyuki, the younger brother, was born in 1930), he dressed up as Cleopatra; he had seen the Queen of Egypt on the stage, making her entry into Rome, "her half-naked, amber-colored body coming into view from beneath a Persian rug."

Mishima learned to read when he was five. He read every fairy story he could lay his hands on, but he "never liked the princesses." He was fond only of the princes. "I was all the fonder of princes murdered or princes fated for death. I was completely in love with any youth who was killed." He read works by Japanese authors such as Mimei Ogawa, and also the tales of Hans Christian Andersen. "Only his 'Rose-Elf' threw deep shadows over my heart, only that beautiful youth who, while kissing the rose given him as a token by his sweetheart, was stabbed to death and decapitated by a villain with a big knife . . . My heart's leaning was for Death and Night and Blood." (This sentence sums up Mishima's aesthetic.) He was also fascinated by a Hungarian fairy tale in which a prince, clad in tights and a rose-colored tunic, was torn to pieces by a dragon, miraculously revived, "caught by a great spider and, after his body had been shot full of poison, eaten ravenously"; the prince was once more brought back from the dead, only to be "flung bodily into a pit completely lined with there is no saying how many great knives." Mishima also imagined himself dying in battle—here were shades of the fantasy which led him to his own death—or being murdered. "And yet I had an abnormally strong fear of death . . . One day I would bully a maid to tears, and the next morning I would see her serving breakfast with a cheerfully smiling face . . . Then I would read all manner of evil meanings into her smiles . . . I was sure she was plotting to poison me out of revenge. Waves of fear billowed up in my breast. I was positive the poison had been put in my bowl of broth."

All his life, Mishima was worried about being poisoned. A friend who was with him in Bangkok in 1967 told me that he was forever on the lookout for danger. "He would never eat anything more than an omelette in the local restaurants. No Thai food. And he brushed his teeth with soda water in the hotel. Vigorously." His grandmother, who put him on a strict diet after his illness, may have created his phobia about poisoning: "Of fish, I was allowed only such white-flesh kinds as halibut, turbot, or red snapper; of potatoes, only those mashed and strained through a colander; of sweets, all bean-jams were forbidden and there were only light biscuits, wafers, and other such dry confections; and of fruit, only apples cut in thin slices, or small portions of mandarin oranges." His mother, Shizue, has described Natsuko's strict rules:

"When he was about five or six, I was allowed to take him out of doors, but only if there was no wind. This was a concession won by my husband, who had great arguments with her about the matter on a number of occasions.

"Mother arranged for a group of three girls to come to the house to play with Kimitake. They were ushered into her room and were allowed to play only such games as ma-magoto (house), origami (folding paper), and tsumiki (blocks).

"I almost gave up everything in the end and would read to him and draw pictures. That is how he became interested in drawing . . . and he started to write, too, at the age of five, much to our surprise."

Mishima says in *Confessions of a Mask* that "the slightest noise affected my grandmother's neuralgia—the violent opening or closing of a door, a toy bugle, wrestling, or any conspicuous sound or vibration whatever—and our playing had to be quieter than is usual even among girls." No wonder the boy took refuge in his fairy tales and preferred to be by himself reading a book or playing with his building blocks or "indulging in my willful fancies or drawing pictures." Shizue thought him a little odd: "We brought him a small record player and he put on the same tune over and over again for two hours." But Kimitake may just have been unmusical. Certainly Natsuko must have been out on the day the child received the record player; she would never have tolerated the noise. Kimitake had learned by this time to obey her in every detail. A photograph taken in the summer of 1930, when he was five, shows the boy standing with a small cart while Natsuko looms above him, her hand on his shoulder. The grandmother has a somber expression, no doubt her illness was severe; she has a strong jaw and powerful eyes—it is a frightening face. But little Kimitake stands there grinning, his eyes sparkling, seemingly at ease with her. His sister and brother were not given over to his grandmother's care and were reared with the freedom befitting children. "And yet I did not greatly envy them their liberty and rowdiness."

In the early spring of 1931, when the boy was six and was about to start school, he went on a visit to his cousins' house. They were two little girls and Natsuko allowed him to play freely with them. "I had many times more freedom at the house of Sugiko [his cousin] than at my own. As the imaginary enemies who must want to steal me away—my parents, in short—were not present, my grandmother had no qualms about giving me more liberty." It was a difficult experience. "Like an invalid taking his first steps during convalescence, I had a feeling of stiffness as though I were acting under the compulsion of some imaginary obligation. I missed my bed of idleness. And in this house it was tacitly required that I act like a boy. The reluctant masquerade had begun." Kimitake proposed that he and his cousins play war, and the trio ran about the garden shouting, "Bang bang," until he escaped into the house and collapsed on the floor. "I was enraptured with the vision of my own form lying there, twisted and fallen. There was an unspeakable delight in having been shot and being on the point of death. It seemed to me that since it was I, even if actually struck by a bullet, there would surely be no pain."

Mishima's comment on this scene is a reflection on his entire life, and on his death. "What people regarded as a pose on my part was actually an expression of my need to assert my own true nature and . . . it was precisely what people regarded as my true self which was a masquerade. It was this unwilling masquerade that made me say: 'Let's play war.'"

4

School and Adolescence

The 1930's was a decade of violence in public affairs in Japan, but the Hiraokas were little affected by the events of these years. Mishima's father continued in his ministry post and received a promotion; and the boy knew little of the upheavals which took place in Tokyo. One morning in 1936, when he was on his way to school, he heard bugles in the far distance—the start of the Ni Ni Roku Incident, the greatest of the numerous coups that shook Japan in the 1930's. The boy remembered that there was snow on the ground—it was in February; and later in life Mishima associated snowy streets with revolution. The Hiraokas, however, were secure in their upper-middle-class existence; life went on as before.

Mishima began school in April 1931, when he entered the Gakushuin, the Peers School. He was still under the control of his grandmother; Natsuko showed no inclination to surrender him to his mother. According to Shizue: "After Kimitake had entered elementary school, I was allowed to take him there myself every day. I was so happy to be with him, picking up acorns in the park and singing songs with him in the park at Yotsuya." She bought him ice cream, to which he was partial; and she induced him to go to the dentist, by offering him ice cream before each visit. Natsuko set the daily program of her grandson; when he came back from school with his mother he had to have his osanji (three o'clock tea) with Natsuko, and he must then do his homework by her bedside. She was particular about being given priority over his mother. "If he called out to me 'Okasama' [Mother] before speaking to her first, addressing her as 'Obasama' [Grandmother], she would be most unpleasant. At other times she would criticize both of us if he showed an inclination to do something with me."

The Gakushuin, a school for the children of the rich and the aristocracy—it was also attended by members of the Imperial family—had a liberal tradition. There was swimming at the beach in the summer, a luxury by the austere standards of prewar schools. But Natsuko would not allow the boy to go on these excursions; he expressed his disappointment in a composition he wrote in 1932:

ENOSHIMA EXCURSION

I did not go on the school outing.

When I woke up that day I thought: "Now everyone must be at Shinjuku Station, on the train."

I easily think of things like that.

I went to my grandmother and my mother. I wanted so much to go. Just at that moment they would all have arrived at Enoshima.

I wanted to go so much because I had never been there.

I was thinking of it from morning until evening.

When I went to bed I had a dream.

I *did* go to Enoshima with everyone else, and I played there very happily. But I could not walk at all. There were rocks.

Then I woke up.

According to his mother, his first school excursion was to Kashima Shrine. "He was so happy that time. He sent a card to Mother, but he rarely sent cards to me." All his life Mishima was to take delight in going to places that he had never visited before; he loved to go to newly opened restaurants, to climb to the top of new skyscrapers in Tokyo—if possible, before anyone else he knew. His childlike enthusiasm, suppressed when he was a child, burst out in later years. When teased about this, he would become angry. "Oh, don't say that!" he would say and turn away.

Life at home was often difficult. The boy, as told in Mishima's autobiographical short story "Isu" ("Chair," 1952), which describes the unhappy home life of a nine-year-old, would run crying to his mother when scolded by his severe grandmother. Ruthless scolding terrified and depressed him; but his grandmother would not let him stay with his parents and would insist that he return to her sickroom. Shizue could hardly bear the situation; on the morning of one such day she drew up her chair to a window on the second floor of the house and looked down at the sickroom where she knew her son must be sitting obediently beside his grandmother's bed. "I saw his small head for a moment while he was waiting for his grandmother and her nurse to return from the lavatory." The boy's attitude was a little different from his mother's: her sympathy for him (he must long to run about and be active like other children) was mistaken in some ways; he liked being with his ill grandmother, who loved him so desperately. He had many of the instincts of a child, "but something within me responded to the darkened room and the sickbed—even now I work at my desk all night long and wake up around noon." As Mishima has it, while his mother was looking down at him and the nurse from the floor above, he was not sad; in fact, he was content. Only sometimes he felt a sudden hatred of the nurse, who "would play obscene jokes on me" (he does not say what these were); it frightened him that his mother might see. "It is hard for me to account for my hatred, for we usually want those close to us to know our pains and sorrows. I tried to hide the pleasure which I took in my pain."

Shizue resolved to take her son back from his grandmother, who was increasingly bedridden; and one day she asked a manservant to smuggle the boy out of Natsuko's room while she was sleeping. It was late December 1934 and there was a cold wind; these were conditions under which the boy was not supposed to go outside, as he was still frail. Shizue took him to a photography studio to have his picture taken. "Afterward her hands were clammy with sweat and she spoke in an unusually pathetic voice. It seemed that she had made a plan to do something and then changed her mind on the way home." A picture taken of the boy at nine shows a little fellow with a shaven head and the look of a wizened old man, prematurely aged; he has a sweet, sad expression.

The following year, the Hiraokas moved. The family split up. Mishima went with his grandparents to one house, and the rest of the family moved into a separate residence a few streets away. The practice in Japan is for grandparents to move out of their children's homes at a certain age; Jotaro and Natsuko were following this tradition, known as inkyo. The time was approaching, however, when Natsuko's health would no longer permit her to care for the boy. Two years later, in March 1937, when he completed the elementary school of the Gakushuin, he rejoined his parents. They had moved to another house closer to the middle school of the Gakushuin, which is in a different part of Tokyo from the elementary school. Natsuko fought to the last. "Day and night my grandmother clasped my photograph to her bosom, weeping, and was instantly seized with a paroxysm if I violated the treaty stipulation that I should come to spend one night each week with her. At the age of twelve I had a true-love sweetheart aged sixty."

After moving away from his grandmother, the boy honored the arrangement that he come and stay with her once a week; he was also taken out on outings by her. Natsuko invited him to accompany her to the theater, and for the first time he went to the Kabuki, where he saw *Chushingura*, the story of the Forty-seven Ronin who committed hara-kiri in 1704. They also went to the No. Mishima had an instinct for the theater which his family had encouraged, but until this time Natsuko had refused him permission to go to the Kabuki or to the No, on the grounds that they were unsuitable for a young boy; the scenes of bloodletting in the Kabuki may have been what she had in mind. These visits to the theater taxed Natsuko's strength; she was in her early sixties and years of illness had taken their toll. Gradually her health declined and Mishima's visits to her home became less frequent. In the autumn of 1938, her condition became serious, and she died early the following year, at the age of sixty-four.

Her influence on her grandson had been great. She

had brought him up like a little Japanese girl but she had also taught him to be proud, instilling in him the samurai spirit of her ancestors. One of her sayings was: "You must be as haughty as you can be." Mishima showed her influence in his formal manner. Even later in life he found it hard to unbend; he taught himself to smoke and trained himself to drink but he did not greatly enjoy tobacco and alcohol, which perhaps reflected Natsuko's wish to see him a paragon. But her enormously strong personality also repressed him: even as a successful adult, Mishima was vulnerable and sensitive behind his samurai mask. He was easily injured and easily influenced by others, and although apparently unable to love, he demanded love from other people; yet, when there was a response, he sheered away.

His grandmother shaped a dual personality. One Mishima had a strong character, with a capacity for making decisions; he directed his body like a machine, made plans for it, sought sexual gratification, and pursued material success. The other Mishima was in retreat from life. I knew a little of both sides of him, but nearly always it was the strong Mishima that one saw, not the shy, retreating child. On the last day of his life, he cast himself in the role of the strong samurai-like figure, but of course there was another side to his personality, or he would not have written *Confessions of a Mask,* a work which reveals weakness, a morbid imagination, and a decadent sense of beauty in which eroticism and "blood" are joined.

Mishima's account of his aesthetic has a quality of desperate humor. He suffered in his adolescence "the anguish of a child provided with a curious toy." At the age of twelve or thirteen he began to have erections, and Mishima's "toy increased in volume at every opportunity and hinted that, rightly used, it would be quite a delightful thing." He was excited by muscular men, by the sight of swimming teams at Meiji pool, and by "the swarthy young man a cousin of mine married." One is reminded of his summary of his aesthetic "Death and Night and Blood," by many later passages in *Confessions of a Mask,* such as the series of images which

excited his adolescent imagination: "Gory dueling scenes
. . . pictures of young *samurai* cutting open their bellies, or
of soldiers struck by bullets, clenching their teeth and dripping blood . . . photographs of hard-muscled *sumo* wres-
tlers of the third rank, and not yet grown too fat."

The young Mishima turned his talent for drawing to
strange ends when he was alone at home: "When the composition of a picture in an adventure-story magazine was
defective, I would first copy it with crayons and then correct
it . . . Then it would become the picture of a young circus
performer dropping to his knees and clutching at a bullet
wound in his breast; or a tight-rope walker who had fallen
and split his skull open and now lay dying, half his face covered with blood." The boy hid these illustrations in a
drawer at home, but sometimes, as he sat in class at the
Gakushuin, he had the horrifying idea that someone in the
house might discover them; this blotted out all thought of
schoolwork.

Mishima moved back into his mother's house at a delicate stage in his life. A family friend who has known the
Hiraokas for thirty years described to me the effect upon the
boy of being handed over to his mother at the very moment
that his adolescence was beginning: "When Mishima started
to live with his mother he fell in love with the poor, beautiful woman who had been so cruelly treated by her awful
mother-in-law. As they had been separated for such a long
time, the reunion between mother and son was scarcely normal. Mishima was at a most sensitive age, the start of his adolescence." Later in life Shizue would refer to her son as a
"lover." (After his suicide she said, "My lover has returned
to me.") Mishima reciprocated her feelings; he loved her
deeply and probably never had a really close relationship
with any other person. His mother, he said, "protected me
ever since I was a child," taking his manuscripts to established writers and giving him secret encouragement to
pursue his writing. She hid her actions from her husband, as
Azusa wanted his sons to follow the family tradition of government service and thoroughly disapproved of literature as

a career for the boy. Shizue, the protector, aroused these feelings in her son: "My mother has been very good-looking since her youth. It may sound odd if I say so, but I was proud of her youth and beauty. I felt superior to others, when I compared my mother to those of my friends" ("Ajisai no Haha," "Hydrangea Mother," 1953).

After his death, Shizue wrote these impressions of her son's relationship with her after World War II:

"If ever I was in bed with flu or something, Kimitake really worried about me, as if I were on the point of dying. He brought hanebuton [feather cushions] and ordered dishes from Hamasaku and Fukudaya [the best restaurants in Tokyo], proposed that I should have a Western-style lavatory or wanted to buy a new air-conditioner instead of the noisy one we had. While he was still single, he would sit by my bedside, working at his papers and taking care of me.

"Whenever flowers were sent to him, he would have the maid bring them over to me [from his house next door]. One day he admired one of my flower arrangements greatly; it was 'Seven Flowers of Autumn.'

"If he went on a trip he would never fail to bring back omiyage [presents] for the family and for the maids. When he was traveling in Japan he would phone from wherever he was, on arrival, chat about the trip and say exactly when he was coming back.

"Once he proposed that we should go to Nara for the Saegusa Matsuri [a festival] saying that there would be masses of sasayuri [lily decorations]. [I could not go and] I was delighted when he brought back a single, thin, pink lily all the way from Nara, carrying it himself although he had masses of luggage that day.

"Kimitake invited me to plays, foreign operas, interesting exhibitions and so on, every month, and also to new restaurants. I saw all these places thanks to him."

His mother was the first person to see his writing, which appeared regularly in the school magazine, *Hojinkai Zasshi*, after the boy had entered middle school in 1937. He got on there much better than he had in the junior school, where his teachers had regarded his compositions as adventurous (he used rare characters and unusual constructions); and as his health improved steadily, his grades also got better. He was no longer an absentee at the Gakushuin.

His father, however, resisted Mishima's literary ambitions and thus came in conflict with the boy's mother. Azusa's ministry had sent Azusa to Osaka for two years, where he lived apart from his family, and on his return to Tokyo in 1939 he was disturbed to find how quickly his older son's interest in writing had developed. On one occasion Azusa stormed into the young Mishima's room and seized the manuscript he was working on, tearing it into pieces, which he scattered about the room. The boy wept and his mother comforted him with tea; thereafter Mishima hid his stories so that his father could not find them.

Shizue was literally her son's "protector"; it was not just a matter of encouraging him to write. Her own interest in literature stemmed from her scholarly family. She did not write herself but would have liked to, and Mishima was her proxy. Shizue did not have the pronounced character and definite literary taste of her mother-in-law (Natsuko had had a high regard for the ghostly, mysterious tales of Kyoka Izumi, a turn-of-the-century writer), but she was far more attuned to literature and the arts than was her husband. Azusa still wanted his son, who showed intellectual promise, to make a career in government. He could not imagine that anyone could make a living by literature, and in fact, before World War II, this was virtually impossible; writers needed patrons. Relations between father and son were never close, yet Azusa had an influence on the boy and exerted a steady pressure on him in his teens. As the oldest, and most gifted, child, Mishima was intended by his father to take the lead in the family; the other two children— Mitsuko, a strong, cheerful, unimaginative tomboy of a girl, and Chiyuki, a quiet, gentle boy—were supposed to follow. Such is the role of the elder son in a traditional Japanese family.

One may only conjecture what would have been the re-action of his father had he known the thoughts and adolescent dreams of his oldest boy—who was to all appearances a normal, even exemplary, child. Ironically, Azusa played a part in Mishima's discovery of an image that haunted him all his life, St. Sebastian on the tree of martyrdom. "One day, taking advantage of having been kept from school by a slight cold, I got out some volumes of art reproductions, which my father had brought back as souvenirs of his foreign travels. [Azusa had been to Europe, to represent his ministry on fishery problems; and, like most educated middle-class Japanese, he was a sampler of Western culture.] . . . Suddenly there came into view from one corner of the next page a picture that I had to believe had been lying in wait there, for my sake." It was a reproduction of a late Renaissance work, Guido Reni's *St. Sebastian.*

Mishima described the painting in *Confessions of a Mask:* "A remarkably handsome youth was bound naked to the trunk of a tree. His crossed hands were raised high, and the thongs binding his wrists were tied to the tree. No other bonds were visible, and the only covering for the youth's nakedness was a coarse white cloth knotted loosely about his loins . . . Were it not for the arrows with their shafts deeply sunk into his left armpit and right side, he would seem more a Roman athlete resting from fatigue . . . The arrows have eaten into the tense, fragrant, youthful flesh, and are about to consume his body from within with flames of supreme agony and ecstasy." The boy's hands embarked on a motion of which he had no experience; he played with his "toy": "Suddenly it burst forth, bringing with it a blinding intoxication . . . Some time passed, and then, with miserable feelings I looked around the desk I was facing . . . There were cloud-white splashes about . . . Some objects were dripping lazily, leadenly, and others gleamed dully, like the eyes of a dead fish. Fortunately, a reflex motion of my hand to protect the picture had saved the book from being soiled." This was the first occasion on which Mishima had an ejaculation. How deep an impression the image of St. Sebastian made on him! Twenty-five years later, Mishima posed for a photographer as St. Sebastian; he had "a coarse white cloth knotted loosely about his loins" and three arrows planted in his suntanned torso, one of which was embedded in his armpit.

Mishima described his "first love" at the Gakushuin. It was an older boy, Omi; as *Confessions of a Mask* has it, "he surpassed us all in physique, and in the contours of his face could be seen signs of some privileged youthfulness excelling ours by far. He had an innate and lofty manner of gratuitous scorn." Omi, according to a school rumor, had "a big thing"; Mishima duly reflected on this report: "It was like fertilizer poured over the poisonous weed of an idea deeply planted in me." Mishima, who was fourteen, looked forward impatiently to summer: "Surely, I thought, summer will bring with it an opportunity to see his naked body. Also, I cherished deeply within me a still more shamefaced desire. This was to see that 'big thing' of his." He could not be the only admirer of Omi's person; the older boy filled his school uniform, a "pretentious" copy of a naval officer's uniform, "with a sensation of solid weight and a sort of sexuality." And "surely I was not the only one who looked with envious and loving eyes at the muscles of his shoulders and chest . . . Because of him I began to love strength, an impression of overflowing blood, ignorance, rough gestures, careless speech, and the savage melancholy inherent in flesh not tainted in any way with intellect." He worshipped all "those possessors of sheer animal flesh unspoiled by intellect—young toughs, sailors, soldiers, fishermen"—but he was doomed to "watching them from afar with impassioned indifference."

One encounter with Omi led to Mishima's discovery of a fetish: white gloves. It was the custom at the Gakushuin to wear white gloves on ceremonial days. "Just to pull on a pair of white gloves, with mother-of-pearl buttons shining gloomily at the wrists and three meditative rows of stitching on the backs, was enough to evoke the symbols of all ceremonial days . . . the cloudless skies under which such days always seem to make brilliant sounds in midcourse and then collapse." In the grounds of the Gakushuin stood a swinging log and the boys often had fights for possession of the log. One day Omi stood on the log waiting for someone to challenge him; he seemed "like a murderer at bay" to Mishima, rocking back and forth and wearing his white gloves. Mishima was drawn toward the log: "Two contrary forces were pulling at me, contending for supremacy. One was the instinct of self-preservation. The second force—which was bent, even more profoundly, more intensely, upon the complete disintegration of my inner balance—was a compulsion toward suicide, that subtle and secret impulse." He darted forward and attacked and the two boys struggled, white-gloved hands interlocked, and crashed to the ground together; during that brief struggle they exchanged a single look and Mishima felt that Omi had surely understood that he loved him. The two boys sat close together in the school ceremony that followed and time after time Mishima looked across at Omi, his eyes resting on the stains on his gloves; both boys had dirtied their white gloves on the ground. Mishima, however, after a short time, looked forward to the ending of this Platonic affair; he even felt an intense pleasure deriving from the foreknowledge that his love would be short-lived.

The end came in the late spring (of 1939). There was a gymnastics class outside, from which Mishima was excused because of ill health—he had had a touch of tuberculosis and had a continual cough. The boy went out to watch the class, in which Omi, a favorite of the gym instructor, was the star. He was called upon to show the class how to swing on a horizontal bar. The day was warm and Omi wore only a light undershirt. Mishima reflected that his strong arms were "certainly worthy of being tattooed with anchors." A surge shot through Omi's body and in a moment he was suspended from the bar, on which he did a series of push-ups. There were admiring exclamations from the class and from Mishima, who had observed with astonishment that Omi had a plentiful growth of hair under his arms: "This was probably the first time that we had seen such an opulence of hair; it seemed almost prodigal, like some luxuriant growth of troublesome summer weeds . . . Life-force . . . it was the sheer extravagant abundance of life-force that over-powered the boys . . . Without his being aware of it some force had stolen into Omi's flesh and was scheming to take possession of him, to crash through him, to spill out of him, to outshine him."

Mishima, sensing the reaction of the other boys, was filled with consuming jealousy; he told himself that he was no longer in love with Omi. The boy then felt the need for a Spartan course of self-discipline and became obsessed with a single motto: "Be strong!" Riding to school by tram in the morning, he fixed other passengers with his gaze and stared them down, to prove his "strength." And yet the spectacle of Omi on the bar had made a deep impression on him; the sight of armpit hair became erotic and when he took a bath the young Mishima would look for a long time in the mirror, surveying his scrawny shoulders and narrow chest and will-ing that one day he too would have luxuriant armpits. He was still small and undeveloped, weighing less than a hundred pounds at the age of fourteen. But slowly his arm-pits budded, "becoming darker and darker," and soon be-came bushy enough to serve as an erotic image for the boy; when he indulged in his "bad habit" (masturbation), he would gaze fixedly on that portion of his anatomy.

Toshitami Bojo, a senior student at the Gakushuin when Mishima arrived in middle school, remembered him as "a rather puny, pale boy. He already had his famous laugh. He read the classics and we were struck by his ability. Despite the difference of eight years in our ages, Mishima could follow everything that I said, and would point out weak-nesses in my remarks. In a sense he has been ageless since then." Bojo was a member of the Bungei-bu, a literary circle at the school, and he became acquainted with Mishima when the boy submitted his first pieces for the school maga-zine, which the Bungei-bu controlled. Mishima's poems and short compositions won the admiration of his seniors in the

Bungei-bu and he sought out their company. He was a snob and befriended boys from good families: Bojo, whose ancestors had served at the Imperial Court for generations; Takashi Azuma, who was his closest friend at the school; and Yoshiyasu Tokugawa, a descendant of the family which had ruled Japan between 1603 and 1868, the Tokugawa era in Japanese history.

Academic brilliance—his grades had continued to improve greatly since he left the junior school—and precocious literary ability enabled Mishima to stand almost on an equal footing with these older boys, who published his work in every issue of *Hojinkai Zasshi,* their magazine. One can see in these writings—in the short story "Sukanpo" ("Sorrel," 1938)—the characteristics of Mishima's mature work: irony and elegance; alienation from the working class and preoccupation with the upper classes; and an insane delight in cruelty. Bojo was right when he said: "In a sense he has been ageless since then"; his tastes changed little after his early teens. The white gloves which he wore on the last day of his life, and which became slightly soiled with blood during the battle in General Mashita's office (one can see it in the photographs of Mishima speaking from the balcony on that day), were like those he and Omi wore the day of their fight on the swinging log.

The descriptions of Omi in *Confessions of a Mask* remind me of Masakatsu Morita, the student leader of the Tatenokai. "Something about his face," wrote Mishima of Omi, "gave one the sensation of abundant blood coursing richly throughout his body; it was a round face, with haughty cheekbones rising from swarthy cheeks, lips that seemed to have been sewn into a fine line, sturdy jaws, and a broad but well-shaped and not too prominent nose." The fate suffered by Omi in the book is not so different from that of Morita; he was made a human sacrifice, according to Mishima's fantasy. "Omi . . . had been betrayed and then executed in secret. One evening he had been stripped naked and taken to the grove on the hill . . . The first arrow had pierced the side of his chest; the second, his armpit." The deaths of Omi (in the style of St. Sebastian) and Morita both offered the spectacle of blood pouring forth, and so did the hara-kiri of Mishima. Blood gave him a sexual thrill—this was one of his most important "confessions" and the core of his aesthetic. The beauty of the spilt blood of the samurai has been endlessly poeticized by the Japanese, who liken the short-lived blossom of the cherry tree to the life of the samurai. Mishima, however, romanticized death and blood in a manner foreign to the Japanese classical tradition.

The young Mishima's taste for the decadent is evident from his work "Yakata" ("Mansion," 1939). In this story, almost the only one he left uncompleted during his life, he describes, in the setting of medieval Japan, a struggle for power between a satanic aristocrat, whose sole pleasure is murder, and his wife, who represents God. In "Yakata," Mishima attempted to develop his idea of a "murder theater," a fantasy that he subsequently described in *Confessions of a Mask:* "There in my murder theater, young Roman gladiators offered up their lives for my amusement; and all the deaths that took place there not only had to overflow with blood but also had to be performed with all due ceremony. I delighted in all forms of capital punishment and all implements of execution. But I would allow no torture device nor gallows, as they would not have provided a spectacle of outpouring blood. Nor did I like explosive weapons such as pistols or guns. So far as possible I chose primitive and savage weapons—arrows, daggers, spears. And in order to prolong the agony, it was the belly that must be aimed at."

In Mishima's aesthetic, blood was ultimately erotic. His imagination was aroused by images of blood and death: "The weapon of my imagination slaughtered many a Grecian soldier, many white slaves of Arabia, princes of savage tribes, hotel elevator boys, waiters, young toughs, army officers, circus roustabouts . . . I would kiss the lips of those who had fallen to the ground and were still moving spasmodically." He contrived a special machine for executing his victims: "A thick board studded with scores of upright daggers, arranged in the shape of a human figure, which

would come sliding down a rail upon a cross of execution."
He also had a fantasy of cannibalism; his most terrible
dream was of the sacrifice of a boy—he chose an athletic
contemporary from the Gakushuin—who was stunned, stripped, and pinned naked on a vast plate, on which he was
carried into a banqueting room. There, Mishima began the
feast: " 'This is probably a good spot to begin on.' I thrust
the fork upright into the heart. A fountain of blood struck me
full in the face. Holding the knife in my right hand, I began
carving the flesh of the breast, gently, thinly, at first . . ."

    This aesthetic owed as much to the West as to classical
tradition in Japan—perhaps much more. In *Confessions of a
Mask* Mishima says that he took his idea of the "murder theater" from the descriptions of the Colosseum in *Quo Vadis*.
Some Western rock music reflects the same influences;
for example, in the song called "Peace Frog" by The Doors,
which is about race riots in America, one of the lines is
"Blood on the rise." Mishima sought to incarnate a similar
vision and found himself on a path that could lead only to
death: to save himself, he would have had to abandon his
romantic notion of beauty.

THREE

The Making of
Yukio Mishima

(1940–49)

I shuddered with a strange delight at the thought of my own death. I felt as if I owned the whole world.

Yukio Mishima, *Confessions of a Mask*

1
Child of Ancient History

Mishima's main interests at fifteen were schoolwork and literature. He was still very much a "puny, pale" boy, as Bojo had described him at thirteen, and he suffered from anemia—an illness which he privately attributed to his "bad habit"; but his health had improved immeasurably since his days in the junior school, and his concentration was good. He was almost at the top of his class of sixty boys, and he excelled in all subjects. But he stayed apart from his contemporaries; they had little to offer him, for his precocious intelligence put him in a different class from them. And his parents, who, pleading his ill health, insisted that he not spend the regulation two years boarding at the Gakushuin dormitory, encouraged his tendency to remain apart. Just as he had done when he first entered middle school, he sought the company of older boys and teachers. Takashi Azuma, who was three years older, was already a close friend, and Fumio Shimizu, his kokugo (Japanese) teacher, encouraged him in both schoolwork and composition. Shimizu, who in 1938 had come to the Gakushuin from Seijo Gakuen School, was his best teacher, and the boy visited him at lunchtime and in the evenings when he had free time.

The young man's taste in literature had developed. He was reading the work of Junichiro Tanizaki, a leading Japanese novelist, and Rainer Maria Rilke, Raymond Radiguet, and Oscar Wilde. He hoped one day to emulate Radiguet, and Wilde's decadence—the play *Salomé* was a favorite of his—intrigued him. Mishima's aesthetic—the beauty of Death (the handsome youth who dies at his physical prime, as did Radiguet at twenty) and the beauty of Blood (the severed head of St. John the Baptist, kissed by Salomé)—was firmly established. And in the angels of Rainer Maria Rilke he found his Night. His "heart's longing for Death and Night and Blood" would not be denied.

His literary taste was extraordinary for a boy in Japan at that time; but then he was an exceptional schoolboy at an untypical school. No one at the Gakushuin forbade him to read Wilde or Radiguet because they were authors of inferior races (the official creed at that time was that the Japanese were inherently superior to all other peoples and destined to rule them). Tanizaki, of whom the militarists disapproved because of his interest in "bourgeois" life, was not criticized at the Gakushuin. Mishima also took instruction outside the school. His mother had obtained an introduction for him to a renowned romantic poet, Ryuko Kawaji, and the boy called on him regularly to show him his compositions; he was still writing mostly poetry. Mishima liked working with Kawaji, for, as he mentions in his book *Shi o Kaku Shonen* ("The Boy Who Wrote Poetry," 1956), "I had feelings of rapture, of rich loneliness, of pure intoxication and of the fraternity of the external and inner worlds." Most of his poems were cheerful little works in which the boy celebrated his enjoyment of a sensuous world of imagination. An exception was "Magagoto" ("Evil Things"), an evocation of Night:

> Standing by my window
> I waited each evening
> For strange events.
> I watched for evil omens
> A sandstorm surging across the street
> A rainbow at night.

After his death, a critic, Jun Eto, maintained that this nihilistic work "held the clue to all Mishima's literature."

The young Mishima, it seems, remained passively homosexual. He had admired Omi from afar, and he did not embark on affairs at the Gakushuin; he was too timid, and as he did not board at the school, his opportunities were much more limited than those of other boys. There was a good deal of adolescent homosexuality at the Gakushuin, as at any boys' boarding school; but the main interest was heterosexuality, as Mishima made clear in *Confessions of a Mask:* "The period called adolescence—I had my full share of it so far as burning curiosity was concerned—seemed to have come to pay us a sick visit. Having attained puberty, the boys seemed to do nothing but always think immoderately about women, exude pimples, and write sugary verses out of heads that were in a constant dizzy reel." He realized that he was different from other boys; they seemed to derive unusual excitement from the mere word "woman." "I, on the other hand, received no more sensual impression from 'woman' than from 'pencil.'" But he did not appreciate how different he was: "In short, I knew absolutely nothing about other boys. I did not know that each night all boys but me had dreams in which women—women barely glimpsed yesterday on a street corner—were stripped of their clothing and set one by one parading before the dreamers' eyes. I did not know that in the boys' dreams the breasts of a woman would float up like beautiful jellyfish rising from the sea of night." Mishima was uneasy about his own sexual feelings. He became "obsessed with the idea of the kiss," and to delude himself that this desire was animal passion, he had to undertake an elaborate disguise of his true self. An unconscious feeling of guilt stubbornly insisted that he play "a conscious and false role."

Schoolwork, literature, and adolescent passions—he maintained an emotional correspondence with Azuma—preoccupied Mishima. Meanwhile, the international situation was rapidly deteriorating; Japan was moving swiftly toward war with Britain and America. In July 1940, numerous British residents in Japan were imprisoned as "spies," and in the autumn Japan entered into the Tripartite Pact with Germany and Italy. This was followed by a neutrality treaty with Russia, which was concluded in April 1941. There had been two conflicting views in the Japanese military establishment during the 1930's. One side believed that the main threat to Japan was from the Soviet Union, and they advocated a strike north; but they had been virtually eliminated after the Ni Ni Roku Incident of February 1936. Their opponents, who favored a strike south against Britain, Holland, and France, gained control of the government. After the success of Nazi Germany in 1940, events played into the hands of the strike-south party; their strategy seemed correct. America, however, was a problem. To inflict a military defeat on the United States was impossible. The Japanese hoped that the Roosevelt Administration would settle for a stalemate in the Pacific, that Britain would be crushed by Hitler and Japanese forces would penetrate as far as Australia and India to complete the destruction of the British Empire. With this aim in mind, the Armed Forces, which had dominated all governments after 1930, planned to deliver an initial crushing blow against the U.S. Navy by making a surprise attack on Pearl Harbor. The enemy was to be put off-guard by diplomatic negotiations right up to the eve of the attack. Following the appointment in October 1941 of General Tojo as Prime Minister, Home Minister, and Defense Minister, the stage was set for war.

At this moment Mishima, aged sixteen, was publishing his first work, *Hanazakari no Mori* ("The Forest in Full Bloom"), in installments in a literary magazine, *Bungei*

Bunka, which his teacher, Shimizu, helped to edit. *Hanaza-kari no Mori* was the first flowering of Mishima's talent; he displayed a gift for language—he wrote a rich, romantic Jap-anese—which astounded his elders. Zenmei Hasuda, a schoolteacher friend of Shimizu, commented in the Sep-tember 1941 edition of *Bungei Bunka*: "The author of *Hana-zakari no Mori* is a very young man. We want to keep his identity secret for a while . . . This young writer is the blessed child of Ancient History." *Hanazakari no Mori*, praised by Hasuda in this Hegelian manner, is a remarkable work. Its theme is ancestry; it consists of five parts, in which Mishima described the lives of "ancestors" of aristocratic lineage from widely separated historical periods. One sec-tion, for example, relates the experiences of a duchess of the Meiji period (the late nineteenth century) who divorces her husband and spends the ensuing forty years of her life in retirement. Another part describes the religious experiences of a lady of the court who has visions of God. What appealed to Hasuda, a vehement nationalist, was Mishima's evocation of a historical Japan totally different in character from the crude modern age, in which the philistinism of the military leaders of Japan was sweeping all before it. The beauty of his language—full of nostalgia for the past—was the more striking in view of Mishima's youth. His Japanese was more distinguished than that of his elders—and all his life Mi-shima was to display a love of rare characters which distin-guished him from his contemporaries.

Hanazakari no Mori was not merely Mishima's first published work and one which contained the seeds of all his writing; it also marked the evolution of his mature thinking, which was pessimistic. At the end of the book, an old ac-quaintance comes to visit an aged friend, a woman of aristo-cratic family who lives alone in her retirement. The visitor attempts to revive their common memories of the past, but the aged woman will have none of it. "It's strange," she remarks, "but it's all gone away somewhere." The scene is very similar to that at the end of Mishima's last work, *The Decay of the Angel*, written almost thirty years later.

In *Hanazakari no Mori*, Mishima adopted the nom de

plume he was to use for the rest of his life: Yukio Mishima. The decision was taken at Shimizu's house in Mejiro, at a meeting in the late summer of 1941. Shimizu proposed that the boy use a pen name, as he was still so young. He suggested the name Mishima: the view of the snowy summit of Mt. Fuji is best seen from the town of Mishima, which lies directly between Mt. Fuji and the sea to the south. Shimizu derived the first name, Yukio, from the Japanese for snow— yuki. The two then discussed which characters they should use to write the name; there is a considerable choice. "Mishima" was easy; they chose the characters used in the place name: 三島 . "Yukio" was more difficult. The young writer proposed 由紀雄 . And Shimizu suggested a literary flourish: changing the third character to 夫 . His idea was to give the pen name a romantic flavor; and 夫 had been selected by a romantic poet, Sachio Ito, as the last syllable of his first name. (Mishima's hostile father later said that his son had selected the pen name by flicking through a telephone directory and making a stab with a pencil. He was wrong.)

In the month in which the last installment of *Hanazakari no Mori* was published, the war started. The root causes of the Pacific War, which began on December 7, 1941, when carrier-borne aircraft attacked the American fleet in Pearl Harbor, remain a matter for debate. Mishima once told me: "We were forced to go to war." This is a view with which many Japanese would agree today, though at the time that Mishima said it—early 1966—it was still hard to find a Japanese who spoke openly about the war, such was the trauma of the defeat of 1945, following the first and only use of nuclear weapons in battle. Many Japanese believe that the attack on Pearl Harbor was a "defensive measure" intended to break the siege of the ABCD alliance (America, Britain, China, and the Dutch). President Roosevelt had announced that he would cut off Japan's oil, and the response was a "defensive" assault on Hawaii and on British colonies in the Far East. Whatever the causes of the war, its effect on the career and the suicide of Yukio Mishima was profound. As

Bunzo Hashikawa, a contemporary of Mishima's and a historian, remarked: "The easiest way to explain Mishima's suicide is by reference to his experiences during the war, when he was in his teens." The war brought no immediate change in the boy's situation, but he and the other students at the Gakushuin lived in the belief that conscription and almost certain death awaited them at the end of their school years.

2

The "Irony" of It All

The war at first made little difference to the Hiraoka family. Azusa Hiraoka was forty-seven, too old to be drafted, and when he resigned from his ministry job in March 1942—he had risen in rank as far as he could—he began a small law practice. His father, Jotaro, aged eighty, died in August, and this was the most important event in the Hiraoka family that year.

Mishima, who was seventeen, moved up from the middle to the senior school at the Gakushuin in March 1942. His record had been excellent academically. For three years he had ranked second out of sixty boys in his class; he had top grades in all subjects but physics, in which he had dropped a grade in a single term. His school report showed:

	First Term	*Second Term*	*Third Term*	*Average*
Rank	2	2	—	2
Average	Excellent	Excellent	—	Excellent
Ethics	A	A	A	A
Japanese	A	A	A	A
Composition	A	A	A	A

He also scored straight A's for calligraphy, English, history, geography, math (geometry and algebra), and chemistry.

Only in sports was he lower down the class, scoring A– in taiso (physical education), kyoren (drill), and budo (martial arts). His record of attendance was good, by comparison with that of his early years in the school. Ill health rarely kept him from his studies any more.

He experienced a disappointment when he entered the senior school in April 1942. "With the beginning of the war"—he remembered in *Confessions of a Mask*—"a wave of hypocritical stoicism swept the entire country. Even the higher schools did not escape: all during middle school we had longed for that happy day of graduation to higher school when we could let our hair grow long, but now, when the day arrived, we were no longer allowed to gratify our ambition—we still had to shave our heads." Mishima, however, was treated as a star pupil by his senior teacher, Ryozo Niizeki, under whose direction he began German studies (literature and law). He was made a member of the committee of the Bungei-bu, the literary club, and was soon to be its chairman; he was also to be a monitor. The exemplary student published patriotic poems, tanka (thirty-one-syllable poems), in the school magazine. In "Omikotonori" ("Imperial Edict"), which appeared in April, Mishima dedicated himself to the Sun Goddess and to service of the Emperor. His interest in the classics increased. He studied the *Kojiki* ("The Record of Ancient Matters"), and he read the *Manyoshu* ("Journal of a Myriad Leaves"), the eighth-century-poetry anthology, for which there was a vogue in wartime. In the summer he published a study of the *Kokinshu*, the tenth-century anthology whose reflective, melancholy poems were more to his taste than the robust *Manyoshu* lyrics. Also, Mishima and Takashi Azuma started a little magazine of their own, *Akae* ("Red Picture"), in which they published their own work.

Meanwhile, the war was developing—in the Emperor's famous words—"not necessarily to Japan's advantage." The first American bombers appeared over Tokyo in April 1942: the raid was a small one, but it was clear that the homeland would be threatened if Japanese military momentum was lost. In June the sea battle of Midway took place. By good fortune, the U.S. Navy sank four Japanese aircraft carriers, destroying a large fighter force in the process; this was a blow from which the Japanese Navy did not recover. Plans for advancing across New Guinea and invading northern Australia were aborted; after Midway, in effect, the war was lost. It continued for another three years, with immense loss of life and destruction of property, but after the Guadalcanal campaign of late 1942 the Japanese were on the defensive in the Pacific.

Mishima associated at this time with a group of writers who believed that the war was holy. Hasuda, the leading spirit in the Bungei Bunka group, and twenty-one years Mishima's senior, encouraged the boy to believe in the ideal of death in the service of the Emperor. A scholar with an exceptional capacity for interpreting the Japanese classics in contemporary terms, Hasuda wrote a study of Otsu-no-Miko, a tragic prince of the seventh century. The moral was, in Hasuda's words: "I believe one should die young in this age. To die young, I am sure, is the culture of my country." Hasuda had a great regard for the young Mishima; a friend, Masaharu Fuji, recorded this impression (in an article in *Shincho* magazine, February 1971) of Hasuda saying goodbye to the boy: "When we visited Hasuda he went out to see Mishima off at the station, and he stared after the departing train for a long time. His attachment to the boy was obvious; he regarded Mishima the prodigy as his own precious jewel."

Hasuda was a slim, tense schoolteacher from Kyushu, the traditional home of priests in Japan. He had served in China and been invalided back to Japan, but in 1943 he was to be drafted again—to Malaya. In 1970 Mishima wrote a preface to a biography of Hasuda in which he remarked: "His enemies [in Japan] had not tried to understand nor wanted to know the source of Hasuda's fierce anger and uncompromising conduct. They were the pure product of his stern tenderness . . . I received Hasuda's tenderness and affection when I was a boy. I saw the grand spectacle

of his anger, suddenly coming and then evaporating . . .
For me Hasuda was a poet who had a scholarly knowledge of Japanese literature. He loved classical lyrical poetry
and injected the quality of the classics into his own work.
I could not understand his anger . . . Hasuda placed his
confidence in me when he was drafted for the second
time [in 1943] and set out on his journey to shishi [death
granted by the favor of the Emperor], but, naïve as I was, I
could not understand his feeling even after I heard of his
death . . ." Though as a schoolboy Mishima did not fully
understand Hasuda, he did sympathize deeply with his
ideals.

The Bungei Bunka was a small, little-known band of literary nationalists. Hasuda encouraged Mishima to get in
touch with the leading intellectuals, who believed in the holiness of the war their country had embarked on. They had
formed a movement known as the Nippon Roman-ha (Japanese Romanticists), led by Yojuro Yasuda, a critic with a rhe-
torical gift, a highbrow agitator for the "sacred" war. In 1942
Mishima collected Roman-ha works, including the poetry of
Shizuo Ito, the best artist in the Roman-ha, with whom he
corresponded. Ito's work was more to his taste than Yasuda's, but this did not keep him from visiting Yasuda in 1943.
Yasuda's ideas, however, were too extreme for the young
Mishima, and his language obscure—a characteristic of
Roman-ha writers with the exception of Ito. Jun Eto, a
scholar with an interest in the Roman-ha, summed up the
ideals of the movement in conversation with me: "They
believed in the value of destruction and ultimately in self-
destruction. They valued 'purity of sentiment,' though they
never defined this; and they called for 'preservation of the
nation' by purging selfish party politicians and zaibatsu
[business] leaders. They believed that self-destruction would
be followed by reincarnation, linked mysteriously with the
benevolence of the Emperor. The Japanese, they considered, were superior to all other peoples."

The young Mishima was intrigued by the Roman-ha.
The movement, which derived its name from *Nippon*

Roman, a magazine edited by Yasuda from 1935 to 1938, took its ideas from the nineteenth-century German romantic movement. (Hence Roman; "ha" in Japanese means "group.") It had great influence in Japan during the war, incorporating elements of the traditional kokugaku (the nationalistic thought of the great eighteenth-century thinker, Norinaga Motoori), and also Marxism; it was eclectic, in a peculiarly Japanese way. The Roman-ha was encouraged by the military leaders of Japan, and Yasuda gave the movement an inspired leadership. His statements now seem unintelligible, however, and even at the time his notion of irony, a key Roman-ha concept, was vague. His well-known, ironic prewar comments include: "I am saying this purely as an observer. I think it would be more *interesting* if Germany were to win the war, I want her to win. I look at culture from a historical point of view, and it seems to me that the Gods seek to make history more interesting and amusing as one epoch succeeds another." "Even if this war [the Sino-Japanese War] should end with defeat, Japan will have succeeded in accomplishing the greatest step forward in world history. From an ideological point of view, to imagine defeat is the greatest romance." Yasuda held that historical reality was unimportant and that the emotion aroused by events was more "interesting" than the events themselves. He argued that it was irrelevant whether a hero was righteous or not. The enlightened man would not commit himself. For such a being, there could be neither decisive defeat nor complete victory; he would be both winner and loser in any game.

Mishima was attracted by the Roman-ha emphasis on death and destruction. The conclusion of "irony" was that death—the world's destruction—was the ultimate value. His own fantasies had run on similar lines since childhood. However, he was not influenced solely by the Roman-ha in his thinking. The young Mishima had a highly rational side to him—and an ideology tailor-made for a nation plunging toward catastrophe was insufficient for him. He was attracted at this time not only by the Roman-ha but also by a stoic moral tradition, that of the early twentieth-century Japanese writer, Ogai Mori.

Mishima imitated Ogai Mori as a man and as a writer, especially after 1950, as he recounted in his essay *Sun and Steel* (published by Kodansha International in a translation by John Bester). This book-length essay was finished in 1968, and Mishima, discussing his literary style, then clarified his debt to Mori: "In my style, as hardly needs pointing out, I progressively turned my back on the preferences of the age. Abounding in antitheses, clothed in an old-fashioned weighty solemnity, it did not lack nobility of a kind; but it maintained the same ceremonial, grave pace wherever it went, marching through other people's bedrooms with precisely the same tread as elsewhere. Like some military gentleman, it went about with chest out and shoulders back, despising other men's styles for the way they stooped, sagged at the knees, even—heaven forbid!— swayed at the hips."

That the young Mishima had an inclination toward the Roman-ha is suggested by some passages in *Confessions of a Mask:* "During this time [the early war years] I learned to smoke and drink. That is to say, I learned to make a pretense at smoking and drinking. The war had produced a strangely sentimental maturity in us. It arose from our thinking of life as something that would end abruptly in our twenties; we never even considered the possibility of there being anything beyond those few remaining years." This was a state of affairs with which Mishima was perfectly "happy": "My journey into life was postponed day after day, and the war years were going by without the slightest sign of my departure. Was this not a unique period of happiness for me? Though I still felt an uneasiness, it was only faint; still having hope, I looked forward to the unknown blue skies of each tomorrow. Fanciful dreams of the journey to come . . . the mental picture of the somebody I would one day become in the world and of the lovely bride I had not yet seen, my hopes of fame . . ." And he thoroughly approved of the war, from the safety of the Gakushuin: "I found childish delight in war, and despite the presence of death and destruction all around me, there was no abatement of the daydream in which I believed myself beyond the reach of harm by any bullet. I even shuddered with a strange delight at the thought of my own death. I felt as though I owned the whole world."

Mishima's "hopes of fame" depended on publication of *Hanazakari no Mori*. He sought out literary men. From Shizuo Ito, the poet of the Roman-ha, he obtained an introduction to a literary editor, Masaharu Fuji of Nanajo Shoin, a small but influential publishing house in Tokyo. Fuji later recalled their meeting in 1943: "Mishima was a very polite young man with dead pale skin. He had a large head and dark eyebrows. I introduced him to Fujima Hayashi [a poet] and Hayashi took an instant liking to him when Mishima rejected his offer of a beer in a polite but stiff way." Mishima hoped that Fuji would publish his book; but this proved impossible. Censorship, which was handled by the military authorities, was not the problem—though many leading Japanese writers were running into trouble at that time; Mishima had backing from the establishment. The difficulty was shortage of paper. All resources were devoted to the war effort and there was no paper to spare for *Hanazakari no Mori*.

In October 1943 Mishima had bad news. His friend, Azuma, with whom he was publishing the little magazine *Akae*, had died. Mishima closed the magazine and published an obituary in the Gakushuin quarterly. His own future was unpredictable; the authorities were drafting university students and he had only a year left at the Gakushuin.

At nineteen, Mishima remained a romantic. And yet his fantasies had become more grandiose and narcissistic. As Hashikawa later remarked: "He thought of himself as a genius, he believed that he could become whatever he liked —the Emperor of Japan, a literary genius, even the kamikaze of beauty. He thought his potential unlimited." The reality was somewhat different, however. Mishima was a frail youth, "ashamed of my thin chest, of my bony, pallid arms," and he only just passed his army medical in May 1944. He was still at the Gakushuin at the time and took his medical at Shikata, the home town of Jotaro, where the Hiraokas had retained a honseki, a registered place of residence, though they no longer owned land there. The army doctors laughed when Mishima failed to lift a hay bale in a test of strength (the local farm boys easily lifted it above their heads any number of times), but they classified him 2-B, just qualifying him for service. He would eventually be drafted into a rough local regiment and serve in the ranks. (Had he volunteered in Tokyo, he would have become an officer in a unit there, but Azusa hoped, by registering the boy at Shikata, to delay the time when he would be called to active military service. With luck, the war would be over before Mishima was drafted.) In July 1944, Mishima and the rest of the class were sent to a naval engineering school at Maizuru on the Japan Sea, to train for a fortnight. This was his first experience of military life, and in the next month he was mobilized again for thirty days, to serve at a naval dockyard at Numazu near Tokyo. The Japanese were steadying themselves for a final assault against the Allies, and every schoolboy had duties. The resignation of the Tojo Cabinet in July 1944 signaled that the leaders of Japan, including the Emperor, believed the war was lost; but there was no thought of surrender. In June, proposals had been put forth for kamikaze attacks on U.S. naval vessels; these proposals were secretly being considered in the late summer of 1944.

Mishima's outstanding ability was recognized at the end of his years at the Gakushuin. He passed out of the school in September 1944 at the top of his class and was awarded a gindokei, a silver watch, by the Emperor. Accompanied by the principal of the school, "a cheerless old man with mucus clotted in the corners of his eyes," Mishima went by limousine to the palace to receive the prize. Years later he remarked, in debate with Tokyo University students in 1969: "I watched the Emperor sitting there without moving for three hours. This was at my graduation ceremony. I received a watch from him . . . My personal experience was that the image of the Emperor is fundamental. I cannot set this aside. The Emperor is the absolute." After the presentation ceremony at the palace, Mishima returned home to celebrate. Photographs taken with his family show him with a shaven head, the rule for schoolboys and students during wartime. His appearance had changed in the war years; he was no longer the cheeky boy of fifteen with shining eyes, heavy black eyebrows, and pallid face, but a mature-looking youth with a thickened and rounded jaw and a look of assurance. The rest of the family sat beside Mishima for the photograph. Chiyuki, his younger brother, dressed in shorts, was at fourteen in the early stage of adolescence, a spotty child. Next to him sat Mitsuko, sixteen; she had a strong face and broad cheeks—not a beauty. Azusa was the most handsome member of the family. His hair, cut short in military style, had turned silver. Shizue had aged greatly. At thirty-nine she was a thin matron with a sharp expression. The main worries of the family—including the provision of food, which had become difficult at this stage of the war—were hers. She bore the family burdens, while Azusa enjoyed his retirement.

Mishima's father had a special reason for looking pleased with himself. He had won a victory. For the first time in his life he had compelled the young Mishima to do something against his will; he had obliged the boy to enlist in the law department at Tokyo Imperial University, where he was to study German law. Mishima had wanted to study literature, but Azusa insisted that for his career it was essential that he study law; his father wanted Mishima to join the civil service. Mishima later commented: "The only thing I have to be grateful to my father for is that he compelled me to study law at the university." Azusa's choice was correct, not for the reasons he thought but because Mishima found law intellectually stimulating.

University uniforms were in short supply, and following a custom of the time, Mishima borrowed a uniform from a senior student, promising to return it. The university was in danger of disruption, however. "The air raids were becoming more frequent. I was uncommonly afraid of them, and yet at the same time I somehow looked forward to death impatiently, with a sweet expectation" (*Confessions*). Mishima "sensuously accepted the creed of death that was popular during the war" but with reservations. "I thought that if by any chance I should attain 'glorious death in battle' (how ill it would have become me!), this would be a truly ironical end for my life, and I could laugh sarcastically at it forever from the grave . . . And when the sirens sounded, that same me would dash for the air-raid shelters faster than anyone."

The university was the best in the land. The Gakushuin had not been a first-class school academically. It had been chosen by Jotaro because it was attended by children of the aristocracy, to which Mishima's grandmother aspired to belong; but the Tokyo Kaisei school, which Shizue's father ran, would have been a better choice, academically. So too would the Tokyo First School, another secondary school with high academic standards. To pass out of the Gakushuin into Todai, Tokyo University, was an achievement. Since its establishment in the late nineteenth century, Todai had produced a majority of the leaders of the nation; its prestige had been enhanced by its being named an Imperial University in 1886 under an ordinance Article I of which stated that the function of the university was "to master the secrets of and to teach the arts and sciences in accordance with the needs of the state." Todai was a state university and a passport to the civil service and thence to politics or the upper reaches of the world of business. It had drawbacks as an institution of higher education, however. Close links with the state prevented Todai from serving as a center of the arts and of liberal thought; Todai had led the way in the early twentieth century in terminating the practice of employing professors from overseas. Despite these drawbacks, it was the leading university in Japan, and other universities, including private ones, were mostly smaller versions of Todai.

Mishima started at Todai in October 1944. Normally he would have left the Gakushuin in March the following year and entered the university in April, but the war had disrupted university administration. The war also interrupted Mishima's university career. As soon as he entered Todai, he was drafted to work in an aircraft factory in the Tokyo region, the Koizumi plant of Nakajima Aircraft Company. The plant was situated in Gumma prefecture, fifty miles north of the capital. Mishima had been drafted twice before, while at the Gakushuin. These had been brief assignments, however, and the posting to Nakajima Aircraft Company was for an indefinite period of time. Like other universities, Todai had virtually ceased to function in deference to the government's demand that everyone participate in the war effort.

Mishima described the factory at Koizumi, which manufactured kamikaze planes—the kamikaze strategy, a last, desperate move, had been initiated in October—in *Confessions of a Mask*. The factory was a strange one. The management might have been Roman-ha purists: "This great factory worked on a mysterious system of production costs: taking no account of the economic dictum that capital investment should produce a return, it was dedicated to a monstrous nothingness. No wonder then that each morning the workers had to recite a mystic oath." This was a vow to the Emperor. "I have never seen such a strange factory. In it all the techniques of modern science and management, together with the exact and rational thinking of many superior brains, were dedicated to a single end—Death. Producing the Zero-model combat plane used by the suicide squadrons, this great factory resembled a secret cult that operated thunderously—groaning, shrieking, roaring."

The factory was a possible target for American bombers, and when the air-raid sirens sounded, everyone would rush to the shelters in a nearby pine grove. As he hurried with the others, Mishima clutched a manuscript. He was working on a new book, *Chusei* ("The Middle Ages"). He had finally succeeded in having *Hanazakari no Mori*, his first book, published. It was brought out in October 1944 by Shichijo Shoin, the publishing house for which his friend Fuji worked. Four thousand copies were printed, with an elegant cover showing a fan with blossoms, and the first edition had sold out in a week. A party had been held at a restaurant in Ueno (Tokyo) to celebrate publication. To have published a book in the last year of the war was a phenomenal achievement, and Yukio Mishima won fame among his contemporaries.

In his autobiographical work, *Watakushi no Henreki Jidai* ("My Wandering Years," 1964)—like so many of his books, it remains untranslated—Mishima said that he expected to be drafted and not live very long thereafter; he wanted to have a book published as a "memorial" to himself. "I admit," he said, referring to criticisms made against him, "that I was an opportunist then and I feel disgusted when I see the opportunism of the introduction of my first publication." *Hanazakari no Mori* sold rapidly: this "meant that I could die at any moment." Nonetheless, Mishima still felt that he had work to do. "I decided to write a very last novel—I might be drafted at any moment"; this was *Chusei* ("The Middle Ages," 1946). His choice of Yoshihisa (1465–89) as the subject of his "very last" book was intriguing; Yoshihisa was the son of a ruler of Japan, the Shogun Yoshimasa, who built the Silver Pavilion at Kyoto—and ignored problems of government, bequeathing countless problems to his successors. Yoshihisa attempted to seize power from his uncle, an appointee of his father, but the coup misfired and he was killed in battle at twenty-four. The civil wars which followed, the Onin Wars, were the most destructive in the history of warfare in Japan. Kyoto was razed to the ground in the course of this Japanese version of the Hundred Years' War in Europe. It was typical of Mishima that he chose to write about an earlier period of Japanese history in which the capital had been reduced to ashes, at a time when the process was being repeated in Tokyo; he had an eye for striking parallels.

Mishima felt that a disaster comparable to the Onin Wars was about to overtake Japan once more. Whether he received his akagami, the "red paper," or conscription summons, or not, he felt sure that disaster—ichiokugyokusai ("Death to the hundred million! No surrender!"), as the war-time slogan had it—waited the entire nation. "The reason I now feel that total nuclear warfare is certain," he wrote in *Watakushi no Henreki Jidai*, "probably goes back to the emotional experiences I had at that time. Now, seventeen years after the end of the war, I cannot be sure of reality; it is temporary and fleeting. Perhaps I have an inherent incli-nation to think that way, but it may be that the war, during which things were there one day and gone the next, influ-enced me a great deal." Mishima's way of dealing with the situation was "to cling to my sensitivity"; in retrospect, he could see that he had been foolish, but at the time it had been unavoidable.

From the factory Mishima wrote a card to Fumio Shi-mizu. He was hard at work translating a one-act play by Yeats, he said, and was rendering it into a No play. But he gave up the project; his English was not up to the task of translating *At the Hawk's Well*, the Yeats play in question. "It is not easy to relate Yeats to the end of the war period," he wrote. "Now I would say that I was not trying to relate these two things. I wanted to put reality aside and wrap myself up in my own world, the world of my tiny, lonely, aesthetic hobby."

3
Fearful Days

Early in 1945, the fighting crept closer to Japan. American naval forces bombarded Leyte in the Philippines and a land-ing was effected; the U.S. Armed Forces overran the coun-try. The Emperor's advisers made secret preparations for surrender, while the Imperial Armies struggled on against overwhelming Allied forces, suffering heavy casualties. Waiting for his draft call, Mishima continued working at the kamikaze factory in Gumma prefecture, and he continued writing. In February 1945 he published part of *Chusei* in a magazine. "I was probably happy at that time," he wrote in *Watakushi no Henreki Jidai;* he had no worries about examinations or employment. "I had a little food—not much—and no responsibilities. I was happy in my daily life and in my writing. I had neither critics nor competitors to contend with . . . I felt no slightest responsibility for myself. I was in an anti-gravity environment."

Late in the evening of February 15, 1945, when Mishima, on leave from the factory, was visiting his parents in Tokyo, his akagami (the "red paper") arrived. He was to report for duty at Shikata, and prepared to leave the following morning. He composed a traditional isho, a farewell note for his family:

> Father, Mother, Mr. Shimizu, and my other teachers at the Gakushuin and at Tokyo Imperial University, who were so kind to me, I thank you for your blessings bestowed upon me.
>
> Also, I shall never forget the friendship of my classmates and seniors at the Gakushuin. May you have a bright future!
>
> You, my younger sister Mitsuko and younger brother Chiyuki, must discharge your duties to our parents in my place. Above all, Chiyuki, follow me and join the Imperial Army as soon as possible. Serve the Emperor!
>
> *Tenno Heika Banzai!*

When he left the next morning, his mother wept bitterly at the gate of their home as she saw him off. "Even my father seemed no little dejected," Mishima wrote. The youth boarded a train for the Kansai (the Osaka-Kobe area), and during the long ride, three hundred miles, a cold he had caught at the factory became much worse. By the time he reached the home of close family friends in the village of Shikata, their legal residence, he had such a high fever that he was unable to stand. After a night's rest, dosed with med-

icine, he made his way to the barracks the following morning. "My fever, which had only been checked by the medi-
cines, now returned. During the physical examination that
preceded final enlistment I had to stand around waiting
stark naked, like a wild beast, and I sneezed constantly. The
stripling of an army doctor who examined me mistook the
wheezing of my bronchial tubes for a chest rattle, and then
my haphazard answers concerning my medical history further confirmed him in his error. Hence I was given a blood
test, the results of which, influenced by the high fever of my
cold, led to a mistaken diagnosis of incipient tuberculosis. I
was ordered home the same day as unfit for service." Once
beyond the barracks gates, he broke into a run down the
bleak and wintry slope that descended to the village.

Mishima paid a short visit to Shizuo Ito, the poet who
had helped him achieve publication of *Hanazakari no Mori,*
who lived in Osaka; and that night he got on a train for
Tokyo. He recorded this journey in *Confessions:* "Shrinking
from the wind that blew in through a broken window glass,
I suffered with fever chills and a headache. Where shall I go
now? I asked myself. Thanks to my father's inherent inability to make a final decision about anything, my family still
remained unevacuated from our Tokyo house. Shall I go
there, to that house where everyone is cowering with sus-
pense? To that city hemming the house in with its dark
uneasiness? Into the midst of those crowds where all the
people have eyes like cattle and seem always to be wanting
to ask each other: 'Are you all right? Are you all right?' "
Mishima also reflected on his medical: "What I wanted was
to die among strangers, untroubled, beneath a cloudless sky
. . . If such were the case, wasn't the army ideal for my purpose? Why had I looked so frank as I lied to the army doctor? Why had I said that I'd been having a slight fever for
over half a year, that my shoulder was painfully stiff, that I
spit blood, that even last night I had been soaked by a night
sweat? . . . Why had I run so when I was through the barracks gate?"

Mishima's statement that he lied to the army doctor is

crucial to his whole career. By doing so, he avoided military service; yet, had he served in the army, even for a short while, his view of life in the ranks would have been less romantic, later in life. Mishima's own comments on his action at the army medical were clear; a voice within him announced that he would "never attain heights of glory sufficient to justify my having escaped death in the army." A second inner voice held that he "had never once truly wanted to die"; he had been looking forward to army service because "I had been secretly hoping that the army would provide me at last with an opportunity for gratifying those strange sensual desires of mine . . . I alone could never die." A third voice: "I much preferred to think of myself instead as a person who had been forsaken even by Death . . . I delighted in picturing the curious agonies of a person who wanted to die but had been refused by Death. The degree of mental pleasure I thus obtained seemed almost immoral."

The end of the war approached swiftly. The Hiraokas, Azusa having finally made up his mind to evacuate, moved out of their Shibuya house to stay with cousins at Gotokuji, beyond Shinjuku, comparatively far from the center of the city. The air raids had been getting worse and the devastating raid of March 9, in which over a hundred thousand people died, had persuaded Azusa to move. The spring was a dry one and the main hazard—the American B-29's dropped incendiaries—was fire. The wooden houses of Tokyo, packed closely together, went up in flames like kindling. Mishima described the scene in Tokyo after the giant raid: "The passageway over the railway tracks was filled with victims of the raid. They were wrapped up in blankets until one could see nothing but their eyes or, better said, nothing but their eyeballs, for they were eyes that saw nothing and thought nothing . . . Something caught fire within me. I was emboldened and strengthened by the parade of misery passing before my eyes. I was experiencing the same excitement that a revolution causes. In the fire these miserable ones had witnessed the total destruction of every evidence that they existed as human beings. Before their eyes they had seen human relationships, loves and hatreds, reason, property, all go up in flame. And at the time it had not been the flames against which they fought, but against human relationships, against loves and hatreds, against reason, against property . . . In their faces I saw traces of that exhaustion which comes from witnessing a spectacular drama . . . They were loud and boastful as they related to each other the dangers they had undergone. In the true sense of the word, this was a rebellious mob; it was a mob that harbored a radiant discontent, an overflowing, triumphant, high-spirited dissatisfaction" (*Confessions*).

The young Mishima had little to do. University classes had ceased and students no longer worked at the kamikaze factory. He stayed at home with his family, reading No plays, the dramas of Chikamatsu, the mysterious tales of Kyoka Izumi and Akinari Ueda, even the *Kojiki* and its ancient myths. "How dearly indeed I loved my pit, my dusky room, the place round my desk with its piles of books" (*Sun and Steel*). He believed that he would die in the final cataclysm at the end of the war. On April 1 the Americans invaded Okinawa, the large island to the southwest of the main islands of Japan. Kamikaze attacks inflicted great damage on the fleet off Okinawa, and the fighting went slowly; but there was no doubt who would win. At the last moment the Japanese commanders committed hara-kiri and many officers jumped to their deaths from the cliff where they had made a last stand. Mishima, who had been mobilized once more and sent to a naval dockyard at Koza near Tokyo, heard rumors that invasion of the mainland was imminent. "I was free. Everyday life had become a thing of unspeakable happiness. There was a rumor that the enemy would probably make a landing soon in S Bay and that the region in which the arsenal stood would be overwhelmed. And again, even more than before, I found myself deeply immersed in a desire for death. It was in death that I had discovered my real 'life's aim' " (*Confessions*).

From an air-raid shelter on the outskirts of Tokyo, Mi-

shima watched one of the greatest air attacks of the war, on
the night of May 24. "The sky over Tokyo turned crimson.
From time to time something would explode and suddenly
between the clouds we could see an eerie blue sky, as
though it were midday . . . The futile searchlights seemed
more like beacons welcoming the enemy planes . . . The
B-29's reached the skies over Tokyo in comfort." Mishima
saw other men who had been watching from the caves
where they had taken shelter applaud when a plane was hit
and fell, without knowing whether it was American or Japanese. "The young workmen were particularly vociferous.
The sound of hand-clapping and cheering rang out from the
mouths of the scattered tunnels as though in a theater . . . It
seemed to make no essential difference whether the falling
plane was ours or the enemy's. Such is the nature of war
. . ." (*Confessions*).

At the dockyard camp Mishima worked on a new manuscript, "Misaki nite no Monogatari" ("Story at a Cape"), a tale
based on a childhood visit to the sea. In June, *Bungei*, a
leading literary magazine, published another story of his,
and in that month he received his first zasshigenkoryo, his
first magazine fee. He wanted to find more allies in the Bundan, the literary establishment, and he met older writers
whenever he had leave from the camp. Two new acquaintances were the novelists Junzo Shono and Toshio Shimao.

In July the Japanese government made overtures of
peace, secretly, via the Moscow Embassy, hoping that Stalin
would serve as intermediary with America. The Potsdam
Conference was about to take place, following the collapse
of Germany; it was attended by Stalin, Truman, and Churchill and was an opportunity to end the war. The Japanese
initiative, however, was ignored by Stalin, who had plans of
his own: an attack on the Japanese positions in Manchuria
and elsewhere in the Far East. He was about to end the
neutrality treaty the two powers had signed in 1941. The
Japanese would not make a direct approach to the United
States, and the war dragged on. Following the Potsdam
meeting, a communiqué was issued which repeated the Al-

lied demand for the unconditional surrender of Japan. The communiqué gave no assurances about the Emperor's future, and the Japanese could not respond without them.

The summer was unusually hot. Mishima wrote in *Sun and Steel:* "My first—unconscious—encounter with the sun was in the summer of the defeat, in the year 1945. A relentless sun blazed down on the lush grass of that summer that lay on the borderline between the war and the postwar period—a borderline, in fact, that was nothing more than a line of barbed wire entanglements, half broken down, half buried in the summer weeks, tilting in all directions."

On August 6, Mishima learned that Hiroshima had been obliterated by a monstrous bomb. A second atom bomb destroyed part of Nagasaki three days later. "It was our last chance. People were saying that Tokyo would be next. Wearing white shirt and shorts, I walked about the streets. The people had reached the limits of desperation and were now going about their affairs with cheerful faces. From one moment to the next, nothing happened. Everywhere there was an air of cheerful excitement. It was just as though one was continuing to blow up an already bulging toy balloon, wondering: 'Will it burst now? Will it burst now?' " (*Confessions*).

Nothing happened for almost another week. "If it had gone on any longer there would have been nothing to do but go mad," Mishima wrote. Then, on August 14, U.S. aircraft appeared over Tokyo and dropped leaflets outlining the surrender proposals of the Allies, including a small concession on the status of the Emperor, who would be subordinate to the Supreme Commander of the Allied Powers (SCAP)— General Douglas MacArthur—but would remain on the throne. Tokyo lay in ruins and there was no possibility of repelling an Allied invasion of the main islands. The terms were accepted by the Japanese government.

Mishima was in bed with a fever at his relatives' house at Gotokuji when he heard the news of the surrender. "For me—for me alone—it meant that fearful days were beginning. It meant that, whether I would or no, and despite everything that had deceived me into believing such a day would never come to pass, the very next day I must begin life as an ordinary member of society. How the mere words made me tremble!" (*Confessions*).

The Emperor's surrender broadcast was made at noon on August 15. It could not be heard clearly; the squeaky voice of the monarch was partly drowned by static. In his first radio address, the Emperor said: "We declared war on America and Britain out of Our sincere desire to ensure Japan's self-preservation and the stabilization of East Asia, it being far from Our thought either to infringe upon the sovereignty of other nations or to embark upon territorial aggrandizement. But now the war has lasted for nearly four years. Despite the best that has been done by everyone . . . the war situation had developed not necessarily to Japan's advantage . . . Moreover, the enemy has begun to employ a new and most cruel bomb."

Five hundred military officers, including General Anami, the Minister of War, committed suicide at the surrender, to "take responsibility" for the defeat and to "apologize to the Emperor." Anami committed hara-kiri alone in his residence in Tokyo, refusing the offer of a coup de grâce; he bled slowly to death. Many officers overseas took their lives; among them was Zenmei Hasuda, Mishima's friend, who murdered his commanding officer for criticizing the Emperor and then put into effect his principle, "To die young, I am aware, is the culture of my nation," by blowing out his brains. A handful of civilians also took their lives, including a dozen members of a fanatical right-wing organization, the Daitokuju, who disemboweled themselves in Tokyo; two of the group acted as kaishaku-nin, beheading their comrades with swords.

Mishima began his "life as an ordinary member of society." "I passed the next year with vague and optimistic feelings. There were my law studies, perfunctorily performed, and my automatic goings and comings between university and home . . . I was not paying attention to anything nor was anything paying attention to me. I had acquired a worldly-wise smile like that of a young priest. I had the feeling of being neither alive nor dead." His former desire for the "natural and spontaneous suicide of death in war" had been completely eradicated and forgotten. The twenty-year-old was in a state of shock. "True pain can only come gradually. It is exactly like tuberculosis in that the disease has already progressed to a critical stage before the patient becomes aware of its symptoms." Later Mishima would often refer to the experience of living through the end of the war. "My life was cut in two," he said. "Misfortune attacked me." The death sentence on Mishima and his contemporaries had been lifted, but their whole system of values had been shattered. For Mishima the experience was even more traumatic. During the war he had been made to feel a genius, the representative spirit of his age; after the war he was merely a student. In Hashikawa's words: "When the pressure of war was eliminated, he lost his balance."

Mishima was in utter misery, and his agony was increased by the death of his sister, whom he loved. Mitsuko died in October 1945 of typhoid contracted from well water. Mishima looked after her in the hospital; he would stay by her bedside for hours, reading his law books. "I shall never forget the way she said, 'Thank you, brother,' when I gave her water," Mishima told his mother. Mitsuko, a student at the Sacred Heart School in Tokyo, died at the age of seventeen. A family friend later remarked: "It was a shame for Kimitake that she died. She gave him a different idea of women to that which he derived from his grandmother and his doting mama. She was tomboyish and critical. He would say of her: 'Can she really be a woman at all?' He could not understand a normal woman."

Mishima withdrew into himself and ignored the chaotic world about him. "I would see no evil, hear no evil, speak no evil." He paid no attention to the important changes in government. Although he was a law student, he did not interest himself in the "five reforms," General MacArthur's programs for industrial, land, election, union, and educational law reform which were to lay the foundations for demokurashi in Japan. Nor did Mishima concern himself with social problems, although he was surrounded by them. The plight of the people of Tokyo, whose homes had been destroyed and who had little food, was acute; a roaring black market rose up and profiteers flourished. The suffering of ordinary people was immense; suicide by drinking methylated spirits was common. Mishima clung to his own little world—his "castle," he sometimes called it, his "dark cave." He paid little heed to the outside world, ignoring even developments that affected the Emperor, whom General MacArthur had decreed should remain on the throne and should not be put on trial with the "war criminals"; as a condition, however, the Emperor had to make a statement disavowing the wartime ideology. The ningen sengen (human declaration)—with its implication that the Emperor was a mere mortal—was delivered on New Year's Day 1946 and contained this key passage: "The ties between Us and Our people have always stood on mutual trust and affection. They do not depend on mere legends and myths. They are not predicated upon the false concept that the Emperor is divine and that the Japanese people are superior to other races and fated to rule the world."

Mishima picked up the threads of his literary career. He took his manuscripts to the editors of the monthly magazines. Utaro Noda, the editor of *Bungei,* later recalled in the magazine (February 1971): "He brought to me the manuscript of *Chusei.* Reading it through, I felt that he was brilliant, but that I could not praise him one hundred percent. He struck me as like a strange plant which had skipped the natural process of maturing and had bloomed straightaway with no more than a couple of leaves on its stem." Noda criticized Mishima's "evil narcissism." Naoya Shiga, one of the best-known writers of the day, was also approached by Mishima, and shared Noda's critical opinion of the youth: "Shiga remembered Mishima as a boy who had been at school with his daughter for a while. He said that Mishima had often slipped manuscripts and letters into his post box. But he criticized Mishima's works: 'His stories are all dreams. They have no reality. They are no good.'" Noda passed on these criticisms to Mishima and encouraged him to write still more romantic tales, hoping that the boy would cure himself of his romanticism through an overdose: "He wrote two romantic short stories and brought the manuscripts to me one day when Tokyo was covered with fresh snow. I remember his seriousness that snowy day."

But Noda was disappointed in Mishima's next manuscripts. The young man had brought him "Misaki nite no Monogatari," the story he had written at the Koza naval dockyard just before the surrender. "It was merely a clever professional work. I told Mishima this and he answered that he had much confidence in the story. I asked, then, if he wanted to be an original novelist or a well-known popular writer, and he replied categorically that it would be the latter." The literary editor expressed his disappointment and Mishima then began to look for another sponsor. He wanted to break though quickly into the postwar literary world, and he needed the help of an older man with an established reputation as a writer. By himself he would not be able to attain his ambition immediately. From Noda, Mishima obtained an introduction to Yasunari Kawabata, one of the foremost writers in Japan.

Noda remembered: "After his work had appeared in *Bungei* . . . he came to see me only once. That was when he wanted my introduction to Kawabata." Mishima had a way of dropping people who were no longer useful to him, and in Noda he made an enemy. "After the war he became a popular novelist, just as he had hoped he would do, but the fresh, serious young Mishima vanished. I felt that Mishima lived only in his pen name and not as Kimitake Hiraoka. That pen name became a narcissistic shadow of the real man, something like Hong Kong flowers." "Hong Kong flowers" were the cheap plastic flowers which used to flood into Japan, much as Japanese goods flooded America, and were regarded as imitations—as "shadows" of the real thing.

4

Kawabata's Protégé

Yasunari Kawabata, the first Japanese writer to win the Nobel Prize (in 1968), was forty-six when he first met the young Mishima. Born in 1899, Kawabata had first wanted to become a painter and then had established his reputation in Japan in the nineteen-twenties as a young writer with a classical background and modern tastes. He was one of the handful of eminent literati who came through the Pacific War with their names unblemished by association with the militarists. A man of independent means, married and living at Kamakura, where he did his writing—he is best known in the West for his novels *Snow Country* and *A Thousand Cranes*—Kawabata was generous by nature and was disposed to help young writers whose work he liked. When Mishima, an almost unknown law student, brought him some manuscripts during the New Year holiday in 1946, he liked a short story about homosexual relationships at the Gakushuin well enough to recommend it to a magazine editor. "Tabako" ("Tobacco") was published in *Ningen* magazine that summer, introducing the young Mishima to the postwar literary world.

Mishima was overjoyed by Kawabata's decision to sponsor him, and rightly so. In the inbred world of the Japanese Bundan, as the literary establishment is called, a young writer needed the backing of an older man, and no one could have been better suited for this role than Kawabata, who instinctively understood the formal, sensitive Mishima. But the young man's dreams of becoming famous overnight were not fulfilled. The publication of "Tabako" caused no sensation. The lack of reaction, even among the other writers he knew, gravely disappointed him, and he decided that his father was right and that he should not concentrate on a literary career.

He made plans to sit for the civil-service examination, the Kobun, and to start his working life as a government official. Obviously a writer had to be better known in the Bundan before he could hope for any real success. But, while he pursued his studies, he also tried to further his literary associations. He continued to meet with Kawabata, and the older writer made him a member of the Kamakura Bunko, an exclusive lending library Kawabata had founded with his literary friends. He also tried to meet as many of the other established writers as he could, with the aim of shifting eventually from government service to a literary career.

One of the writers he met in the early postwar years was Osamu Dazai, and his single encounter with this famous romantic writer made a deep impression. The meeting took place in 1947 when a friend of Mishima's, another young man with literary aspirations, who knew Dazai and his circle personally, took him along one evening to meet the writer at a party in the Ginza. Dazai, who was only thirty-eight, was at that time the most popular novelist with the younger generation in Japan. In his best-selling novel *The Setting Sun* he portrayed a mood of hopelessness they identified with, and this reflected a quality in his work as a whole, for it was often dark and depressing, and had something in common with Mishima's own writing.

Mishima, however, was unnerved by the similarities between Dazai and himself, which were at that time personal, and not obviously literary. Both men were snobs; both desired to create a sensation and be heroes of the general public; and both were obsessed with suicide. Mishima, in advance of his meeting with Dazai, made up his mind to be aggressive, to be a "literary assassin," as he once said. When he and his friend joined them, Dazai and his group of admirers were sitting in an upstairs room in their Ginza restaurant. It was a squalid room, with dirty tatami (rice-straw mats), just the kind of place Mishima disliked, and the company was drinking low-quality saké, the only alcohol that could be obtained in Japan then, unless one bought imported liquor at black-market prices. Mishima did not drink in those days; and he sat a little apart from Dazai and his disciples, listening tensely to their conversation—waiting for an opportunity to pounce. When there was a brief silence, Mishima broke in. "Mr. Dazai," he said, "I hate your work." The novelist, as Mishima told it, paused for a moment before replying, seemingly surprised (not unnaturally). Then he remarked to those sitting close by: "I know he loves me, though; otherwise, he wouldn't have come here." The remark stung Mishima, presumably because it had an element of truth; and he remembered the taunt for the rest of his life. He would often tell his "Dazai story"; twenty years later he was still obsessed with the memory of the remark: "I know he loves me, though . . ." Dazai was one of the very few men who "put down" Mishima, and he never had an opportunity to retaliate, as Dazai committed suicide in 1948; he drowned himself in a river in Tokyo with his mistress.

It is interesting to contrast Mishima's relationship with Dazai and with Kawabata. He met Dazai only once and had a very strong reaction to him; the long-haired, pale-faced writer could have been close to Mishima had he lived: even his suicide seems to stress an element they had in common. Mishima's friendship with Kawabata, though it lasted for almost twenty-five years, was far less intense. Mishima kept his distance from everyone and made no exception for Kawabata; they had, in a sense, a literary alliance, based on mutual understanding and appreciation rather than friendship. Kawabata was much less tense than Mishima—or Dazai—and seemed unlikely ever to contemplate suicide (in fact, he gassed himself eighteen months after Mishima's death).

Although his interest was in literature, Mishima read his law books with a wholehearted concentration typical of him. He studied hard, displaying stoic virtue. In the spring of 1947, "the time for preparing for the civil service examination was at hand and I had to devote all my energies to dry-as-dust study." Mishima described in *Confessions of a Mask* how "spring came and a frantic nervousness built up behind my façade of tranquillity." At odd moments he would go out for a walk to exercise his body a little, and "often I became aware that people were looking questioningly at my bloodshot eyes." He was exceedingly self-conscious.

He wrote at length in *Confessions of a Mask* of an abortive love affair with a girl named Sonoko, but Sonoko was a composite character drawn from the experiences of Mishima's friends and several young women in upper-middle-class families he knew. The young law student occasionally went to a party, but found it impossible to relax with other young people. Going home alone—he was still living with his parents, who had returned to their house in Tokyo immediately after the war—he would play at mental self-torture: "You're not human. You're a being who is incapable of social intercourse. You're nothing but a creature, non-human and somehow strangely pathetic." Was he also incapable of sexual love? It is almost certain that he had no real relationship with a woman until at least his early thirties. His Japanese biographer, Takeo Okuno, speaks of having received a call late one night, at about 2 a.m., in which Mishima enthusiastically reported that he had slept with a girl (this was 1957, many years later). He was homosexual, as is clear from *Confessions of a Mask*. Yet he certainly attempted to have relationships with women as well as men, in the early postwar years; he even made marriage proposals, at least twice. But he was an uncertain prospect, not least because of his closeness to his mother, to judge by the comments that one of the women to whom he proposed made to me: "I couldn't see myself marrying him, because he was too close to his mother. She was very nice to me and there was nothing wrong, but I feared that I would come between mother and son if we were married. Besides, I wasn't sure that I felt a passion for him."

Mishima took his kobun examination in the autumn of 1947 and was accepted by the Ministry of Finance, much to his father's delight (this ministry is the power center of the Japanese bureaucracy). He worked hard in the Banking Bureau of the ministry during the day and then would sit up half the night writing short stories. He was beginning to get more of his work published. A colleague remembers him as "a stylish official who tried his utmost to combine literary work with his labors in the office." In the ministry he had a reputation for literary knowledge, joined the group which edited the ministry magazine, *Zaisei*, and gave lectures to his colleagues on classical literature. "Once," according to his fellow civil servant, Minoru Nagaoka, "he made a speech to junior officials on the subject of 'Women in the Literature of the Heain Period.' " Mishima was naturally gifted as a bureaucrat and could have risen to the top of the ministry had he chosen. He had powers of organization of a rare order and was an amusing colleague who attracted attention. "He wrote a witty speech for the Minister, and his kacho [section chief] had to cut out a great deal of it, as it was far too funny for the Ministry of Finance." But Mishima did not fancy a career in government. He continued to devote himself to short-story work at home, often staying up until 2 a.m. or later, to fulfill the growing stream of requests from magazine editors. A writer establishes himself in Japan by writing short stories and then goes on to novels or plays. Mishima's output was formidable, as one may see from this representative list of his publications during 1948, up to September:

		MAGAZINE
January	*Sakasu*	*Shinro*
	Somon no Genryu	*Nihon Tanka*
February	Preface to *Tozoku*	*Gozen*
March	*Jushosha no Kyoki*	*Ningen*
	Chapter 5 of *Tozoku*	*Shinbungaku*
April	*Junkyo*	*Tancho*
	Kazoku Awase	*Bungaku Kikan*
May	Commentary on Radiguet	*Sekai Bungaku*
	Ayame	*Fujin Bunko*
June	*Kashira Moji*	*Bungaku Kai*
	Jizen	*Kaizo*
	Hoseki Baibai	*Bungei*

July	*Koshoku*	*Shosetsukai*
	Tsumibito	*Fujin*

September 22   Resigned from the Ministry of Finance

As the titles of his works suggest—*Koshoku* means "Sensuality"; *Junkyo* is "Martyrdom"; and *Hoseki Baibai* translates into "Traffic in Precious Stones"—Mishima's writing was sensational.

Mishima was now doing well enough as a writer to resign from the ministry. Azusa was enraged by his decision, but he no longer had the power to control his son. Mishima was earning a good income from his writing and could certainly support himself for several years, especially as he was saving money living with his parents. Shizue naturally took Mishima's side in the family quarrel over his resignation, and Azusa was no match for mother and son, so gave in with a typical remark: "All right, if you absolutely insist, you may go ahead and leave the ministry. But you'd better make yourself the best writer in the land, do you hear?"

Mishima was often melancholy. He wrote in his diary: "What does it matter to me if A-bombs rain down on us again? All I desire is beauty." When he embarked on *Confessions of a Mask*, on November 25, 1948, his intention was to analyze his "aesthetic nihilism"; also, to purge himself of a "monster" within. Twenty-two years later, to the day, he committed suicide.

Almost half of *Confessions of a Mask* is taken up with a description of the relationship between the narrator and the young girl Sonoko, whom I have mentioned. These Sonoko scenes are not reliable as autobiography, but they are nevertheless revealing. At one point the narrator goes to his mother—just before the end of the war—and asks whether he should marry Sonoko, for the girl has concluded from his fumbling approaches that he has matrimony in mind. It seems somehow natural that the narrator of *Confessions,* when faced with this decision, should consult his mother and accept her verdict (which is *not* to marry). The scene is greatly in character with what one knows of Mishima himself; he depended on his mother for protection.

The second passage, probably the most well-known scene in the book, is the encounter between Sonoko and the narrator, with which *Confessions of a Mask* ends. It is a sweltering summer day in Tokyo and the pair have entered a cheap dance hall to while away time. The narrator sees a group of yakuza, of gangsters, who are seated close by, and he is hypnotized by the sight of a young man among them. "He was a youth of twenty-one or -two, with coarse but regular and swarthy features. He had taken off his shirt and stood there half naked, rewinding a bellyband about his middle . . . The hot mass of his smooth torso was being severely and tightly imprisoned by each succeeding turn of the soiled cotton bellyband. His bare, suntanned shoulders gleamed as though covered with oil. And black tufts stuck out from the cracks of his armpits . . ." At this point, "above all at the sight of the peony tattooed on his hard chest," the narrator is beset by sexual desire. He forgets Sonoko's existence: "I was thinking of but one thing: of his going out onto the streets of high summer just as he was, half-naked, and getting into a fight with a rival gang. Of a sharp dagger cutting through that bellyband, piercing that torso. Of that soiled bellyband beautifully dyed with blood . . ." The book closes on a note characteristic of Mishima's writing: "It was time [to leave] . . . The group [of thugs] had apparently gone to dance, and the chairs stood empty in the blazing sunshine. Some sort of beverage had been spilled on the table top and was throwing back glittering, threatening reflections."

Confessions of a Mask was hailed by the critics as a work of genius. The book established Yukio Mishima, as he was known thereafter, as one of the foremost writers of the younger generation. Few of the critics, however, sensed the existence of the profound conflict within the personality of Yukio Mishima, and the nature of his struggle against weakness—a struggle out of which *Confessions of a Mask* was born.

Among the many comments on Mishima's work, one searches in vain for a criticism with the accuracy of a remark of Yasunari Kawabata's in his introduction to an earlier, unsuccessful novel by Mishima, *Tozoku* ("Robbers," 1948). "I am dazzled by Mishima's mature talent," Kawabata wrote. "And at the same time I am disturbed by it. His novelty is not easy to understand. Some may think that Mishima is invulnerable, to judge from this work. Others will see that he has deep wounds." Kawabata had seen into the young writer's being; he knew how vulnerable his protégé was. In this he was almost alone among Mishima's associates and friends. No wonder, then, that when Mishima put an end to his life twenty years later, Kawabata felt an overwhelming responsibility for his death. Who knows, though, whether it was within his power to have helped Mishima to avoid disaster? The wounds were so deep and the end had been so well rehearsed.

Confessions of a Mask had another revealing aspect: Mishima had nothing to say in it about political events that had influenced his life. He made no attempt to analyze the crucial event of his youth—his experience during the war and the collapse of Japanese imperialism in 1945. He was regarded as apolitical by his contemporaries, although an emissary from the Japanese Communist Party, Hajime Odagiri, did once try to persuade him to join the party. It was not until the 1960's that Mishima attempted to write about the Emperor and the defeat of 1945. His long silence on these great national topics may be interpreted as a sign that he was not politically involved or as evidence of his depth of feeling. I believe that both theories are tenable: Mishima felt no involvement in politics in a mundane day-to-day sense; but his experience during the war—and the teaching of the Nippon Roman-ha—made a deep impression on him. He *was* an imperialist of a kind.

FOUR

The Four Rivers
(1950–70)

I want to make a poem of my life.
Yukio Mishima

Suicide is something planned in the silence of the heart, like a work of art.

Albert Camus

1
Pictures at an Exhibition

Shortly before he killed himself, Mishima organized an exhibition devoted to his life. It was held at the Tobu department store at Ikebukuro in Tokyo between November 12 and 19, 1970. In an introduction to the catalogue of the exhibition, he wrote: "Just as I was about to complete my tetralogy, *The Sea of Fertility,* after six years of work, the Tobu department store asked me for permission to do a retrospective exhibition on my literary life. I have been writing for nearly a quarter of a century and should like to reexamine the paths I have trod. A writer, once he begins looking back on his past works, drives himself into a dead end, but what is wrong with letting others arrange his past? I made only one suggestion: that was to divide my forty-five years of life—a life so full of contradictions—into Four Rivers, 'Writing,' 'Theater,' 'Body,' and 'Action,' all finally flowing into *The Sea of Fertility.*"

The exhibition was a great success. There were one hundred thousand visitors, the great majority of whom were men. "It seems that I am not popular with the ladies," Mishima wrote in a letter to his old teacher from the Gakushuin, Fumio Shimizu. Among the visitors was Shizue Hiraoka. She was astonished to see so many materials on display which Mishima had not previously shown to the public—pictures, for example, of Shizue herself as a young woman. She was also surprised by the exhibition as a whole; the hall was hung with black curtains.

"What does it mean?" Shizue asked her son at home. "Why are all the pictures surrounded by black?"

"It's just so that you can see them properly, to provide contrast," he replied.

The exhibition was Mishima's farewell to the general public. In a prominent position was the sword made by Seki no Magoroku, the two-handed, three-foot-long weapon with which Masakatsu Morita was to cut off Mishima's head on November 25.

In the black-bound catalogue, Mishima wrote: "The visitor will be able to choose just those Rivers that interest him and avoid being swept away into a River that he dislikes. I shall be grateful to those who follow all four Rivers of my life but I cannot believe there will be many such visitors."

2

The River of Writing

This River helps me to cultivate my fields with the mercy of its waters, supports my living and at times floods and nearly drowns me in its prolific streams. The River also demands from me infinite patience and daily hard labor through the changing seasons and passing time. How alike are writing and farming! One's spirit must be on guard at every moment against storms and frosts. After such a long and vigilant watch over my field of writing, and after such endless toil of imagination and poetry, can I ever be sure of a rich harvest? What I have written departs from me, never nourishing my void, and becomes nothing but a relentless whip lashing me on. How many struggling nights, how many desperate hours, had to be spent on those writings! If I were to add up and record my memories of such nights I would surely go mad. Yet I still have no way to survive but to keep on writing one line, one more line, one more line . . .

Yukio Mishima, Catalogue to the Tobu Exhibition

PART ONE   1950–54

Yukio Mishima described his first years as a professional writer in his untranslated autobiographical work, *Watakushi no Henreki Jidai* ("My Wandering Years," 1964). He was not the kind of writer who "rushed ahead with his work on inspiration." He had gained confidence personally, gave an impression of extraordinary liveliness, and attracted a great deal of attention to himself, but in his method of work he considered himself to be like a banker. (Perhaps he had been influenced by his year in the Banking Bureau at the Ministry of Finance.) Imagine, he wrote, a bank with a large, cheerful display in its window—there are such banks in Japan—and that would give a picture of his style. Mishima regarded Thomas Mann, who had remarked that "writers should look like bankers," as his model. Mann's "Teutonic stubbornness and unnecessary meticulousness" were far from Mishima's original character, but he had been "captured by the dramatic quality" of Mann's writing and had been attracted by "the unique character of tragedy in German literature." Mishima, like other Japanese writers, sought to incarnate the style of the Western writer whom he most admired at this time. When he gave lectures to literary societies, he dressed in three-piece suits, had his hair cut short, and looked every inch the prosperous, able young banker or Japanese industrialist.

And yet he was not at peace with himself. "In 1950 I went up and down, from a peak of happiness down to the pit of melancholy." During this period, and up to the time of his departure on his first world trip at the end of 1951, he was "emotionally more unstable than at any other time of my life." The smart young Mishima was "constantly lonely, and I was jealous of the mediocre youth of others"; he thought of himself as "a peculiar, grinning old man aged twenty-five." And he was ill. He had taken up riding, shortly after leaving the ministry, as he felt that he was in need of exercise. He had joined an exclusive riding club which used the grounds of the Imperial Palace, and there he had his photograph taken, sitting astride a white mare. But this exercise was insufficient to bring him back to health. "I was continually troubled by stomach ache." Mishima decided that he must at all costs get out of Japan; he made inquiries about booking passage on an Antarctic whaler; even this proved impossible to arrange. The degree of his nervousness is evident from *Watakushi no Henreki Jidai:* "I decided to divide my energy between two worlds: my work and my everyday life. I would no longer trouble myself with the intermediate existence, 'association with others.' " He hated "others."

Early in the autumn of 1950, as he was standing outside a large bookshop in Tokyo inspecting a poster for an exhibition of mummies from the Chuson temple, it suddenly crossed his mind that the people he saw entering and leaving the bookshop were themselves mummies. "I detested their ugliness. How unattractive intellectuals are!" Out of this experience came a bold resolution. Spurred by "uncontrollable hate," he decided that he must travel to Greece, "the land of my dreams." This classical aspiration, he related, was generated by "a keen passion for harmony and a deep antipathy to disharmony and exaggeration." Later, with the benefit of hindsight, he changed his self-diagnosis: "I was probably mistaken. My antipathy for intellectuals was a reaction against my own enormous, monstrous sensitivity. That is why I wanted to become a classicist." "Travel," he said, not without self-contradiction once more, for he was ignorant of nature, "consoled me and I experienced a sensual attraction toward scenery . . . Descriptions of nature have an importance in my literature similar to that of love scenes in the work of other men."

Mishima, who was Western in many respects, was encountering in his mid-twenties the difficulties of many young romantic writers of the same age in the West. It was a crisis period that affected his work. During 1950–1 he wrote a novel that he described as a failure: *Mashin Reihai* ("Worship of Evil"). And he wrote a second novel, *Ao no Jidai* ("Blue Period"), the construction and style of which he analyzed as "miserable." A third novel, *Forbidden Colors,* was "unnecessarily confused." Others thought he was writing well, but the pace of his work had been disturbed: "I don't like to write like that." His successful novel of this time (Mishima was writing two or three books a year) was *Thirst for Love.* It was written, he said, under the influence of François Mauriac. "Surely," wrote Mishima, "there can be no foreign author as much to Japanese taste as Mauriac." According to Donald Keene, who wrote the first long essay on Mishima's writing to be published in the West (it is in his collection *Landscapes and Portraits,* published by Kodansha International in 1971): "He explained this [the influence of Mauriac] in terms of a Japanese fascination for details— the expression on a woman's face when, on the point of weeping, she holds back her tears; just how far back one can see in a woman's mouth when she smiles; the pattern the wrinkles make in her dress when a woman turns round. Mauriac is a master of such details, but, according to Mishima, American novels afford little pleasure of this nature and therefore have never had much appeal for the Japanese." *Thirst for Love,* Keene observes, "abounds in such details; they suggest not only Mishima's indebtedness to Mauriac but his place in the tradition of Japanese literature."

The central character in *Thirst for Love* is Etsuko, a woman in her early thirties, who has gone to live with the family of her husband, in the country near Osaka, after his death. The novel is set in the immediate postwar period, a

time of great social upheaval. Mishima describes Etsuko in a
scene at the beginning of the book: "Etsuko passed her
hand through the handle of her shopping bag. The curving
bamboo scraped down across her forearm as she lifted her
hands to her face. Her cheeks were very warm. That was a
common occurrence with her. There wasn't any reason for
it; of course, it wasn't a symptom of any illness—it was just
that suddenly her cheeks would start to burn. Her hands,
delicate though they were, were calloused and tanned, and
because of that very delicacy seemed rougher. They
scratched her cheeks and intensified the burning." Etsuko
walks "as if she were pregnant," with "an ostentatiously
indolent walk. She didn't realize it; she had no one who
might see it and set her right; but like the slip of paper that
a mischievous boy has surreptitiously affixed to a friend's
back, that walk was her involuntary sign and seal." She
comes from a middle-class family in Tokyo and does not like
the rural life about her. As she walks home from a shopping
expedition: "Lights were burning in the rows of government
housing. There were hundreds of units—of the same style,
the same life, the same smallness, the same poverty. The
road through this squalid community afforded a shortcut that
she never took." (In this description, Mishima's own feelings about postwar demokurashi are evident.)

Etsuko is secretly in love with a farm boy, Saburo, who
also lives with the family. And in the autumn there is a festival which gives her a chance to come physically close to
him after months of longing. Saburo and the other village
youths, wearing only fundoshi (loincloths), dash about in
front of the village Shinto shrine, in pursuit of a lion's head
borne on a standard. For this, Etsuko prepares herself as if
she were going to a chic reception in Tokyo: "She wore a
scattered-chrysanthemum silk kimono, of a kind rare outside
the city, under a shiny, black haori, tailored slightly short.
The scent of her treasured Houbigant wafted faintly about
her—a cologne that had no place at a country festival, obviously put on for Saburo alone." On the way to the festival
she tears her haori, her jacket, but does not notice. Her

thoughts are on the fiery scene ahead. She arrives at the shrine and sees the young men dancing around the lion's head, back and forth, as bamboo firecrackers explode, and suddenly rushes toward them, having recognized Saburo in their midst. "Etsuko stumbled forward, pushed by the throng, and collided with a bare back, warm as fire, coming from the opposite direction. She reached out her hands and held it off. It was Saburo's back. She savored the touch of his flesh. She savored the majestic warmth of him. The mob pushed again from behind her, causing her fingernails to gouge into Saburo's back. He did not even feel it. In all the mad pushing and shoving he had no idea what woman was pressing against his back. Etsuko felt the blood dripping between her fingers."

Thirst for Love ends with a scene in the genre of the "murder theater," in which Etsuko drives a mattock through the neck of Saburo. Her love for him turns to panic when she discovers that Saburo is attracted to her. As Flaubert was Madame Bovary, Mishima was Etsuko. He, too, felt a compulsion to love and to hurt the object of his love; he, too, was repelled when the other responded to his approaches. His thirst, like that of Etsuko's, could not be quenched with love; to accept the love of another was the hardest thing that could be required of him.

The "basic proposition of the modern novel," wrote Mishima, "is, as Dostoevsky said . . . the expression of diametrically opposed attitudes within human beings." In his other major work of this period, *Forbidden Colors*, Mishima attempted to show "the discrepancies and conflicts within myself, as represented by two 'I's.' " The first "I" is Shunsuke, a writer of sixty-five, a celebrated novelist whose *Collected Works* are being published for the third time. Shunsuke is the "grinning old man" whom Mishima feared to find in himself: "This new collection of *The Works of Shunsuke Hinoki* would be his third. The first one was assembled when he was forty-five. At that point in time, I recall, he thought to himself that in spite of the great accumulation of my works acclaimed by the world as the epitome of stability and unity, and, in a sense, having reached the pinnacle, as many predicted, I was quite given over to this foolishness . . . a wild ability to handle abstractions, which threatened to make me misanthropic." Shunsuke studies a brochure advertising his *Collected Works,* on which his photograph appears: "It was a picture of an ugly old man. That was the only way to put it. However, it was not difficult to see in it certain dim and delicate traces of the spiritual beauty so acclaimed by the world. The broad forehead; the clipped, narrow cheeks; the broad, hungry lips; the willful chin: in every feature the traces of long, hard work and of spirit lay open to the light. His face, however, was not so much molded by spirit as riddled with it . . . In its ugliness his face was a corpse emaciated of spirit, no longer possessing the power to retain its privacy." (Mishima, in his disgust with old age, was ahead of his years, yet in touch with the mood of his time, as represented by the work of Tanizaki and Kawabata, whose books *The Diary of a Mad Old Man* and *The House of the Sleeping Beauties* expressed a horror of old age more vividly than did *Forbidden Colors.*)

The second "I" of *Forbidden Colors* is Yuichi, a youth of exquisite beauty, first seen by Shunsuke as he emerges from the sea after a swim: "It was an amazingly beautiful young man. His body surpassed the sculptures of ancient Greece. It was like the Apollo molded in bronze by an artist of the Peloponnesus school. It overflowed with gentle beauty and carried such a noble column of a neck, such gently sloping shoulders, such a softly broad chest, such elegantly rounded wrists, such a rapidly tapering, tightly filled trunk, such legs, stoutly filled out like a heroic sword." Shunsuke sees Yuichi's face: "Quick, narrow eyebrows; deep, sad eyes; rather thick, fresh lips—these made up the design of his extraordinary profile. The wonderful ridge of his nose, furthermore, along with his controlled facial expression, gave to his youthful good looks a certain chaste impression of wildness, as if he had never known anything but noble thoughts and starvation." Yuichi, unlike the protagonist of *Confessions of a Mask,* is an uncomplicated homosexual who enjoys the act of love. He is, however, much more of a narcissist than he is a homosexual—true to Mishima's own character in this respect. When Yuichi makes his first appearance at a gay bar in Tokyo, "Yuichi floated on desire. The look they gave him was like that a woman feels when she passes among men and their eyes instantly undress her down to the last stitch. Practiced appraisers' eyes usually do not make mistakes. The gently sloping chest . . . the potential lovely harmony between what one saw and could not see seemed as perfect as a product of the ratio of golden section."

The novel was strongly misogynist; Shunsuke uses Yuichi to wreak his revenge on several women whom he hates. In one scene Shunsuke, confronted with the drowned body of his third and last wife, who has committed suicide with her lover, presses a No mask onto the swollen face of his dead spouse, "until it buckled like ripe fruit." The novel was also chauvinistic; the foreigners in the book are deliberately absurd. One such character has the custom of shouting "Tengoku! Tengoku!" (Paradise! Paradise!) when he reaches a sexual climax; another makes an assault on Yuichi and, when repulsed, weeps and kisses the cross which hangs from a chain about his own neck.

Mishima's private life at this time resembled Yuichi's. "He knew far more about boys than we did," remarked one of his literary friends. He patronized Brunswick, a gay bar in the Ginza; there he met the seventeen-year-old Akihiro Maruyama, who had just begun a golden career in the gay bars—from which he was to graduate to the theater, where he became the most celebrated female impersonator of his day. The two men danced together; but they did not have an affair, according to Maruyama, who "did not think him [Mishima] handsome, he was not my type." Mishima had reservations about the gay bars, which are the haunts of scandal-seeking journalists and blackmailers and, like the whole of the Ginza, are under the protection of yakuza, of gangsters. He particularly disliked effeminate men (his own ideal was a masculine type), as is clear from this description of a gay bar in *Forbidden Colors:* "Men dancing together—this uncommon joke. As they danced, the rebellious smiles beaming from their faces said: 'We aren't doing this because we are forced to; we are only playing a simple joke.' While they danced, they laughed, a spirit-destroying laugh." Mishima wrote to a friend a little later: "I am not going to Brunswick any more."

Like Yuichi in *Forbidden Colors,* Mishima sought both male and female company. One of his girlfriends told me: "He liked women with long necks and round faces and he was very particular in some ways. When we went out together, he would specify what I was to wear. For the Comédie Française I had to wear a gown from Paris." He was, in the Japanese phrase, a "bearer of two swords"; but he preferred men.

Shizue remained the center of his life. At night she would set out in the tatami room in which her son lived in their new home in Midorigaoka—a fashionable suburb of Tokyo—the things he needed in the evening: fresh paper, pen and pencils, tea, fruit, blankets, glasses, and so on. And Shizue was always the first person to see her son's writing. The family home was quiet and a good place to work. Chiyuki, Mishima's younger brother—an entirely different kind of man, unassuming and lacking in great ambition— had decided to take the diplomatic-service examination; he never disturbed his busy older brother. Only his father, still a grumbler, enjoyed disputes; Azusa picked quarrels over the domestic pets, and, as a lover of dogs, tried to insist that Mishima do away with his cats. Mishima had cut a little door in the wall of his room so that his cats could come and go. And when he traveled abroad, he would send postcards to the cats, adding postscripts in which he urged his father to be more considerate to them. "Sometimes he would work away for hours with a cat sitting on his lap, it would drive me mad," Azusa said. "Your brain must be like a dog's, Father," Mishima would reply. "You can't understand the delicate psychology of cats."

Late in 1951, with his father's assistance, Mishima made arrangements to travel abroad. Azusa had a friend at the *Asahi Shimbun,* the leading Japanese newspaper; and with this journalist's help Mishima obtained an appointment as a special correspondent without reporting duties but entitled to an issue of foreign exchange, available from the Ministry of Finance, his old ministry, only under the rarest circumstances (Japan was desperately short of foreign exchange). He left Yokohama on Christmas Day on the *President Wilson,* seen off by his parents, who waved goodbye from the pier. Mishima had been looking forward to this chance to travel overseas; as he recalled in *Watakushi no Henreki Jidai:* "I felt the strong necessity of traveling abroad . . . I was in the midst of an emotional crisis, I had to discover a new man within myself."

On board ship he was happy. He mixed with the other passengers, abandoning "my long-held claims to the solitude of a writer and my contempt for the world." He attended New Year fancy-dress parties with some Americans, tying a hachimaki, a headband, on his head, and during the day he sat on deck reading. Sitting in the sun, which he had been unable to do earlier in life, when his lungs were delicate, opened up a new world to him. "I found the sun for the first time. I had come out of a dark cave. How long I had suppressed my love of the sun! All day long, sunbathing on deck, I wondered how I should change myself. What did I have in excess? What did I lack?" (*Watakushi no Henreki Jidai*). He concluded that he had quite enough sensitivity. "What I lack is an existential awareness of myself and of my body. I know how to despise mere cool intelligence. What I want is intelligence matched by pure physical existence— like a statue. And for this I need the sun, I need to leave my dark, cave-like study."

Mishima's baptism in international travel was not unlike that of other Japanese. He tended to look back over his shoulder at Japan rather than at the life about him. In Honolulu he was struck by the calm manner in which Nisei (American Japanese) who lived there received a concert by

Yehudi Menuhin and Jascha Heifetz; by contrast, in Tokyo, there had been an enormous fuss over the musicians (to the amusement of people in Hawaii). In San Francisco, Mishima went to a Japanese restaurant and was given food of poor quality; he was "reminded of Japan in the most miserable fashion possible." Traveling on to Los Angeles, visiting museums, he came across a work by Turner borrowed from London, and he greatly admired a first edition of William Blake's *Songs of Innocence;* he was also much intrigued by a case full of minutely detailed old cameos. New York made a deep impression on Mishima. This was "Tokyo five hundred years from now," but Tokyo and New York had something in common: "in both cities, artists have a nostalgia for Paris." He was shepherded about by a guide from the Congress for Cultural Freedom, on the introduction of Herb Passin, the American scholar, a friend of Mishima's in Japan. In New York he visited the museums (at the Museum of Modern Art, he admired Picasso's *Guernica*) and went to the theater and to the opera. Richard Strauss, he said, after seeing *Salome* at the Metropolitan Opera, was the "Wagner of the twentieth century." And he was taken up to Harlem late in the evening for a round of the bars.

In New York he also met Meredith Weatherby, the American who was working on the translation of *Confessions of a Mask.* According to Weatherby's account in the *Asahi Shimbun* (1956): "We spent a whole day going over only two or three points. Mishima showed no sign of irritation. The translation was not published, but I learned a great deal from Mishima on that occasion. Translation of his works is harder than translating classical No. Sometimes it took me three hours to translate a single sentence. He always expressed the most subtle things in the most condensed sentences." The translation was of course published eventually; its homosexual theme may have put off some American publishers twenty years ago.

From America Mishima traveled to Brazil: "During a stay of one month in Rio de Janeiro at carnival time I was captured by the tropical sunshine. I felt as if I had finally come home." Leaving Brazil, he continued his journey to Paris, where he was cheated by a currency dealer on the street, and compelled to stay in a small pension for almost a month, with hardly any money. The pension was owned by a Japanese, and an acquaintance, the film director Keisuke Kinoshita, was also there; his situation was not desperate. While Mishima waited for news of his purloined traveler's checks, he wrote a play, *Yoru no Himawari* ("Sunflower at Night"). Then, after getting his money back, he traveled to Greece, alone. This was an important journey for him. Unlike other Japanese writers, Mishima had long been interested in Greek literature and in the classical tradition of Europe. Four years before, he had written a short story, "Shishi" ("Lion"), based on Euripides' *Medea*. Though Mishima's contemporaries in Japan paid little attention to Aeschylus, Sophocles, and the Homeric epics, Mishima knew the classical literature well, having read it in translation. His interest in the Greek classics—and also in the authors of the grand siècle, notably Racine—matched his love of the Japanese classics, also a most uncommon taste for one of his generation in Japan.

When at last Mishima reached Greece, he "fell in love with the blue seas and the vivid skies of that classical land." He traveled to all the famous places (Cape Sounion was an exception) and "felt completely intoxicated all day long." He formed a theory about classical Greece. In ancient times there had been no "spirituality" (a "grotesque outgrowth of Christianity"), but there was an equilibrium between the body and the mind. It had been only too easy for the ancient Greeks to lose their equilibrium, and the very effort required to maintain a balance had helped them create beauty. Tragedy, in which arrogance had invariably been punished by the gods, had aided men to understand how to maintain an equilibrium. "My interpretation may have been wrong, but that was the Greece of which I stood in need." Mishima found that which he had come to discover: "an ethical criterion according to which I could produce beautiful work and also make myself beautiful." His visit to Greece, he maintained, healed him of "my self-hatred and liking for solitude." In their place, he discovered a "will toward health"—this phrase he adapted from the Nietzschean expression, "will toward Power." He returned to Japan "in good humor, full of confidence in myself, sure that I could no longer be hurt by others." (He was guilty, so he would discover, of naïveté in this respect.)

Back in Japan in May 1952, Mishima felt that "one part of my career was coming to an end, and I was entering a new phase of my life." The transition period lasted for a year; he had a backlog of plays, novels, and short stories to write, works which he had already planned in his mind. In the summer he published "Death in Midsummer," a haunting (but misogynist) story about a woman whose two young children are drowned. And early in 1953 he completed a sequel to *Forbidden Colors*. In the second volume of *Forbidden Colors*—both volumes were later published as one novel—the story of Shunsuke, the aging author, and Yuichi, the beautiful boy, winds to a conclusion. Shunsuke takes an overdose of drugs after giving Yuichi a long and meaningless lecture. Yuichi remains precisely the same person throughout this long novel: a "doll" . . . "Yuichi was a doll." Asked by his wife to be present at the birth of their first child, he witnesses the Caesarean delivery: " 'I must look. No matter what, I must look,' he told himself, attempting to control his nausea. 'That system of countless, gleaming, wet red jewels; those soft things under the skin, soaked in blood . . .' " Yuichi attempts to persuade himself that the insides of his wife are "just so much pottery," and he fails. For once, he has been moved.

In the summer of 1953, Shinchosha, his main publishers, brought out Mishima's *Collected Works*, in six volumes. It was an honor for one so young. The publishers gave a party, to which Mishima escorted his mother; Kawabata was a guest of honor. "Young Mishima," as he was known, looked about eighteen—a bright child whom his

mother had brought along to a school prize-giving ceremony. He was recognized, however, as the ablest of the
postwar writers—his collected works were published much
earlier than those of his contemporaries: Kobo Abé, Yoshie
Hotta, and Shohei Ooka. His forte was style.

Edward Seidensticker, the translator of Kawabata (and
of Mishima's last novel, *The Decay of the Angel*), wrote in
the magazine *Pacific Community* (1971): "So decorated as
sometimes to seem mannered and contrived [his language]
shows a concern which the rest of the nation seemed to be
abandoning for the beauties of the Japanese language. A language that lends itself generously to the uses of mannerism
and decoration, it is rather like English in its way of enrich-
ing a native essence with imported sauces and spices." Mishima was "delighted" with the richness of Japanese vocab-
ulary: "Of numbers of writers of Mishima's age and younger
it may be said that the style is difficult . . . Only of Mishima can it be said that the subtlety and richness of vocab-
ulary and phrase and allusion force even the fairly erudite
reader to keep a reference shelf at hand." Professor Seidensticker compared Mishima to Joyce: "He was master of a variety of styles, and was perhaps unique among his peers in
being able to use the classical literary language . . . with
ease, confidence and indeed elegance. In this respect he
might be called Joycean." Joyce "could be many different
people, and so could Mishima."

In 1954 Mishima's *The Sound of Waves* was published,
a novel which indeed revealed a "different" person. The
book was written under the influence of his visit to Greece
two years before. It was a classical idyl of love, for which
Mishima transported Daphnis and Chloë to the island of
Uta-jima (Kamishima, in reality) and reincarnated them as a
simple fisherman and a young girl who dives for abalone.
The novel, which was translated by Meredith Weatherby
and published by Alfred A. Knopf, begins: "Uta-jima—Song
Island—has only about fourteen hundred inhabitants and a
coastline of something under three miles. The island has

two spots with surpassingly beautiful views. One is Yashiro Shrine, which faces northwest and stands near the crest of the island. The shrine commands an uninterrupted view of the wide expanse of the Gulf of Ise, and the island lies directly in the straits connecting the gulf with the Pacific Ocean . . . By climbing the two hundred stone steps that lead up to the shrine and looking back from the spot where there is a *torii* guarded by a pair of stone temple-dogs, you can see how these distant shores cradle within their arms the . . . Gulf of Ise, unchanged through the centuries." The hero and heroine of the story are almost children. The boy wears the same clothes every day, "a pair of trousers inherited from his dead father, and a cheap jersey"; and the girl works on the beach wearing the cotton-padded jacket and baggy trousers of fishing folk. Jealous rivals keep the lovers apart, but the story ends happily. The morbid sexuality of *Forbidden Colors* and *Thirst for Love* is quite absent in *The Sound of Waves*.

The book was a best seller in Japan in 1954, and Shinchosha gave Mishima a prize for the work; it was adopted by the Ministry of Education as a standard text, and made into a film by Toho, the production company, whose team Mishima accompanied to Kamishima for the filming on location. The critics paid little attention to the novel, however, and Mishima had doubts about the book. "Its success cooled my passion for Greece," he said. The descriptions of nature in *The Sound of Waves* were somewhat artificial, "in the style of the Trianon" at Versailles. A common criticism of the work was that Mishima did not know the mood of rustic spots. He had difficulty, in fact, in distinguishing the most elementary forms of natural life; he could not remember the names of trees, confusing pines and cedars.

Donald Keene has described to me a journey through the countryside with Mishima in 1966 in the course of which Mishima's ignorance of country life was revealed. One evening the travelers, while resting at an inn, heard a noise from a nearby valley—a chorus of frogs in a river bed.

MISHIMA: What can that dreadful racket be?
KEENE: Oh, there are some frogs, surely?
MISHIMA: Ah, yes, I see.
   (*A dog barks.*)
KEENE: That would probably be a dog barking, you know.
   (*Mishima chuckles ruefully.*)

Classicism was a major influence on Mishima. Keene—in *Landscapes and Portraits*—has described the "shift of emphasis in his works to structure, theme and intellectual content, as opposed to the baroque lushness of, say, *Forbidden Colors*. His style had already shifted from the archaisms of the early period and the heavy influence of translated literature, particularly the works of Radiguet and Stendhal, in his first novels, to the leanness of style of Ogai Mori (1862–1922). Ogai's masculine, intellectual diction often suggests a translation from the Chinese; the favored tense is the historical present, and there is a rigorous insistence on purity of language . . . He followed Ogai in the unhesitant use of rare characters and words when they corresponded exactly with the desired nuance of meaning . . . The use of the Japanese language for intellectual rather than emotional expression is an aspect of his classicism." He was nonetheless still the decadent romantic, to judge by his short story "Kagi no Kakaru Heya" ("The Room with the Locked Door," 1954). An Okurasho official has a love affair with a married woman, who dies in bed; he leaves the room, locking the door behind him, and outside in the passage meets the nine-year-old daughter of the woman. The two play together for a while, and the man dreams of ripping the frail body of the little girl to shreds, to make himself a "free inhabitant of this disorderly world."

Looking back on the early 1950's, Mishima commented, from the vantage point of the 1960's, that he "felt like destroying everything, as soon as possible." He did not, he stated in *Watakushi no Henreki Jidái*, believe in the "classicism" for which he had had so great a passion at the age of twenty-six. "It may sound merely clever if I say so, but I exploited and used up my sensitivity entirely; I know that my sensitivity dried up." He thought of youth and the period of youth as foolishness: at the same time he felt no attachment to age and experience. "Thus," he wrote, "in a sudden flash, the idea of Death is born within me. This is the only truly vivid and erotic idea for me." He had suffered, he concluded, from "an incurable romantic illness" since the day of his birth. "I, twenty-six years old, I, the classicist, I, the one closest to life—all of these 'I's' may have been fakes."

PART TWO   1955–63

Man gives his seed to woman. Then commences his long, long, nondescript journey toward nihilism.

Yukio Mishima, *Han-Teijo Daigaku*
("The Book of Anti-chaste Wisdom," 1966)

Like Etsuko, the protagonist of *Thirst for Love,* Mishima had a compulsion to love, but when he gained the attention of another person, he would take flight. A rare exception was his friendship with Utaemon, the well-known onnagata (the actor in the Kabuki theater who takes the female roles). The experiences and insights he gained from this friendship are reflected in his short story "Onnagata," published in 1957. In the story, Mangiku, a famous onnagata, falls in love with a young man of the contemporary theater. The development of their relationship is jealously observed by Masuyama, a member of the Kabuki theater staff. Masuyama's tribute to Mangiku begins the story (which was translated by Donald Keene and published in the collection *Death in Midsummer and Other Stories* in 1966): Mangiku Sanokawa "was a true *onnagata,* a species seldom encountered nowadays. Unlike most contemporary *onnagata,* he was quite incapable of performing successfully in male roles. His stage presence was colorful, but with dark overtones; his every gesture was the

essence of delicacy. Mangiku never expressed anything—
not even strength, authority, endurance or courage—except
through the single medium open to him, feminine expression, but through this medium he could filter every variety
of human emotion. That is the way of the true *onnagata*, but
in recent years this breed has become rare indeed."

Mishima had been a visitor to Utaemon's dressing room
at the Kabukiza since 1951 and knew the off-stage onnagata:
"Mangiku faithfully maintained the injunctions of the eighteenth-century *onnagata*'s manual *Ayamegusa*, 'An *onnagata*, even in the dressing room, must preserve the attitudes of an *onnagata*. He should be careful when he eats to
face away from other people, so that they cannot see him.'
Whenever Mangiku was obliged to eat in the presence of
visitors, not having the time to leave his dressing room, he
would turn toward his table with a word of apology and race
through his meal so skillfully that the visitors could not even
guess from behind that he was eating." Mangiku's body,
when he had removed his costume, "was delicate but un-
mistakably a man's. Masuyama found it rather unnerving
when Mangiku, seated at his dressing table, too scantily clad
to be anything but a man, directed polite, feminine greetings toward some visitor, all the while applying a heavy
coating of powder to his shoulders." The make-believe of
his daily life "supported the make-believe of his stage performances. This, Masuyama was convinced, marked the true
onnagata. An *onnagata* is the child born of the illicit union
between dream and reality."

The world of the onnagata was totally different from
that of women, in Mishima's experience: "Anyone pushing
apart the door curtains dyed with the crest of the Sanokawa
family and entering Mangiku's dressing room was certain to
be struck by a strange sensation; this charming sanctuary
contained not a single man. Even members of the same
troupe felt inside this room that they were in the presence
of the opposite sex. Whenever Masuyama went to Mangiku's
dressing room on some errand, he had only to brush aside
the door curtains to feel—even before setting foot inside—a

curiously vivid, carnal sensation of being a male. Sometimes Masuyama had gone on company business to the dressing rooms of chorus girls backstage at revues. The rooms were filled with an almost suffocating femininity and the rough-skinned girls, sprawled about like animals in the zoo, threw bored glances at him . . ."

"Onnagata" threw light on Mishima's private life. *The Temple of the Golden Pavilion* (1956), regarded by some as the best of his novels, illuminated his values. *Kinkakuji*—as the book is entitled in Japanese—is the story of a young monk, Mizoguchi, who serves at the renowned Kyoto temple of Kinkakuji (the Golden Pavilion), a fifteenth-century Zen temple. The young acolyte is the son of a priest and has a chronic stutter which "placed an obstacle between me and the outside world." He believes that the whole of Kyoto—its citizens, its 1,500 temples and shrines, and its many treasures—will be destroyed at the end of the war (he has taken up residence at Kinkakuji in the closing year of the war). As did Mishima, living in Tokyo in 1945, Mizoguchi regards this wholesale destruction as inevitable and desirable; he has no compunction about dying. The novel is a parable. Mizoguchi, unable to accept the continued existence of Kinkakuji, his ideal of beauty, burns the ancient pavilion to the ground one night; so Mishima, having created his own temple of beauty, his "Greek" body, was to destroy that temple. Mizoguchi says: "Beauty, beautiful things, those are now my most deadly enemies"; and he speaks with the voice of Mishima. The destruction of beauty is more beautiful than beauty itself.

The Temple of the Golden Pavilion contains a wealth of philosophical discussion, which Mishima described in *Watakushi no Henreki Jidai* (in a section translated by Donald Keene in *Landscapes and Portraits*): "With respect to the conversations in my novels, I believe I have already freed myself to a considerable extent from Japanese fastidiousness. Japanese writers enjoy displaying their delicate skill at revealing in an indirect manner, by means of conversations, the personalities, temperaments and outlook on life of their characters; but conversations that are unrelated to the personalities and temperaments of the characters, conversations that are read for their content alone, and, finally, long conversations that fuse into the same tempo with the descriptive passages, are the special quality of the novels of Goethe, and of the German novel in general." Mann, he said, had inherited from Goethe "the epic flow of conversation"; and the style of *The Temple of the Golden Pavilion* he characterized as "Ogai plus Mann."

The long conversations in *The Temple of the Golden Pavilion,* translated by Ivan Morris and published by Alfred A. Knopf in 1958, are dominated by Kashiwagi, a fellow student of Mizoguchi at a Buddhist seminary, an evil man. "His most striking characteristic was that he had two rather powerful-looking clubfeet. His way of walking was most elaborate. He always seemed to be walking in mud: when finally he had managed to pull one foot out of the mud, the other foot would appear to be stuck. At the same time there was a sprightliness about his whole body. His walk was a sort of exaggerated dance, utterly lacking in anything commonplace."

Kashiwagi harasses Mizoguchi, using the aggressive conversational technique of a Zen priest:

" 'Stutter!' he said. 'Go ahead and stutter!'

"I listened in sheer amazement to his peculiar way of expressing himself.

" 'At last you've come across someone to whom you can stutter at your ease. That's right, isn't it? People are all like that, you know. They are all looking for a yoke fellow. Well now, are you a virgin?' "

The clubfooted fellow follows up this attack on Mizoguchi with a reference to his physical ailment and his use of the deformity to intrigue women and lure them into bed. Mizoguchi, who is a virgin, is hypnotized by Kashiwagi's aphorism: " 'The special quality of hell is to see everything clearly down to the last detail. And to see all that in the pitch darkness.' "

Kashiwagi gives a demonstration of his technique of

seducing women. As the two students walk along a path, Kashiwagi catches sight of a beautiful girl approaching them. At the critical moment he lurches and falls with a pitiful cry, attracting the attention of the girl, who helps him to his feet and takes him to her home, close by, to bandage his (unhurt) leg. The two have an affair. Kashiwagi later gets rid of the girl, after teaching her how to disguise the fact that she has lost her virginity—she is going to marry.

One day Mizoguchi steals some irises from the garden at Kinkakuji and brings them to Kashiwagi's lodging as a gift. While the latter makes a flower arrangement in a dish in his room, Mizoguchi questions him about the girlfriend he has just disposed of. Kashiwagi replies:

" 'Do you know the famous words in the chapter of Popular Enlightenment in the *Rinsairoku?* "When ye meet the Buddha, kill the Buddha! When ye meet your ancestor, kill your ancestor! . . ." '

" ' "When ye meet a disciple of Buddha," ' I continued, ' "kill the disciple! When ye meet your father and mother, kill your father and mother! When ye meet your kin, kill your kin! Only thus will ye attain deliverance." '

" 'That's right. And that was the situation, you see. That girl was a disciple of Buddha.'

" 'And so you delivered yourself?'

" 'Hm,' said Kashiwagi, arranging some of the irises that he had cut, and gazing at them, 'there's more to killing than that you know.' "

Kashiwagi then introduces the Zen koan (riddle), "Nansen Kills a Kitten." One day a beautiful kitten is found in the neighborhood of two temples. The monks of the two temples dispute among themselves as to who should look after it. Nansen ends the dispute by asking them to tell him why he should not kill the kitten, and when they cannot reply, he kills it. When his chief disciple, Joshu, who has been out, returns to the temple, Nansen tells him what has happened. Thereupon Joshu takes off his muddy shoes and places them on his head. "If only you had been here," Nansen says, "then the kitten could have been saved!" " 'You see,' continued Kashiwagi, 'that's what beauty is like. To have killed the kitten seemed just like having extracted a painful decayed tooth, like having gouged out beauty. Yet it was uncertain whether or not this had really been a final solution. The root of the beauty had not been severed, and even though the kitten was dead, the kitten's beauty might very well still be alive. And so, you see, it was in order to satirize the glibness of this solution that Joshu put those shoes on his head. He knew, so to speak, that there was no possible solution other than enduring the pain of the decayed tooth.' "

Mizoguchi is very much frightened by this "completely original solution" of the koan. He asks:

" 'So which of the two are you? Father Nansen or Joshu?'

" 'Well, let's see. As things are now, I am Nansen and you're Joshu. But some day you might become Nansen and I might become Joshu. This problem has a way of changing—like a cat's eyes.' "

As Mizoguchi watches Kashiwagi at work on his arrangement of irises, he has a premonition of approaching disaster: "There was something cruel about the movement of his hands. They behaved as though they had some unpleasant, gloomy privilege in relation to the plants. Perhaps it was because of this that each time that I heard the sound of the scissors and saw the stem of one of the flowers being cut I had the impression that I could detect the dripping of blood."

The story ends with Mizoguchi's destruction of Kinkakuji—Mishima's story is based on a real event, the burning down of Kinkakuji by a psychopathic monk in the summer of 1950.

The Temple of the Golden Pavilion won high praise. The *Asahi Shimbun* said that Mishima had "outgrown the smart young writer and has evolved as a mature observer of human nature." The *Yomiuri* newspaper awarded Mishima a prize; and Kon Ichikawa, one of the best of the postwar directors, filmed the book. Its publication in the translation by Ivan Morris was to seal Mishima's reputation overseas. (Only one criticism was made. Hideo Kobayashi, probably the most powerful critic in postwar Japan, said he doubted if *The Temple of the Golden Pavilion* was a novel; it was a poem, he said, which revealed the author's attitudes too directly. A photograph taken of Kobayashi and Mishima having dinner together in January 1957 shows Mishima with his head uncharacteristically bowed, as he listens to his critic.)

To many writers their reputation is secondary. To Mishima it was cardinal. With the publication of *The Temple of the Golden Pavilion*, he established himself as the leading writer of his generation in Japan. His claim to this title, as novelist, playwright, and critic, was strong: his style was superior to that of his contemporaries. Mishima was not content with this success, however. As Keene has remarked: "He wanted to conquer the world with his books." By 1956–7 this ambition was within the realm of the possible. There was a boom in the West in Japanese literature—many of the leading authors of the twentieth century were being published in America; this was essential for Mishima's success. Moreover, Mishima was in a better position than any other writer to exploit the surge of interest in Japanese literature: his books were Western in structure, unlike, for example, those of Kawabata, in which mood is all-important and which are often difficult for a Western reader to appreciate. Also, Mishima's work was very varied—over forty books of his had been published—and from this wide range could be selected half a dozen books with appeal to the West. Finally, Mishima was personable and eager to communicate with Western audiences, whereas other Japanese writers either were too elderly to care much or were simply indifferent. His major problem was that he was not fluent in English.

Early in 1957 he received two invitations which sealed his determination to overcome this handicap. The first came from Alfred A. Knopf, his publisher in New York, who asked him to travel to America for the publication of *Five Modern Nō Plays*, a collection translated by Keene. (The previous

year, Knopf had brought out *The Sound of Waves,* which
had been successful for a Japanese author: 10,000 copies
were sold.) The second invitation was to deliver a speech at
Michigan University, on the subject of modern Japanese literature. Mishima accepted both invitations, and settled
down to learn English with characteristic determination. A
friend told me: "He bought tapes and earphones for his tape
recorder, and sat down with the machine for hours every
day. He went over the same tapes again and again, battering
the unfamiliar sounds into his head."

On July 1, Mishima boarded a plane at Haneda to begin
his second world trip. Anyone who saw him that day would
not have taken him for a writer. He had his hair cut short,
and he wore a blazer and white shirt and tie; he radiated
good health. One might have thought he was a sports coach,
with his thick neck and physical flamboyance. For two years
he had been working at building up his body and he had
transformed his physical appearance. In place of the
spindly, white arms of his youth, he had strong, muscular
arms and shoulders. He had turned into a healthy, suntanned specimen of Japanese manhood.

In the lecture which he gave at Michigan, Mishima discussed the work of Kawabata (the heir to the Japanese classical tradition), Ooka, Takeda, and Ishihara. He also spoke
of himself, his association with the Nippon Roman-ha during the war—he referred to the movement's uyoku kokusui-
shugi, its right-wing chauvinism—and his love of the classics. In the future, he said, there would be "an entirely new
kind of reunion between modern literature and the classics"
in Japan, and in it, he implied, Mishima would play a role.

His stay in America lasted nearly six months. He traveled in the South, visiting New Orleans, and then on to the
West Indies—in Port-au-Prince he saw a voodoo ceremony—arriving in New York in late summer. He wished to
see his No plays—which were free adaptations, in modern
settings, of the classical plays and were exciting interest in
many parts of the world—performed in New York.

He stayed in a first-class hotel and waited. Weeks went

by, his money began to run out, and he received no news. He moved to a third-class Greenwich Village hotel, which he likened to a yoroin, an old people's home; it had many elderly, permanent residents. Waiting in vain for a performance of his No plays, and with little money (Japan still had severe foreign-exchange control), Mishima became very gloomy. He was not good at managing abroad by himself. He described his feelings in an untranslated autobiographical essay "Ratai To Isho" ("Nakedness and Clothing"): "In a foreign country everything is a source of fear. You cannot go to the post office or to the bank, as you are frightened of going by yourself. You don't know how to get about, whether by bus or by underground. All around you is a mystery, so much so that you cannot tell one man from another, who is good and who evil."

Donald Keene was in New York at the time—he was then an assistant professor of Japanese literature at Columbia University. He remembers: "I wanted to see him and to encourage him, but I was busy with lectures and did not invite him out. One day Mishima came to my apartment, unannounced, and said, proudly, that he had taken the subway. I was about to go out and told him this. Then, in a hesitant manner, speaking in a low voice, he asked if I would permit him to stay behind a little longer, alone." Mishima lacked self-confidence and was unable to stop himself from showing his weakness to others. "It was an incredible scene," remarked Keene, "if one considers the man he was in the 1960's." In the end there was a private performance of one No play, *Hanjo,* and Mishima left for home, dispirited, at the end of the year, returning by way of Europe. He arrived just before his thirty-third birthday.

In Japan it is rare for a man to remain unmarried. Most people marry in their twenties, the girls in their early twenties, the men a little later. Not to marry is considered odd, especially if one comes from the upper middle class. That Mishima had not married in his twenties was surprising, for he was guided in what he did by a strong sense of duty, particularly to his parents. He had been held back, however, by his close relationship with his mother; Shizue did not press him to get married. Early in 1958, on his return from abroad, Mishima learned his mother had cancer and would probably die. He immediately made up his mind to find a wife, so that Shizue would see him safely married before she died. Having no particular girl in mind, he opted for an arranged marriage, a common practice in Japan, and he began to take part in many omiai—formal meetings with girls found by family friends and acquaintances.

One of Mishima's first omiai was with Michiko Shoda, the beautiful daughter of a flour-company president—who subsequently married Crown Prince Akihito. Possibly, Mishima's ideas about the person he wished to marry were too much for Miss Shoda and her family. He stipulated that his bride must be neither a bungaku shojo, a bluestocking, nor a yumeibyo kanja, a celebrity hunter. And he had five other requirements: 1. His bride must wish to marry Kimitake Hiraoka, the private citizen, not Yukio Mishima, the writer. 2. She should be no taller than her husband, even in heels. 3. She must be kawaii (pretty) and have a round face. 4. She should be eager to take care of Mishima's parents and capable of running the house efficiently. 5. She must not disturb Mishima while he worked. These were the guidelines given to the intermediaries who had the task of finding suitable candidates.

His choice settled finally on Yoko Sugiyama, the twenty-one-year-old daughter of a well-known traditional painter; Mishima chose her partly because she was the daughter of an artist. And also, according to the magazine *Young Lady:* "I could not help choosing someone from a spot I did not know . . . someone who was not interested in my writing." Yoko was two inches shorter than Mishima— she was just over five feet tall—and she was kawaii and round-faced; and, according to the confidential reports that the Hiraoka family received from the marriage counselor, she was thoroughly competent. Mishima met Yoko in early April and after two meetings made up his mind: they were engaged early in May 1958. He asked Kawabata to act as baishaku-nin—the "go-between" who officiates at the dinner party that follows the marriage ceremony, a Shinto service. He wanted to rush ahead with the wedding—"it is not a good idea to delay, while people whisper advice into one's ear"—and would have liked to get married in May. This proved to be impossible, however, as the couple could not find a taian, a lucky day, and Yoko's three wedding dresses were not ready (the bride at a Japanese wedding appears in kimono, Western wedding dress, and ball dress). They were married on June 1.

After the wedding the couple left for Hakone in the mountains near Mt. Fuji, spending their first night at the old-fashioned Fujiya Hotel. From the hotel Mishima made phone calls to his home to check on Shizue's condition. They continued on their honeymoon to Kyoto and then sailed through the Inland Sea to Beppu. At the end of their honeymoon Mishima and Yoko came back to Tokyo to live with his parents for a short time, until their new houses were ready. Mishima had bought land in Magome, some miles north of the airport, and decided to build two houses, one for him and Yoko, and the other for his parents next door. Shizue, it had been discovered, was no longer in danger—and had never had cancer at all.

Most Japanese homes are small and unpretentious, a mixture of Japanese and Western styles; and the Japanese do not invite friends home. In Japan there is no tradition of entertaining at home, as there is in the West. Mishima, however, decided to be thoroughly Western. He built as large a house as he could afford—he borrowed money from his publishers, Shinchosha. It had a reception room with a high ceiling, and also had a rectangular Western garden with a lawn. In his travels in the West Indies he had been attracted by the sight of decaying colonial mansions, and the design of his house was "colonial," with thick, white, painted walls, the antithesis of Japanese taste. It was, Mishima said, an "anti-Zen house." But the architect had a problem: how to realize Mishima's idea of a "colonial" house on a plot of land sufficient only for a house of normal size. To make room for a garage on one side of the house, a drive, and a garden, he was compelled to cut down the size of the house; the reception room, for example, had a high ceiling level with the second floor but was nonetheless a small room.

Mishima's aim—his fundamental aim in life, it might be said—was to shock. He was determined to create an effect with his new house: unable to build on a grand scale, he fell back on unusual décor. He decorated the reception room of the new house in Victorian style; and he filled it with copies of nineteenth-century furniture. On the walls he put oil paintings with "classical" themes; and he hung the large window which faced the garden with heavy, ornate curtains. "This," he said, "is my dream—or nightmare—of Victorian opulence." To a Western eye the effect was a little unusual; to a Japanese eye it was grotesque. In the garden he placed an outsize statue of Apollo on a plinth: "my despicable symbol of the rational."

This desire to shock others was evident in the articles Mishima wrote for Japanese magazines: "Now I am a dannasama [a family head, a traditional term, here used ironically]. I rule my wife at home, act according to common sense, build a house, am fairly cheerful, love speaking ill of others, rejoice when people remark on my youthful appearance, pursue the latest fashions and favor all manner of things in bad taste. I say nothing serious . . . and do my utmost to live to the age of Methuselah." (He wrote this article in response to criticism by his architect, Hayao Hokonohara, who had condemned Mishima's taste as "ghastly.")

Statements by Mishima about his family were, however, rare. He divided his life into distinct compartments: his family life, and his public career. He had something of the Confucian within him, for all his exhibitionism; in certain circumstances, he regarded his duty to his family as his prime consideration. Photographers who came to his home were not allowed to take pictures of Yoko; nor, later, when the Mishimas had children, could they film them. Mishima's parents were also kept out of the glare of publicity. Mishima the public figure was Mishima the novelist, playwright, and exhibitionist; he was never Mishima the son, husband, and father. The separation between public and private life was complete; he never used any other name than Mishima. Very few members of the public knew him as Kimitake Hiraoka; nor did I know his real name until after his death.

At home to reporters Mishima assumed a pose of insouciance: "My ideal is to live in a house where I sit on a rococo chair wearing an aloha shirt and blue jeans." He was, however, a relentless self-disciplinarian. Early in 1959, six months after his marriage, he embarked on a heroic program of physical exercise. On Mondays and Fridays he trained at kendo, and on Wednesdays, Thursdays, and Saturdays he did body building. He also kept up his writing, working every night until dawn and sleeping in the morning. He commented gloomily that his aim sometimes was a day divided into sleep, work, and physical exercise, twenty-four hours of "solitude and leisure." People would think that he was always busy, and there would be "no more personal associations." But this was only Mishima in a certain mood.

His longing to shock others was apparent in his writing as well as in his daily life. "He would never write two novels in the same style," Keene says. "He would always try to find something new, to surprise his readers." The book which he wrote shortly after his marriage, *Kyoko no Ie* ("Kyoko's House"), reflected this urge; it was his "study of nihilism." "The characters run about in one direction or another as their personalities, their professions and their sexual tendencies command them, but in the end all roads, no matter how roundabout, flow back into nihilism" (*Landscapes and Portraits*). In this novel, Mishima represented himself by four "I's": "When I am developing a single character in one of my novels, I sometimes feel him quite close to my own thinking, but at other times I drive the same character away from myself and let him wander into independent action. The attitudes of the hero change convulsively, as the course of composition dictates. In *Kyoko no Ie*, in order to resolve this contradiction which has always appeared in my novels (and was most extreme in *Forbidden Colors*), I have avoided having a single hero, but have represented various aspects of myself through four different heroes."

The four heroes are:

Shunkichi, a boxer. His principle is "to think about nothing." Through "disorderly" and "free" anarchism he hopes to destroy the social order of postwar Japan. He believes in "might," which he associates with beauty and with death—not with justice and order. He envies his older brother, who died in the war; his brother had sped through life "without fear of boredom and without thinking at all." Shunkichi lives in a hateful epoch of "normality," and in such an era he cannot maintain his "purity." Believing in "might," he sets about making himself a boxing champion. However, his career ends after a beating by some thugs, who break his fingers. Shunkichi believes that his future will be boring and insignificant; he joins a Uyoku (rightist) group, "to oppose the future." In such a group he is "close to death, even in this age of normality." Shunkichi meets his death in a street brawl.

Osamu, a narcissistic actor, who practices body building. Osamu is racked with anxiety: "Do I really exist or not?" He is constantly peering at himself in a mirror. He has a mistress, an elderly usurer, who has bought Osamu's services. The woman loves Osamu, and expresses her love by torturing him. The handsome actor wonders whether the shedding of his blood will prove his existence. He desires to perform in "a complete drama." He and his mistress commit a bloody shinju (double love suicide).

Natsuo, a traditional Japanese painter. He believes that he is an angel, whose pure and gentle existence is protected by a special deity. He has no troubles in life. However, on a trip to Mt. Fuji he has a vision of the destruction of the world. He reflects on his situation; he is well known and successful, but he is the subject of jealous gossip among his contemporaries. He suggests to his friends that one should kill himself while one's body is still beautiful. Natsuo is captured by a strange world of "reality" and "nihilism." In the end he has an existential experience: "what I see and I that see belong to one world." He is saved.

Seiichiro, a capable businessman. He is a shoshain, a trading-company executive. The world, he considers, is doomed; total destruction is inevitable. He is outwardly cheerful and competent, however, and he is successful at work. His motto is to play the role of "somebody else" and to lead a "conventional life." He marries the daughter of a senior director. His company later sends him to New York, where he continues as before. Seiichiro suffers from "an incurable illness"—health.

Kyoko no Ie revealed more about Mishima than any other work of his in the 1950's. Each of the four heroes of the novel suggests aspects of the author's character which had been largely hidden, and which were to emerge clearly in the 1960's. His right-wing inclination, exemplified in the character of the boxer Shunkichi, became conspicuous after 1965. His notion that one must commit suicide while one still has a beautiful, muscular body was another idea that emerged in Mishima's life in the late 1960's. The same may be said of Osamu's desire to prove his existence by shedding his blood, and his wish to perform in "a complete drama." The most interesting feature of *Kyoko no Ie,* however, is the conviction of three of the four heroes that the destruction of the world is inevitable; Mishima's nihilism bore a close resemblance to that of the Roman-ha. A literary critic, Jun Eto, pointed out in an essay published in *The Journal of Asian Studies* that Mishima was "the only possible spokesman for the lost Roman-ha cause. *Expectation of the world's destruction,* the theme that has appeared almost obsessively in his postwar works, is one of the most typical ideas of the Roman-ha group. This theme is clearly recognized in his novels, *Bitoku no Yoromeki* ["Tottering Virtue," 1957], *Kyoko no Ie,* and *Utsukushii Hoshi* ["Beautiful Star," 1962]."

But the novel failed with the public—it was Mishima's

first major critical failure as well. He wrote: "The painter
represents sensitivity, the boxer action, the actor self-
awareness, and the businessman knowing how to get along
with the world. It is naturally to be expected that the personalities of these characters will become abstract and purified. I have for the time being given up any attempt to
create characters as single, coordinated, organic entities"
(*Landscapes and Portraits*). Perhaps it was this intellectual
attitude that undermined his "study of nihilism"—without
character, what could he do? Mishima may have reflected
thus, for his next book, *After the Banquet*, was a triumph of
characterization.

Mishima once remarked: "All my works can be divided
into two categories, *pièces roses* and *pièces noires*, as
Anouilh used those terms." *After the Banquet* was the best
of his *pièces roses*. Kazu, the proprietress of a fashionable
Japanese-style restaurant in Tokyo, the Setsugoan (in real
life, the Hannya-en), is the protagonist of the novel, which
satirizes political life and the mores of the upper class.
Kazu, Angus Wilson has remarked, "is a woman of Balzacian
dimensions and Flaubertian truth." Mishima described her
thus (in the translation by Donald Keene, published by
Alfred A. Knopf): "A streak of rustic simplicity in Kazu's
plump, attractive figure, always bursting with energy and
enthusiasm, made people with complicated motives who
came before her feel ashamed of their complexity. People
with drooping spirits, when they saw Kazu, were either con-
siderably heartened or else completely overpowered. Some
curious blessing of heaven had joined in one body a man's
resolution with a woman's reckless enthusiasm. This combination carried Kazu to heights no man could reach."

Mishima described her taking a stroll in the garden of
her restaurant: "This morning stroll was the poem of Kazu's
security. She was over fifty, but no one seeing this carefully
groomed woman, whose complexion and sparkling eyes had
lost none of their loveliness, as she sauntered through the
huge garden could help but be struck and moved to romantic conjectures. But, as Kazu herself realized better than anyone, for her romantic stories were a thing of the past, her

poem was dead." Her conviction is disproved. She falls in love with a politician, Noguchi, and they get married. Noguchi stands for election to the governorship of Tokyo, and Kazu throws all her energy, and finally all her money, into the campaign. Noguchi, a liberal candidate, loses the election, however, as the conservatives have far more cash than he. Mishima knew a great deal about the functioning of party machines in Tokyo and here he describes party politics to perfection. His knowledge of the nuances of behavior in upper-class society is also evident in *After the Banquet*. After the elections, Kazu runs into a woman she dislikes, Mrs. Tamaki, the widow of a diplomat. The two women meet by chance in a fruit shop, where Kazu discovers Mrs. Tamaki rummaging in a bin of Sunkist oranges:

"Mrs. Tamaki, after much deliberation, selected three oranges. 'Even oranges have become expensive these days. And just think, in America they practically give them away!' Mrs. Tamaki, as part of her brave display of inverse snobbery, deliberately ordered the salesgirl to wrap just three oranges . . .

" 'My husband liked oranges,' Mrs. Tamaki went on. 'Sometimes I offer them at the family altar. That's why I bought them today . . . You know, it suddenly occurred to me that my husband, without realizing it, of course, played the part of cupid for you and Mr. Noguchi.' " (By falling ill in Kazu's restaurant, Tamaki had by chance brought together Kazu and Noguchi.)

" 'In that case I suppose I'll have to offer him some oranges myself.'

" 'I didn't mean it that way.'

"Kazu did not herself understand why she was behaving so rudely. On a sudden impulse she motioned to the salesgirl with the sandalwood fan she had been using, and ordered her to make up a gift box of two dozen oranges." (Presents must be neither too large nor too small, in Japan. By flouting this convention, knowing that Mrs. Tamaki will not have the courage to refuse the offer of the gift, Kazu crushes her enemy.)

Mishima's taste in women was evident in his descriptions of Kazu. He had a traditional Japanese liking for white flesh and a dislike of suntans: "Kazu's rich shoulders and breasts had lost nothing of their beauty, despite all the summer's exertions. Her sunburned neck, however, emerging light-brown, like a faded flower, from the snow-white skin below, showed the effects of the election campaign. The sunlight striking the surface of the mirror still kept a lingering summer intensity, but Kazu's white shoulders and breasts were an icehouse. The fine-grained, saturated whiteness repelled the light, suggesting that it concealed within a cool, dark summer interior."

After the Banquet was a brilliant success for Mishima; it is also the work by him which I like most as entertainment (*Confessions of a Mask* is compelling enough, but it is gloomy reading). But he was never satisfied with his successes. He had been put off by the applause for *The Sound of Waves*, and the great triumph of his career in the 1950's, *The Temple of the Golden Pavilion*, had also not provided him with lasting satisfaction. What did he want of life? 1960 was without doubt a crucial year in his life. He does not appear to have known what he wanted; once more he was deep in a personal crisis, as he had been in 1950–51, just before his first travels abroad. But in the fifties something had changed. Ten years had gone by—his "classical" period lay behind him—and he seemed, to himself at any rate, to have nothing to show for that decade. Worst of all, he had failed as a novelist—with *Kyoko no Ie*. This failure, I believe, made a very deep mark on Mishima. One has to remember that he had had almost no experience of failure—and, at the same time, he set an enormous premium on success. He had thrown everything, he said, into *Kyoko no Ie*. All his accumulated experience—as a man, as a craftsman, and as a novelist—was contained in that long book, the longest novel of his career (the two volumes of *Forbidden Colors* excepted). And he had had the book virtually cast back in his face. The critics were extremely harsh in their treatment of the novel; scarcely anyone—Takeo Okuno was an exception—expressed a liking for it. Some reviewers said that this was

Mishima's "magnificent failure"; he instantly sensed that beneath the sycophancy was a barely concealed sense of triumph: the brilliant young Mishima had fallen flat on his face. Under such circumstances, the success of *After the Banquet* did not console Mishima. What he wanted, urgently, was to reestablish himself; and for the first time in his life, he found that he lacked the thrust, the energy to do so. As a novelist, Mishima experienced his gravest crisis in 1960; it was not until 1965 that he attempted another major novel—when he embarked on his monumental *The Sea of Fertility*.

It may be, however, that he felt a still deeper sense of failure at this time in his life. Not only was he beset by difficulties as a novelist—they may have acted as catalyst—but the position in which he found himself seems to have been far graver than the failure of *Kyoko no Ie* alone would have justified. I do not know exactly what was going on in his mind, but judging by his actions, Mishima was in profound despair. In the autumn of 1959, presumably after he learned the bad news about *Kyoko no Ie*, he decided to play a part in a movie. There was nothing extraordinary about this. Why should he not amuse himself a little? (He said that he would "like to be a jazz singer, to be eighteen again.") But the movie he chose to appear in was bad. It was an ugly, irresponsible, yakuza (gangster) movie in which Mishima played the part of an insignificant hood who gets himself murdered—and is, indeed, a nasty little specimen. Had Mishima chosen to play in a good film, one would not be surprised; this was his first movie and the experience was plainly one that someone of his temperament would enjoy. But why *Karakkaze Yaro* ("A Dry Fellow"), a grubby tale of prison, of betrayed girlfriends and broken trust, with no redeeming features? It is as if Mishima, at the end of *Confessions of a Mask*, in that famous scene with Sonoko in the cheap dance hall, had risen from his seat, leaving his friend at the table, and gone over to the group of yakuza standing in the sun winding their bellybands around their hot torsos, and spent the afternoon carousing with his new friends—

having left his girl to find her own way home, without even saying goodbye.

He had, of course, every reason to lead his life in his own way; he was free. But by taking on the part in *Karakkaze Yaro* Mishima alienated people of good sense (of whom Sonoko stands as a symbol in my parable). What had he to gain? His decision to enter the world of the cinema in this fashion was equivalent to an announcement to society that he no longer recognized the conventions. If the critics did not care for his novel *Kyoko no Ie*, so much the worse for them; he didn't need them. I have no quarrel with Mishima's dislike of the critics; the Bundan strikes me as a pitiful society which is inimical to talent. But Mishima was not simply saying "Boo!" to the critics. He was turning his back on quiet people—friends, family acquaintances, people he had never met but who could have become close to him, people of no great power or influence, whose collective disapproval, however, would go against him in the long run. Ten years before, he could have got away with an action like this (in a sense he did: parts of *Forbidden Colors* are in dreadful taste). At the age of thirty-five, with an enormous critical reputation (despite *Kyoko no Ie*), and a great following from the general public, he could not afford to cut such a caper as his appearance in *Karakkaze Yaro* represented. To be an immature romantic at twenty-five is understandable. At thirty-five? No.

I take Mishima's decision to appear in the yakuza movie—he had the lead—as indicative of his parlous state of mind at this time, as a sign that he was losing control. And it was not the only indication that he was in a serious state. Here let us jump ahead to the summer of 1960. As installment after installment of *After the Banquet* appeared in a monthly magazine, it became apparent that he was satirizing an extremely well-known public man in his portrayal of Noguchi, the lover of Kazu in the book. His target was a former Foreign Minister, a man of liberal views, Hachiro Arita. I do not imagine that Mishima had a personal grudge against the man; still less that he had any objection to his politics. But he made a complete fool of Arita. *After the Banquet* was a thinly disguised, brilliant, witty account of Arita's affair with a restaurant owner, the proprietress of the Hannya-en in Tokyo. Why did Mishima take such a risk? The libel laws in Japan are weak—by Western standards they are a farce—but Mishima was going much too far. Each successive installment of *After the Banquet* sank another, only too accurate shot into a man who had already virtually failed in public life. What the Arita family thought about this can be imagined; and they found much sympathy among friends, influential people in Tokyo, and even editors and publishers in the city.

In the end Arita was provoked to the point where, discarding normal Japanese rules of behavior (in cases of libel it is usual for the disputing parties to settle their quarrel through intermediaries who may not even be lawyers), he brought a suit against Mishima. It was an unprecedented case which came to public notice early in 1961; Arita's complaint was that his privacy had been invaded. The libel suit—for this is what it was in Western eyes, though Japanese law scarcely makes provision for such a thing—attracted much public interest. Puraibashii (or "privacy," as it is spelled in Japanese too—the word has been adapted directly from English into the Japanese language) instantly became a vogue word and was accepted as a neologism by the Japanese at large. And Mishima lost the suit; it took many years, but in the end Arita's lawyers nailed him down. The key factor, I suspect, was that people with influence in Tokyo felt that the novelist had behaved monstrously. In the absence of a precedent, their opinion must have affected the court, which had no specific guide as to the law.

Mishima was succeeding in antagonizing a good number of people at this time. He was, of course, a charming person, when he was in form. He was entertaining, more than a little witty at his own expense, and, above all, intelligent. He had, say what he might about the Bundan, very many friends in the literary establishment. About this time in his life, however, he reached a parting of the ways with one particular group of people that he had associated with happily for nearly a decade; these were the members of a little literary club called the Hachi no Ki Kai (Potted Cherry Tree Club). They were a powerful group: Toson Fukuda, a playwright; Mitsuo Nakamura, the *Asahi Shimbun* critic; Shohei Ooka, the novelist; and Ken-Ichi Yoshida, a rare instance of a Japanese man of letters. Mishima had got on well with these people for many years; when they started a magazine, they printed his work right away (the first installments of *Kyoko no Ie*). But for the most part the Hachi no Ki Kai was a social affair; the members met for dinner, enjoyed drinking together, and indulged in merry gossip at the expense of others. By 1960, however, Mishima's relations with this group had begun to deteriorate. A member of the Hachi no Ki Kai once told me of an incident at one of their dinners: "I had had much too much to drink, I expect, and for some reason I was feeling antagonistic and decided to give Mishima a piece of my mind. I don't know what exactly I said but the others told me afterward that I spoke with unwonted frankness: I suppose I told Mishima he was a snob who took himself too seriously." Whether it was on this or on some other occasion that Mishima finally took offense, I do not know; but certainly the time came when he severed his ties with the Hachi no Ki Kai, the only literary group with which he had ever got on well and with whom he sustained a link over many years. He was foolish; he *was* a snob and he *did* take himself too seriously: he should have listened and not taken umbrage.

These were small matters in their way—the gangster movie, the quarrel with Arita, and the parting with the Hachi no Ki Kai—but it was through such incidents that Mishima found himself increasingly isolated in 1960. And, as luck would have it, this was the year in which political events impinged on his life, for the first time since 1945. Just at a point in his literary career when he was vulnerable, Mishima came under pressure.

The story is a complex one. During the late 1940's, terrible years for Japan, Mishima had paid no attention to political matters. After the end of the Occupation, during which momentous decisions had been made about the future of Japanese society, Mishima still did not respond to events on the political scene. Throughout the 1950's he contented himself with his literary pursuits. He was thought by his contemporaries to be vaguely leftist, a man inclined toward acceptance of the popular creed of political neutrality between the Western world and the Communist bloc. He was even approached once by a critic who belonged to the small Communist Party, and asked if he would become a member. By 1960, however, his interest in politics was coming to life. *After the Banquet* is not a political novel, but it shows that Mishima had learned more about politics in Japan than many of his friends and fellow writers. It is a classic description, in its way, of the alliance between money and power in Japanese society. *After the Banquet* was the first sign that Mishima was curious about the political world. The second was his interest in the huge demonstrations against the government in May and June of that year—the most spectacular political demonstrations in postwar Japanese history. Mishima went out onto the streets to see the "demos" and wrote articles for the press about them.

What was at stake, essentially, was the neutralist vision; intellectuals, students, labor-union leaders—even the opposition parties at last—had finally awakened to a realization that the ruling conservative party, the Liberal Democratic Party, which had governed Japan without a break, almost, since 1945, had all along been making a nonsense of the ideals of the left. While subscribing to neutralist tenets—refusing, for example, to play a direct, military role in the Korean War—the conservatives had given the public the impression that the Liberal Democratic Party would keep Japan on the path of neutralism for the indefinite future. By 1960, however, the conservatives, under the leadership of Nobusuke Kishi, a strong reactionary, had made up their minds to challenge the popular assumption that they were, in effect, prisoners of the ideological left. Kishi and his ministers decided to strengthen the alliance with the United

States—enshrined by the U.S.–Japan Security Treaty—by revising that treaty to make the ties between America and Japan closer, above all in the economic field. Mishima was not interested in these issues. However, he was curious about the demonstrations, which became more violent during the early summer; and he reacted very strongly, it seems, to the new political atmosphere. The story "Patriotism" is evidence of this.

At this point the latent imperialism in him suddenly burst forth. "Patriotism" describes an act of devotion to the Emperor, the hara-kiri of a young army lieutenant at the time of the Ni Ni Roku Incident. It is not so much Mishima's imperialism that impresses, however; it is the re-emergence of his old aesthetic, the longing for "Death and Night and Blood" that characterized his adolescence as described in *Confessions of a Mask*. Gone is his "classical aspiration." In its place is a sensuous, anti-rational, romantic longing. What the object of that longing might be, no one could know; certainly Mishima had no concrete idea, no notion of what he himself would do. The theoretical ideal was clear enough, however; it was death. Thus Mishima resolved the crisis that he faced in 1960, by a reversion to romanticism.

Curiously, he was subject at this time to extraordinary threats of violence. They were issued by Uyoku (rightist) extremists, who warned him that they would burn down his house and kill him because he had supported a fellow writer who had published a short story describing a dream in which leftists attacked the Imperial family. For two months Mishima had a bodyguard. During this time— early 1961—there were threats against other literary figures; and an attack was made on the house of Mr. Shimanaka of *Chuo Koron,* publisher of the magazine which had carried the story offensive to the Uyoku. A maid was killed in the attack, and Mrs. Shimanaka was injured. Mishima himself was not assaulted, however.

Suicide, it is clear from Mishima's writing, had been a theoretical option for him for many years. It was still no more than that; he was fairly young and had many literary projects in mind—particularly in the theater—and he also had a family. Mishima's second child, his son Ichiro, was born in 1961. (Like many Japanese parents, the Mishimas would seem to have decided to have no more children.)

What was the nature of his relationship with Yoko? She is still alive, of course; this is one subject on which I cannot write without inhibition. The evidence, however, is that Mishima treated Yoko with a consideration that far exceeded the kindness shown to their wives by most Japanese husbands of his generation. For example, he took Yoko with him on his foreign travels. She had never been abroad, and when Mishima embarked on a long journey around the world in late 1960, she accompanied him. They were in New York, where they saw the première of Mishima's modern No plays, in an Off-Broadway production. And from America they went on to Europe, where Mishima met publishers. One of the results of his visit was a French translation of *The Temple of the Golden Pavilion*, brought out by Gallimard. The Mishimas went to Greece, to Egypt, where they saw the pyramids, and then returned to Japan via Hong Kong. It must have been a refreshing experience for Yoko to travel freely about the world like this in the company of her husband, leaving the little girl in Tokyo in the care of her family. Life in Tokyo, certainly, was not easy for Yoko; she was very young, just twenty-four on their return from abroad in 1961; but her days were full. She had the house to care for—and Mishima had become very social, giving dinner parties for diplomats, for foreign friends, and for Japanese friends from well-known families. His standards were high and he expected the dinner parties—for which he issued invitations on printed, embossed cards in English—to run smoothly. Yoko also had her child to care for. And in addition she was a kind of secretary to Mishima, taking phone calls, running errands, going out on combined shopping and secretarial missions in the family car (only Yoko drove; Mishima qualified for a license in 1962 but never took up driving a car). Her life was a busy one.

Things were not made easier by her mother-in-law. Shizue as a daughter-in-law had suffered greatly at the hands of Natsuko; and having experienced such treatment, she was able to dispense not a little herself. Shizue was jealous of Yoko. Yoko's response was to adopt a policy of not complaining, at a fairly early stage in her married life. She would be criticized at the slightest opportunity and would not complain; she would do her best. She is a most competent person and her best was more than adequate by her husband's standards. The house ran smoothly, he could concentrate on his work undisturbed, and his one absolute requirement—that his daily program of appointments and physical training in the afternoon, dinner in the evening, and writing at night not be interfered with—was met. Yoko Mishima must be a remarkable person to have been able to live for so many years so close to a man of Mishima's energy, yet show no signs of strain at all. I feel all the more admiration for her, in that there can be no gainsaying Mishima's dark, romantic pessimism, epitomized by his statement: "Man gives his seed to woman. Then commences his long, long nondescript journey toward nihilism."

I do not believe that marriage put Mishima under great strain. His literary career, however, was another matter. His books did not sell well in the early 1960's. He continued to write an enormous amount; some of it was trash, intended purely for the commercial market, the women's slush magazines—I am not concerned with that. He also wrote a succession of serious novels: *Utsukushii Hoshi* ("Beautiful Star," 1962), *The Sailor Who Fell from Grace with the Sea* (1963), and *Kinu to Meisatsu* ("Silk and Insight," 1964). John Nathan, who has made a study of this period in Mishima's work, and who translated the second of these novels, has remarked: "His books were selling only 20,000 or 30,000 copies in some cases, as compared with 200,000 copies or so in the 1950's. At one point he even felt obliged to go to his publishers to make a formal apology." As Mishima's reputation in the West was soaring, he was actually losing ground in Japan, not only in terms of sales but in critical reputation. It is ironical that, while he was regarded overseas as a future Nobel Prize winner, he was being outsold ten times over by many Japanese novelists whom the West has still not heard of. Any novelist, Mishima not excluded, must have lean years; but he did not see it this way. He was deeply concerned; otherwise, I cannot imagine anyone with his pride going cap in hand to his publisher to apologize. But one does not have to look this far for evidence of his uncertainty. The tone of his pronouncements over the years became increasingly pessimistic; Mishima, as always, was his own best guide to himself. In an article written for *Fukei* magazine in 1962, he remarked: "Within two or three years I shall be forty-five years old and will have to make a plan for the rest of my life. I feel better when I think that I have lived longer than Ryunosuke Akutagawa, but then I'll have to make a great effort to live as long as possible. The average life for men in the Bronze Age was eighteen, and in the Roman era twenty-two. Heaven must then have been filled with beautiful youths. Recently, it must look dreadful. When a man reaches the age of forty, he has no chance to die beautifully. No matter how he tries, he will die in an ugly way. He has to force himself to live."

Ryunosuke Akutagawa, to whom Mishima refers in this article, was the most brilliant of the many Japanese writers who have committed suicide in modern times. The high incidence of suicide among writers may be attributed in part to the extraordinary tension and stress of life in modern Japan. A nation cannot evolve from feudalism to an ultramodern way of life in the short space of time granted to the Japanese and not place great stresses on individuals—not least on writers. The well-known novelists who have taken their lives in the twentieth century are Bizan Kawakami (1908), Takeo Arishima (1923), Akutagawa (1927), Shinichi Makino (1936), Osamu Dazai (1948), Tamiki Hara (1951), Michio Kato (1953), Sakae Kubo (1958), and Ashihei Hino (1960).

By the mid-1960's, Mishima was already toying with the idea of adding his name to this doleful list. His obsession was "to make a plan for the rest of my life"; and certain developments—his difficulty with his literary career, among them—were pushing him along the path to suicide.

PART THREE   1964–70

Among my incurable convictions is the belief that the old are eternally ugly, the young eternally beautiful. The wisdom of the old is eternally murky, the actions of the young eternally transparent. The longer people live, the worse they become. Human life, in other words, is an upside-down process of decline and fall.

Yukio Mishima, Postscript to the Ni Ni Roku Incident trilogy

Mishima did not find his "plan for life" for some time. In the summer of 1964 he made a ten-day visit to New York, the purpose of which was described by Faubion Bowers in an article published in *The Village Voice* (December 3, 1970): "One night Mishima flew over to America just for sex. He came up and had dinner with me and described quite bluntly what he wanted and asked could I steer him to the right place. I should have been the hospitable host and taken him on a tour of the gay bars downtown, but I didn't, and didn't want to, and really didn't feel qualified. Maybe I was flat broke or something of the sort. At any rate I took him around the neighborhood, introduced him to anyone we ran into, straight, gay, or in-between. But it was one of those nights. Nothing happened. Nobody around here was interested in 'Japan's greatest novelist.' Even his meticulously expensive suit and tie didn't impress anyone. Finally, I put him in a taxi and I felt both stupid and remiss that I hadn't helped a friend in need. His need for a white man that night was very great, and his specifications were detailed. Afterward, it flashed into my mind that Mishima was impotent." (As other friends of Mishima's pointed out in a letter to *The Village Voice*, published two weeks later, Bowers's article contained many errors. Yet Mishima may have been impotent.)

New York certainly evoked odd moods in Mishima. In pictures taken of him during his stay in the summer of 1964 he looks particularly old and ill at ease. Usually he seemed about a decade younger than his real age, and in these photographs he seemed older than he was. His face is lined and haggard. It may have been the jet lag—the journey by air from Tokyo to New York is a long one; but I think that New York distressed Mishima and left him feeling unusually tense. In his article "Touching New York with Both Hands" (*Mainichi Shimbun*, January 1966), he described his reaction to the city: "In New York there is no direct contact between man and man or man and object. This huge city has lost its instinctive life and turned into a colossal machine. New York is further and further away from being able to be 'touched' by man. I like such a place, though. People there gather together and part. And one cannot be sure that someone who appears on TV actually listens to what he says. You can touch New York with your hands if you visit the gym I used off Times Square . . . This was a big-city gymnasium. The worlds of body building are much the same in Tokyo and in New York. People cracked jokes in Brooklyn accents and were most friendly." There is something pathetic about his discovery that he felt at home only in the gym. As someone who met him in New York remarked to me: "He couldn't get on with foreigners really, or he was confused by Americans." It is well known that Mishima felt that American writers whom he had entertained royally in Japan (Truman Capote, Tennessee Williams) did not reciprocate properly when he visited *their* city.

He had a huge number of friends and acquaintances in America, especially in New York. Among them were scholars whom he had met in Japan and who had translated his works; for example, the leading academics in the field of Japanese literature, Donald Keene and Ivan Morris (for whom he was to leave letters at his death). He also knew a great many people in the arts and in literature in America. His difficulty was that he was very well known in Japan and sure of attention, but not overseas. Mishima liked to be the center of the stage, and his inability to dominate social gatherings outside his homeland troubled him. He would be invited to parties in New York but he would not be the focus of all eyes. In Japan, where he was sure of himself, he developed close friendships with many foreigners. Meredith Weatherby, the American publisher, was a friend of Mishima's for more than twenty years in Tokyo; and he regularly associated with a number of other foreign residents of the city. Abroad, however, the streak of chauvinism that colors his writing—in many of his books foreigners are described as gaudy, strange creatures, and the male foreign characters are often weak-minded homosexuals—gained the upper hand at times; he would return to Japan with very mixed impressions of life in the West.

Back in Japan he had many diversions. In the autumn of 1964 he immersed himself in the task of reporting the Tokyo Olympic Games for the Japanese press and wrote enthusiastic articles about sports "from my own experience." He donned a blazer, put on a press armband, and watched the many events of the Olympics with childlike enthusiasm. He described in his articles how he trained at sports and at body building, "so that today I can move the muscles of my chest in time to music."

Later that year he edited the *Collected Works* of Shintaro Ishihara, a younger and more glamorous novelist friend whose first work, *Taiyo no Kisetsu* ("Season of the Sun," 1955)—a "shocking" après-guerre novel—had made him famous at the age of twenty-three. Mishima admired Ishihara's talent and was at the same time envious of this polished, sophisticated, handsome person, whom he was to criticize harshly toward the end of his life, as a political opportunist. (Ishihara later went into politics, winning a seat in the Upper House as a Liberal Democratic Party member, after gaining the largest number of votes ever won by a candidate for parliament.)

Early in 1965 Mishima accepted an invitation from the British Council to visit England. It was his only long stay in England, and he did not find a great deal to please him—

although he liked the Brighton Pavilion. Among those he
met were Margot Fonteyn, Edna O'Brien, Ivan Morris,
Angus Wilson, and Peter Owen. He wrote: "I was glad to
find Dr. and Mrs. Morris in London . . . The soft side of
Japanese culture has been introduced to the British public
by the late Arthur Waley and now by Dr. Morris, mainly for
the benefit of upper-class intellectuals; and the tough side of
Japanese culture has been shown to mass audiences in films
in which Toshiro Mifune plays the hero . . . During a walk
on the bank of the Thames I was given the interesting information that all swans belong to the Queen."

On his return to Japan, Mishima was caustic about the
quality of the reception he had been accorded in England.
The British Council, he complained, had put him up in sec-
ond-rate hotels. He also complained that the British were
mean, citing the example of a Scottish publisher whom he
traveled to Edinburgh to meet and who had "poured himself a glass of whisky without offering me a drop." Paris,
where he was received by literary members of the Rothschild family—Philippe and Pauline de Rothschild, to whom
he dedicated a collection of translated short stories, *Death
in Midsummer and Other Stories*—had been more to his
taste.

In Tokyo he and Yoko busied themselves with alter-
ations to their house in Magome; they added a top floor
which gave both husband and wife comfortable sitting
rooms where each could receive friends privately. The workmen were in the house for three months, during which
time the Mishimas and their two children lived in the Hotel
New Japan. Mishima amused himself by designing book
covers; he had always been interested in the covers of his
books, especially in the genteibon, the luxury-edition, covers. He designed two covers with the help of experts, one
for *St. Sebastian no Junkyo* ("The Martyrdom of St. Sebastian"), a translation of the work by Gabriele D'Annunzio,
which Mishima had supervised, and one for *Kurotokage*
("Black Lizard"), a play. For the latter he chose a design
which incorporated frontal views of male nudes. Early in

1965 Mishima published one of his strangest short stories, "Kujaku" ("Peacocks"), the story of a man who beats a flock of peacocks to death. He also filmed his short story "Patriotism," acting as producer, director, and chief star—he played the part of the army lieutenant who commits harakiri. In his customary whirl of activity, Mishima found time to produce one of his short "modern No plays," Yuya, in which his friend Utaemon took the lead.

In the summer of 1965 Mishima implemented one of the major decisions of his literary career—to begin a long novel, in four volumes, a work which he expected would take him about six years, into the early 1970's. The novel would cover a span of sixty years in modern Japan, beginning in the early Taisho period, about 1912. Each volume would have a protagonist who would be a reincarnation of the hero of the previous book, starting with Kiyoaki, a peerlessly handsome boy from an aristocratic family. Kiyoaki would be the main character of the first volume, and his closest friend would be Honda, a fellow student at the Gakushuin school. Only one character, Honda, the friend of the protagonists of all four books, would know the secret of their reincarnations. A physical feature common to all four would be three moles under the left arm; by these moles Honda would recognize the reincarnations. The lives of Honda's four friends would also be linked by dreams. Through chance remarks and diary entries Honda would be informed of the dreams and would gain additional clues to the future existences of Kiyoaki. The protagonists of the first three books would die young, at the age of twenty.

For the design of his new, long novel Mishima drew on a Heian romance of the eleventh century, the Hamamatsu Chunagon Monogatari ("The Tale of Hamamatsu"), a not very well-known work in which the Buddhist idea of reincarnation appears and in which there are prophetic dreams. As a religious background to the novel, Mishima used the teaching of the small Buddhist sect known as Hosso, whose yuishiki ron, or theory of consciousness only, affirms that all experience is subjective and that existence cannot be verified. Mishima gave a twist of his own to the teaching of this ancient Buddhist sect, which came to Japan in the seventh century and lost most of its hold in the country in the succeeding five hundred years. As only consciousness existed, there was no telling reality from illusion. This was a favorite theme of Mishima's, as he explained in the speech he gave at the Foreign Correspondents' Club in Tokyo in 1966, which I quoted in the prologue and from which I repeat the last two sentences: "It might be our . . . my basic subject and my basic romantic idea of literature. It is death memory . . . and the problem of illusion."

Mishima, most of whose novels appeared in installments in magazines before they were issued in book form, gave the first part of the first volume (*Spring Snow*) of his long novel to *Shincho* magazine in the late summer of 1965. In the early autumn, following reports from Stockholm that he was a candidate for the Nobel Prize that year, he set off on a world trip with Yoko, traveling to Cambodia, where he visited Angkor Wat—he was to write a play about the temple of Bayon at Angkor—and thereafter on to Western Europe. Following the death of the elderly novelist Junichiro Tanizaki in June 1965, Mishima was considered the leading Japanese contender for the Nobel Prize, and agency dispatches stated that he was among about ninety candidates for the prize. He regarded himself, rightly, as an outsider—the winner in 1965 was to be the Russian, Sholokhov—as he was still comparatively young (forty). But he had faith that he would eventually win the prize and wanted to gauge how soon he would have a serious chance. He made delicate inquiries at Japanese embassies in Europe, to find out if anyone had an inkling when the Swedish Academy would eventually turn to Japan. His conclusion was that it could not be many years before the Nobel Prize for Literature would go to a Japanese for the first time. Unwisely, he shared this information with friends in Japan and he was repeatedly mentioned in the press thereafter as a candidate. Mishima's concern was in part an indication of his excessive self-regard; but it was also a reflection of the extraordinary interest taken by the Japanese in international distinctions, particularly the Nobel Prize.

Returning to Japan, he made a journey to the nunnery of Enshoji, close to Nara. He had decided to use this small, isolated nunnery in a later section of *Spring Snow*. Enshoji was a Rinzai Zen temple, but he converted it, in the book, to Hosso and gave it a different name, Gesshuji. In the autumn of the following year, 1966, Mishima completed *Spring Snow*. It is a love story whose heroine, Satoko, exemplifies what he called tawoyameburi, " 'the way of the graceful young maiden,' an archaic term referring to the traditional beauty and charm of the Japanese girl," according to Donald Keene. Satoko and Kiyoaki, her lover, are the children of aristocratic, powerful families in Tokyo; their passion is inflamed after the betrothal of Satoko to a member of the Imperial family (some Japanese saw in this tale an evocation of Mishima's relationship with Michiko Shoda before her marriage to the Crown Prince, a romantic but slightly far-fetched idea). Satoko is the daughter of a very old family with a long tradition of service at court; Kiyoaki has also been brought up in this tradition, having been sent to the household of the Ayakuras, Satoko's parents, by a proud father who wishes his only son to learn the manners of the aristocracy. Keene has written: "Mishima's long association with the aristocracy, ever since his childhood days at the Peers' School, had led him repeatedly to choose for his characters members of this tiny fraction of Japanese society, and he wrote with a unique knowledge of their speech and attitudes. His account in *Spring Snow* of the aristocrats who built the Victorian mansions still standing here and there in Tokyo is curiously affecting . . . The billiard room, the well-stocked wine cellar, the racks of suits tailored in London, the cut-glass chandeliers and the freshly starched table-cloths obviously attracted Mishima himself, but he did not neglect to describe the Japanese aspects of their lives as well—the spacious garden with its pond and artificial hill, the servants in kimonos eternally dusting and, above all, the elaborate etiquette that revealed itself most conspicuously in the distinctive language" (*Landscapes and Portraits*).

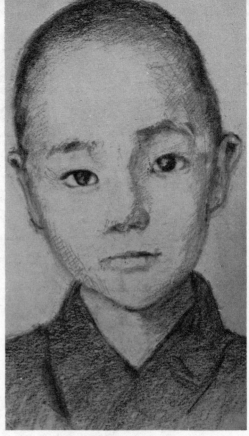

Kimitake Hiraoka—the young Mishima—at eight. A pencil drawing by Akiko Sugiyama. "For many years I claimed I could remember things seen at the time of my own birth. Whenever I said so, the grown-ups would laugh at first, but then, wondering if they were not being tricked, they would look distastefully at the pallid face of that unchildlike child . . ."

Natsuko Hiraoka, Mishima's grandmother, drawn by Akiko Sugiyama. She resolved to take personal responsibility for his upbringing and virtually kidnapped the little boy from his mother.

Photo: Shinchosha

Mishima in 1956 when he carried a portable Shinto shrine through the streets of Tokyo. "Through it all there was only one vividly clear thing, a thing that both horrified and lacerated me, filling my heart with unaccountable agony. This was the expression on the faces of the young men carrying the shrine—an expression of the most obscene and undisguised drunkenness in the world . . ."

The wedding reception at International House. He stipulated that his bride must be neither a bungaku shojo (a bluestocking) nor a yumeibyo kanja (a celebrity hunter), and he had five other requirements . . .

Visiting New York in 1960. Mishima treated Yoko with a consideration that far exceeded the kindness shown to their wives by most Japanese husbands of his generation. For example, he took Yoko with him on his foreign travels. She had never been abroad, and when Mishima embarked on a long journey around the world in late 1960, she accompanied him. They were in New York, where they saw the première of Mishima's modern No plays, in an off-Broadway production.

Photo: Shinchosha

Photo: WWP—Shinchosha

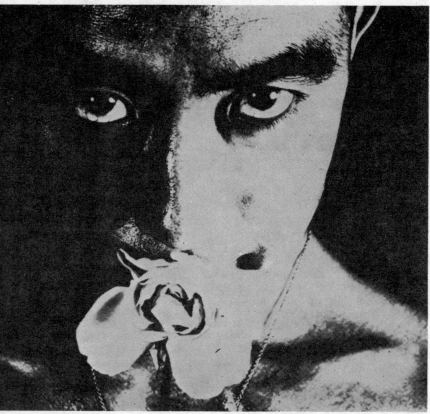

He posed for an album of photographs by the fashionable photographer, Eikoh Hosoe. In these magnificent pictures he appears in a
number of extraordinary poses—lying on his back in his garden against
a baroque ornament, stripped naked, with a white rose in his mouth,
or lying upon his hairy chest. The album, *Barakei* ("Torture by Roses"),
gave Mishima a bad reputation in some quarters. Critics and other
writers who disliked him said he was going off his head at last.

Photo: Shinchosha

In front of his home on the outskirts of Tokyo in 1965. "Surprised by luxury in which Mishima lives," I noted in my diary. "Modern, three-story home set well back from road in quiet suburb of Tokyo . . . Very solid house with solid walls, painted white. Maid at the door in cap and apron!"

Mishima as St. Sebastian, in a photo taken in 1966 by Kishin Shinoyama, the leading young Japanese photographer. It shows Mishima in the pose selected by Guido Reni for the portrait of St. Sebastian which—as Mishima had described in *Confessions of a Mask*—had inspired his first ejaculation. He is standing against a thick tree trunk, the lower foliage of which is visible, acting as a canopy over the man below ...

Photo: Shinoyama

Prime example of his clowning is another picture he sent me: shows him stripped to the waist, chest bulging like mad and beaded with sweat, he's holding a sword, that long sword I saw in his home. He has a pathological expression on his face: brows knotted, eyes popping out. He has a hachimaki (headband) on in the picture, on which is written a medieval samurai slogan: *Shichisho Hokoku* ("Serve the Nation for Seven Lives"). Thank goodness this is not the real Mishima, I thought at the time. Or is it?

Photo: Shinchosha

Photo: Shinchosha

Mishima during his debate with left-wing students at Tokyo University in May 1969. "I was as nervous as if I was going into a lions' den, but I enjoyed it very much after all. I found we have much in common—a rigorous ideology and a taste for physical violence, for example. Both they and I represent new species in Japan today. I felt friendship for them. We are friends between whom there is a barbed-wire fence."

When he gave lectures before literary societies, he dressed in three-piece suits, had his hair cut short, and looked every inch the prosperous, able young banker or Japanese industrialist.

With me on Mt. Fuji in 1969, the year before his death. I had been invited to watch training exercises of the Tatenokai, Mishima's private army, and I noted about this snapshot: "Sitting in snow, having lunch with Mishima (am trying to digest fearful dish called sekihan, glutinous rice with red beans). Picture shows Mishima looking a bit criminal, thuggish: he does sometimes look like that."

In Tatenokai uniform. He wanted to "inspire people with a sense of national pride," he said, as if imagining the sound of brass bands and cheering multitudes of onlookers.

Photo: Eikoh Hosoe—Time/Life Picture Agency

The Mishima family on one of their vacations at Shimoda. When I visited them the last time, I noted: "Two children with us: Noriko, the girl, beautiful and quiet, very feminine at eleven; Ichiro, a barbaric little boy with white teeth and very sunburned—two years younger. Only Yoko can control him. Children teased Mishima about his [swimming] trunks: 'Won't you do a striptease, Dad?', etc. Mishima rolled on his back in sand, narcissism exposed yet again. What a funny man!" His boisterous talk of suicide seemed like an act, but behind his frivolous mask on vacation, Mishima was already plotting his death at secret meetings with members of the Tatenokai.

Masakatsu Morita. The descriptions of Omi in *Confessions of a Mask* remind me of Morita, the student leader of the Tatenokai who was to die with Mishima. "Something about his face," wrote Mishima of Omi, "gave one the sensation of abundant blood coursing richly throughout his body, it was a round face, with haughty cheekbones rising from swarthy cheeks, lips that seemed to have been sewn into a fine line, sturdy jaws, and a broad but well-shaped and not too prominent nose." The fate suffered by Omi in the book is not so different from Morita's; he was made a human sacrifice, according to Mishima's fantasy.

Photo: Kyodo

With members of the Tatenokai; Morita on the right. "I've often heard the glib motto 'The Pen and the Sword Join in a Single Path.' But in truth they can join only at the moment of death."

Photo: Shinchosha

Mishima's private group within the Tatenokai, who helped him stage the hara-kiri. Mishima is seated. Behind him, left to right, are Morita, Furu-Koga, Ogawa, and Chibi-Koga. They had a group portrait taken in full uniform at Tojo Hall, where wedding parties are the usual customers. (Mishima joked to the others that the Tojo Hall cameramen had the art of making everybody look beautiful.)

Photo: *Newsweek* (Bernard Krisher)

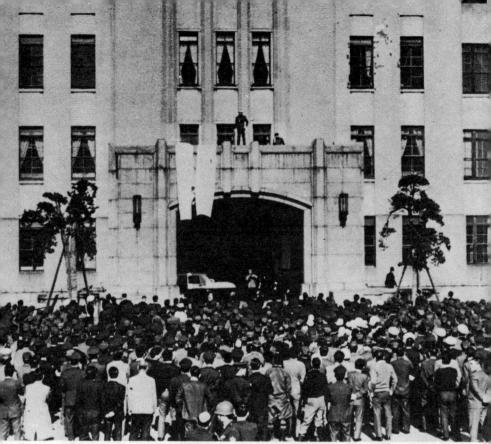

Photo: WWP

(ABOVE AND ON FACING PAGE) Mishima addresses the Jieitai soldiers from the balcony at Eastern Army Headquarters a few minutes before his death. At midday precisely, Mishima appeared on the balcony. He strode forward to the front of the balcony, a small figure in the yellow-brown uniform of the Tatenokai. The men below saw only his head, with a hachimaki bound around it, the symbol of the Rising Sun in the center of the forehead. He leaped up onto the parapet, his small, wiry frame coming entirely into view, the buttons of his uniform shining brightly in the November sun. On his white gloves, blood-stains were visible. He braced himself, shoulders back, his hands on his hips. "It is a wretched affair," Mishima began, "to have to speak to Jieitai men in circumstances like these . . ."

Chibi-Koga led the way out of General Mashita's office carrying Mishima's sword. Also surrendering with him are Ogawa (LEFT) and Furu-Koga, who escort General Mashita between them. An officer rushed to Mashita. "Are you all right, sir?" The general nodded, but he was on the verge of collapse. The police still did not move. "Well," an inspector cried out finally, "arrest them!" The police doctors went into the room. At 12:23 they confirmed that Mishima and Morita had died by hara-kiri and beheading.

Photo: WWP

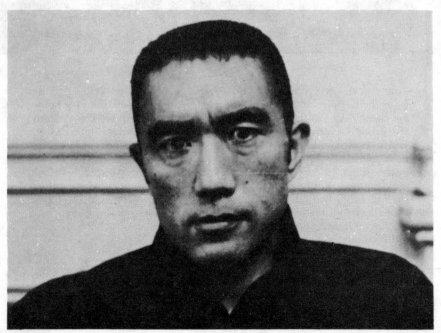

Photo: UPI

One night Kiyoaki, tormented by his feelings for Satoko, tosses and turns on his bed; at last he throws off the bed-clothes and lies naked on his stomach. This is how Mishima describes him, in Michael Gallagher's translation, published by Alfred A. Knopf in 1972: "He lay with his face buried in his pillow, his naked back to the moon and the hot blood still throbbing in his temples. And so he lay, the moonlight washing over the incomparable smooth white of his back, its brilliance highlighting the graceful lines of his body to reveal the subtle but pervasive hint of firm masculinity that made it clear that this was the flesh not of a woman but of a still immature young man. The moon shone with dazzling brightness on Kiyoaki's left side, where the pale flesh pulsed softly in rhythm with his heartbeat. Here there were three small, almost invisible moles. And much as the three stars in Orion's belt fade in strong moonlight, so too these three small moles were almost blotted out by its rays."

Kiyoaki is of two minds about Satoko, who is in love with him. When he compares her charms to those of merely beautiful women, however, as in a scene in which he scrutinizes a crowd of geisha in his father's park, on the occasion of a party given for an Imperial prince, he is sure that Satoko is greatly superior to the professional beauties. He wondered "how these women could laugh and play as happily as if they were bathing in water warmed to their liking. He observed them closely—the way they gestured as they told stories, the way they all nodded alike, as though each had a finely wrought gold hinge in her smooth white neck . . . and of all these many devices, the one that interested him most was their manner of letting their eyes rove incessantly." Kiyoaki finds them "tasteless."

Satoko and Kiyoaki quarrel on the occasion of this garden party, and during the long period which ensues before their next meeting, Kiyoaki will not respond to a series of letters and calls from Satoko; the girl becomes engaged to a young prince. The arranged marriage is not one she would have chosen, and she finds means of meeting Kiyoaki secretly. These encounters lead to a love affair which is connived at and arranged by a scheming lady companion of

Satoko's. While the gentlewoman waits discreetly out of sight in the isolated inn to which she has brought the lovers, Kiyoaki wrestles with Satoko's clothing: "He had no idea whatever how to unfasten a woman's *obi*. Its tightly fastened flared bow at her back defied the efforts of his fingers. But as he groped blindly, trying to undo it by force, she reached behind her and while giving every sign that she was trying desperately to check his fumbling efforts, she subtly guided them in a more profitable direction. Their fingers lay tangled for a few moments in its folds, and then as its clip suddenly fell away, the *obi* uncoiled in a rustle of silk and sprang from her body as though it had a life of its own. It was the beginning of a confused riot of uncontrollable movements. Her entire kimono swirled in revolt as he tore frantically at the folds of silk that bound her breasts, rebuffed at every turn by a whole network of straps that tightened as others came loose. But then right before his eyes, he saw the tiny, well-guarded triangle of white below her throat spread into a rich and fragrant expanse of skin."

Satoko becomes pregnant by Kiyoaki shortly before her marriage is to take place, and the parents of the two lovers desperately hustle her off to Osaka for an abortion. The operation is performed, but Satoko, instead of returning to Tokyo as planned by the parents, takes refuge in a nunnery close to Nara, Gesshuji. Kiyoaki goes to see her and is refused admittance by the abbess. He makes repeated journeys to the nunnery in cold weather, when spring snow is on the ground, and his health begins to suffer. Honda, Kiyoaki's best friend at school (the Gakushuin), comes down from Tokyo too, and pleads with the abbess to allow Kiyoaki to see Satoko. " 'It's a frightening thing to say, but I somehow feel that he's not going to recover. So I am really giving you his dying request. Would letting him see Satoko for just a moment or two be quite outside the scope of the Lord Buddha's compassion? Won't you please permit it?' " At that moment Honda thinks he hears something. "It sounded like a muffled laugh, as faint as the opening of plum blossom. But then, after a moment's reflection, he was sure that unless his ears had deceived him, the sound that had carried to him through the chill convent atmosphere on this spring morning was not a muffled laugh, as he had thought, but a young woman's stifled sob." The abbess remains firm in her refusal to let Kiyoaki see Satoko. To Honda she gives a lecture on the precepts of the Hosso sect: "The Abbess referred to the net of Indra. Indra was an Indian God, and once he cast his net, every man, every living thing without exception was inextricably caught in its meshes. And so it was that all creatures in existence were inescapably bound by it. Indra's net symbolized the Chain of Causation or, in Sanskrit, *pratitya-samutpada*. *Yuishiki* (*Vijnaptimatrata* or Consciousness), the fundamental doctrine of the Hosso Sect, to which Gesshuji belonged, was celebrated in *The Thirty Verses of Yuishiki,* the canonical text attributed to Vasubandhu, whom the sect regarded as its founder. According to the Verses, *Alaya* is the origin of the Chain of Causation. This was a Sanskrit word that denoted a storehouse. For within the *Alaya* were contained the karmic 'seeds' that held the consequential effects of all deeds, both good and evil." After the lecture—only a section of which is given here—Honda returns to the inn where Kiyoaki is staying and then accompanies his friend, now desperately ill, back to Tokyo. In the train Kiyoaki tells Honda a snatch of a dream: "Just now I had a dream. I'll see you again. I know it. Beneath the falls." Two days later Kiyoaki dies; the first volume ends there.

Spring Snow is beautifully written; the romantic lovers—and the lackeys who surround them—are marvelously described. Once the love affair has begun, however, the interest of the book declines, and its ending, the death of Kiyoaki, is not moving. A second difficulty is Mishima's description of religion. He was not a religious man (so Taijun Takeda, a poet and the son of a Buddhist priest, and one who liked Mishima's work, has also testified), and his description of Hosso teaching reads like a doctoral thesis; yet reincarnation is central to the novel. Here was a major problem for the writer: how to make an idea convincing when he did not believe it himself. In later volumes of the novel Mishima was forced to confront this problem.

There is no space here to describe all of Mishima's private and literary activities (I have already bypassed the less interesting novels which he wrote in the early 1960's). He was perpetually in motion; in addition to family matters and an enormous amount of entertaining, he continued to train several times a week at kendo and at body building. And he was also involved in any number of special events ancillary to his main task of committing pen to paper. A review of his schedule during a single year, 1966, gives an idea of his pace through life. In January he was awarded a prize by the Ministry of Education for his play *Madame de Sade.* In the same month he was made a member of the committee which awards the Akutagawa Prize for young novelists—a high award and an important position demanding a good deal of effort, as committee members must read many manuscripts; Mishima's presence on the committee is said to have completely changed the atmosphere there, which had been stuffy. In April the film *Patriotism,* which had made its way to Tours for a festival, received an award; it was also released in Japan and was a colossal success. During the summer Mishima had his holidays as usual, and he found time to be in Tokyo and to rehearse for a cabaret organized by his friend, Akihiro Maruyama, the female impersonator; he composed a ballad for the occasion and himself sang "The Sailor Who Was Killed by Paper Roses." The following month he was off on a tour with Donald Keene, visiting Kyoto, Omiwa Shrine, Hiroshima, and Kumamoto, gathering material for *Runaway Horses,* the second volume of his long novel, and making a donation to the shrine at Omiwa so large that the priests were quite taken aback. In the autumn he finally achieved a reconciliation with the Arita family.

In the midst of these activities he completed a dozen minor literary works. These are listed together with the months in which they were published, or began to appear, in the case of serial works:

Jan.   *Fukuzatsu no Kare* ("A Complex Man")
        in *Josei Seven* until July

Feb.   *Kiken na Geijutsuka* ("Dangerous Artist")
        in *Bungakukai*
        Owari no Bigaku ("The Aesthetic of the End")
        in *Josei Jishin* until August

March   *Hanteijo Daigaku* ("The Book of the Anti-chaste
        Wisdom"), published by Shinchosha

April   *Yukoku* ("Patriotism")
        published by Shinchosha

May   *Eigatekki Nikutairon* ("On the Body in Films")
        in *Eiga Geijutsu*

June   *Eirei no Koe* ("The Voices of the Heroic Dead")
        in *Bungei,* and published by Kawade Shobo

July   *Watashi no Isho* ("My Final Word")
        in *Bungakukai*
        Narcissism Ron ("Essay on Narcissism")
        in *Fujin Koron*

Aug.   *Mishima Yukio Hyoronzenshu* ("Collected Criticism")
        published by Shinchosha

Sept.   *Danzo, Geido, Saigunbi* ("Danzo, Art, and Rearma-
        ment"), in *Niji Seiki*
        Yakaifuku ("Ball Costume")
        in *Mademoiselle* until August 1967
        Mishima Letter Kyoshitsu ("Mishima Letter School")
        in *Josei Jishin*

Oct.   *Koya Yori* ("From the Wilderness")
        in *Gunzo*
        Taiwa Nihonjinron ("On the Japanese"), with Fusao
        Hayashi, in *Bancho Shobo*

Dec.   *Ito Shizuo no Shi* ("The Poetry of Shizuo Ito")
        in *Shincho*

Two of these works, *Eirei no Koe* and *Taiwa Nihonjinron,* belong to Mishima's "committed" literature and will be mentioned later. A great many of the pieces were for women's magazines (*Josei Jishin, Fujin Koron, Josei Seven, Mademoiselle*), publications that paid well and demanded light fare. In this year alone, however, Shinchosha, Mishima's chief publishers, brought out three new volumes and also published an essay in their house magazine, *Shincho*. The list excludes new and luxury editions of Mishima's works. This was the pace which he kept up throughout the 1960's.

Most men would have collapsed after a few weeks of living under this pressure; yet he rarely looked tired. As luck would have it, the only occasion on which I saw him that year—it was the first time I set eyes on him, at the dinner at the Foreign Correspondents' Club at which he was guest speaker—he looked distinctly wan. Usually he had a deep suntan, but on that particular evening he appeared pale and a little nervous. That was an exception. Normally, when he was in public, he affected high spirits and dominated any gathering in which he took part: gesturing, joking, and laughing the raucous, rather ugly laugh which he is said to have been taught by his overbearing grandmother. His mask was firmly in place; a stranger might have classified him as a former amateur boxing champion turned nightclub owner or band leader. For there was something coarse about his mask; he projected an air of deliberate vulgarity which deceived all but those who knew him well. What is truly remarkable is that he was able to go through with this act— that is what it was—although he was under the most terrible strain. This is reflected in his writing; for example, in the autobiographical work *Sun and Steel,* which he began late in 1965 and which appeared regularly over three years in a small magazine, *Hihyo* ("Criticism"), founded by a rightwing friend, the critic Takeshi Muramatsu, and supported among others by Mishima himself. *Sun and Steel* is a work which he classified as "confidential criticism," and it affords glimpses into the inner man of a far more intimate nature than those who knew him only superficially were able to obtain by meeting him and talking to him.

The key to this work—which is central to an understanding of his suicide—is the author's definition of tragedy. From this definition springs the whole of the remainder of *Sun and Steel,* an essay of eighty pages: "According to my definition of tragedy, the tragic *pathos* is born when the perfectly average sensibility momentarily takes unto itself a privileged nobility that keeps others at a distance, and not when a special type of sensibility vaunts its own special claims. It follows that he who dabbles in words can create tragedy, but cannot participate in it. It is necessary, moreover, that the 'privileged nobility' finds its basis strictly in a kind of physical courage. The elements of intoxication and superhuman clarity in the tragic are born when the average sensibility, endowed with a given physical strength, encounters that type of privileged moment especially designed for it. Tragedy calls for an anti-tragic vitality and ignorance, and above all for a certain 'inappropriateness.' If a person is at times to draw close to the divine, then under normal conditions he must be neither divine nor anything approaching it." There is much to criticize in this statement. Mishima's notion of a "privileged nobility" is repulsive; his idea that he must abandon his keen sensibility and settle for a "perfectly average sensibility" is absurd. What matters most, however, is that Mishima yearned to be a hero—so much is clear from his definition of tragedy; he also believed that he must abandon his role as a writer, one "who dabbles in words," in order to become a tragic hero.

In this essay, Mishima described a scene in which he becomes convinced of his aspiration to be a tragic figure. One summer day, heated by training, "I was cooling my muscles in the breeze coming through an open window. The sweat vanished as though by magic, and coolness passed over the surface of the muscles like a touch of menthol. The next instant, I was rid of the sense of the muscles' existence, and—in the same way that words, by their abstract functioning, can grind up the concrete world so that the words themselves seem never to have existed—my muscles at that moment crushed something within my being, so that it was as though the muscles themselves had similarly never existed . . . I was enveloped in a sense of power as transparent as light. It is scarcely to be wondered at that in this pure sense of power that no amount of books or intellectual analysis could ever capture, I should discover a true antithesis of words. And indeed it was this that by gradual stages was to become the focus of my whole thinking."

From this point, it is not a long step to the conclusion that it was death that he desired.

With the aid of "sun and steel"—by sunbathing and weight lifting—Mishima had discovered his body and created his muscles. Thereafter, he "glimpsed from time to time another sun quite different from that by which I had been so long blessed, a sun full of the fierce dark flames of feeling, a sun of death that would never burn the skin yet gave forth a still stranger glow." Mishima's conclusion, as he described it toward the end of 1966, was this: "The goal of my life was to acquire all the various attributes of the warrior." It was thus that he arrived at the romantic idea of death as a samurai. If *Sun and Steel* is to be trusted, Mishima cared nothing for ideology; his was to be strictly a non-political action. And the essay is in fact persuasive, more so than Mishima's "political" writing.

Mishima was well versed in Nietzsche, as one sees from the internal evidence of the passage just quoted. The model which he chose for his life style at this point in his life—and which he faithfully followed for the last four years of his existence—was, however, a Japanese one, which Mishima adapted from feudal times. The ideal samurai pursued his life (and death) according to the ancient practice of Bunburyodo, the dual way of Literature (Bun) and the Sword (Bu); he was expected to cultivate the literary and the martial arts in roughly equal proportions. In practice, very few of the ancient knights of Japan lived up to this demanding standard. Nonetheless, it was the ideal and was encouraged by the authorities from the seventeenth century onward, when peace had finally settled upon Japan and it was desirable that the samurai class no longer unsheathe their weapons at the slightest pretext. Mishima had long been intrigued by the feudal ideal of Bunburyodo—"ryodo" may be translated as "dual way"—as he recounts in *Sun and Steel*: "During the post-war period, when all accepted values were upset, I often thought and remarked to others that now if ever was the time for reviving the old Japanese ideal of a combination of letters and the martial arts, of art and action.

For a while after that, my interest strayed from that particular ideal; then, as I gradually learned from the sun and the steel the secret of how to pursue words with the body (and not merely pursue the body with words), the two poles within me began to maintain a balance, and the generator of my mind, so to speak, switched from a direct to an alternating current . . . [These two poles] gave the appearance of inducing an ever wider split in the personality, yet in practice created at each moment a living balance that was constantly being destroyed and brought back to life again. The embracing of a dual polarity within the self and the acceptance of contradiction and collision—such was my own blend of 'art and action.' "

It is at this point in his essay that Mishima begins to describe the stress under which he lived—the strain which he so faithfully hid behind his mask. "Why," he asks, "should a man be associated with beauty only through a heroic, violent death?" His answer: "Such is the beauty of the suicide squad, which is recognized as beauty not only in the spiritual sense but, by men in general, in an ultra-erotic sense also." He does not argue the point. He states it as a fact of his consciousness (certainly not of "men in general"). Thereafter, he veers out of control—there was indeed "an ever wider split in the personality": "The most appropriate type of daily life for me was a day-by-day world destruction; peace was the most difficult and abnormal state to live in . . . No moment is so dazzling as when everyday imaginings concerning death and danger and world destruction are transformed into duty . . . To keep death in mind from day to day, to focus each moment upon inevitable death, to make sure one's worst forebodings coincided with one's dreams of glory . . . the beautiful death that had earlier eluded me [in the war] had also become possible . . . I was beginning to dream of my capabilities as a fighting man."

His reaction to loss of control was to discipline himself still more rigorously than before. Bunburyodo then became more than a life style for Mishima; it became the "plan for life" for which he had been so anxiously casting about for almost five years. And it had very specific objectives in the fields of art and action. His long novel was his main endeavor in art; and in action his aim became nothing less than "the beautiful death . . . as a fighting man." The greater the stress upon him, the more furiously Mishima fought to control himself. Bunburyodo came to mean for him that every time he completed a stage of his novel, a new volume, he must simultaneously commit himself one step further on the road to martial action—and death. As he completed *Spring Snow* in the autumn of 1966, he submitted an application to the Jieitai for permission to train at army camps.

Not inappropriately, the second volume of Mishima's long novel, which he began early in 1967, depicts what Mishima called masuraoburi, the way of the warrior. Its hero, Isao, is a right-wing terrorist who commits hara-kiri after stabbing an aged businessman to death. The action of this book, entitled *Runaway Horses*, takes place in the early 1930's, twenty years after the death of Kiyoaki; Isao dies, also, at twenty. The young man, who is nineteen at the outset, is a brilliant swordsman and kendo performer who already holds the rank of 3-dan. He is a student at Kokugakuin University in Tokyo—an institution at which many nationalists have been trained—and is the son of Kiyoaki's former tutor, Iinuma, a cunning, corrupt rightist. Isao, a sturdy youth quite unlike Kiyoaki in appearance, has sharp, furious eyes and firm-set lips. He is keen and "pure"; his father, however, takes money from tainted sources (i.e., business). Honda, who is now a judge at an Osaka court, attends a kendo match in which Isao appears; he knows nothing of the boy, apart from the fact that he is the son of Iinuma. After the match, which Isao wins, Honda climbs a nearby hill with a priest; the latter persuades him to bathe in a waterfall on the way down. Isao, too, is bathing there, and seeing him under the falls, Honda suddenly notices, as he raises his arms above his head, that the boy has three moles on the left-hand side of his chest. The youth laughs as he tumbles in the water, but Honda is terrified by what he sees, remembering the last words of Kiyoaki: "I'll see you again. I know it. Beneath the falls." Isao, then, must be Kiyoaki's reincarnation. Honda feels that his way of life, his dry-as-dust rationalism, is threatened.

Isao is reading a pamphlet which impresses him deeply, "The League of the Divine Wind" by Tsunanori Yamao. It describes the Shinpuren Incident of 1877, one of the last times in Japanese history when samurai appeared in action. Mishima gives the pamphlet so much importance in his novel that it takes up nearly fifty pages out of just over four hundred in the translation by Michael Gallagher published by Alfred A. Knopf in 1973. It begins one summer day in 1873 when "four stalwart men of high ideals" gather to pray at Shingai Village close to Kumamoto Castle, led by Tomo Otaguro, adopted son and heir of the former chief priest, the late Oen Hayashi. The four men are Harakata Kaya, "at the height of his powers"; Kengo Ueno, over sixty; and Kyuzaburo Saito and Masamoto Aiko, in their fifties. All have swords with them; all are believers in Sonno Joi ("Revere the Emperor and Expel the Barbarians"), and all hate Western culture. After praying, they wait for the priest Otaguro to perform the Ukei divination ceremony. They wish to put two questions to the gods: whether they might present a petition to the authorities, calling for Kamiyo (the rule of the Emperor) and then commit hara-kiri; and if not, whether the gods would permit them to assassinate the villainous retainers ostensibly acting for the Emperor in their district. All four men eagerly desire the restoration of Kamiyo, the practice of Kodo (ancient morality), and the unity of shrine and state. Their teacher has been Oen Hayashi.

In the Ukei ceremony, one learned the will of the gods with the aid of sacred pendants—Shinto divine symbols—and positive and negative slips of paper. On this occasion both requests gain a negative response. After the ceremony, the men burn the slips of paper and drink the ashes with water. The next year, the Saga Rebellion occurs. Otaguro thinks that this is a chance not to be missed and performs a second Ukei. Once again the gods reply in the negative. The feeling of Sonno Joi is strong among the group and in that year fifteen followers of the four men are made priests. In 1877, on March 18, the government proclaims the decree abolishing the wearing of swords, and shortly afterward comes another decree ordering former samurai to trim off the topknots from their heads. These two announcements convince the group to take action. Alone, Kaya decides to present a petition and then to commit hara-kiri.

Otaguro performs the Ukei ceremony for a third time in May. This time he receives an affirmative reply from the gods. Accordingly, he prepares a plan for the assassination of government officials in the Kumamoto area; some army officers are also added to the list. He gathers men together in secret from the neighborhood. His plan is: (1) One party of thirty men to assassinate the general at the Kumamoto barracks, and also to kill the local governor and the chairman of a local commission in their homes. (2) A second party to attack the artillery camp in the barracks. (3) A third party to attack the 2,000-man-strong infantry garrison at the camp. Kaya decides to join the group again three days before their day of action.

The sole preparation is prayer. They would not arm themselves with guns, because they hate these abominable Western weapons. (When obliged to walk under electric power lines, they cover their heads with white fans.) They arm themselves instead with sword, spear, and halberd. They have oil also, to set fire to the camp. Very few of them wear armor. Their treasured possession is a sacred tablet, the Mitamashiro, and Otaguro carries it on his back. The decision is made to attack on October 24.

The attack begins at midnight. The general is killed and the governor and chairman are injured. But by early morning the majority of the rebels attacking without guns are also dead. The two leaders, Otaguro and Kaya, have been shot. Otaguro asks his brother-in-law to give a coup de grâce by kaishaku. Forty-six survivors of the attack retire to Kinposan, a hill west of the castle, and decide to disperse and hide.

Seven boys are ordered home, and three severely injured men commit hara-kiri.

Thereafter, the rebels commit hara-kiri in a variety of places, some at home, others in the mountains. One is a boy of sixteen. Six men flee by ship to Konoura and wait there for news. After receiving a report of the defeat, they climb Omidake Mountain early in the morning, make a circle with rope and with the sacred pendants and papers on a flat spot, and all commit perfect hara-kiri.

Almost all the rebels commit hara-kiri or are burned to death, but one man, Kotaro Ogata, surrenders. Arrested and in prison, he puzzles over the failure of men with such dedication, purged of impurity: how is it that divine assistance was not forthcoming? The will of the gods is hidden, but Ogata concludes by giving voice to the spirit of the samurai: "Were we to have acted like frail women?"

Isao worships the "purity" of these men who sacrificed their lives in the Shinpuren Incident. Paying a visit to a lieutenant of a regiment stationed in Azabu in central Tokyo, he reveals his wish to commit hara-kiri "on a cliff . . . just at sunrise . . . under a pine tree . . . looking down at the shining sea." At a second meeting, the lieutenant introduces Isao to a member of the Imperial family, a prince, and Isao gives him his copy of the pamphlet on the Shinpuren Incident. Toin no Miya, the prince, has been told in advance of Isao's idea of sacrificing himself for the Emperor, and he asks: "Supposing the Emperor turns down your idea, what would you do?" Isao replies that he would commit hara-kiri. Loyalty, says Isao, using a parable, is to prepare hot nigirimeshi (a simple rice dish) for the Emperor as a present. If the Emperor refuses the food, for whatever reason, Isao would commit hara-kiri. Equally, if he accepts the dish, Isao would commit hara-kiri, for it is a grave sin for a somo, a humble subject, to make nigirimeshi for the Emperor. One kind of loyalty would be to make the food and then not present it, but this would be loyalty without bravery. Real loyalty would be to present the nigirimeshi, without regard to one's life. Prince Toin is greatly moved by the

speech and comments: "With such young men we can have
hope for the future." He gives Isao a cake upon which his
crest has been pressed.

Isao, thus encouraged, plans, with a group of friends, to
assassinate government and business leaders; they will also
blow up the Bank of Japan. His father, however, who is
receiving money from Kurahara, one of the tycoons Isao
plans to murder, informs the police of the plot; the boy is arrested and put in prison. (Honda, meanwhile, has been med-
itating on his discovery of Isao; he has become greatly disturbed and his thoughts have drifted toward romanticism.
When he hears that Isao is to be put on trial, Honda gives up
his judgeship. He makes his way to Tokyo and offers himself as defense counsel for Isao, whom he defends with help
from Prince Toin.) In prison, Isao reads *The Philosophy of
the Japanese Wang Yang-Ming School,* by Dr. Tetsujiro
Inoue, a description of the teaching of the neo-Confucian
school whose maxim is: "To know and not to act is not yet to
know." He is attracted by a chapter on Heihachiro Oshio, a
nineteenth-century hero who sacrificed his life in an attack
on the great merchant houses in Osaka, who were hoarding
rice at a time of famine. There was no fearing the death of
the body, Dr. Inoue summed up; only the death of the spirit.

At his trial, under examination by the judges, Isao gives
an account of the two sources of his inspiration. One has
been Yomeigaku, the teaching of the Chinese Wang Yang-
ming, a soldier philosopher who broke the hold of Confucianism on China in the sixteenth century. Isao says: "Yes,
Your Honor. In the philosophy of Wang Yang-ming there is
something that is called congruity of thought and action: 'To
know and not to act is not yet to know.' And it was this philosophy that I strove to put into practice. If one knows of the
decadence of Japan today, the dark clouds that envelop her
future, the impoverished state of the farmers and the despair
of the poor, if one knows all this is due to political corruption and to the unpatriotic nature of the zaibatsu, the industrial combines, who thrive on this corruption, and knows
that here is the source of the evil which shuts out the light

of our most revered Emperor's benevolence—with such knowledge, I think, the meaning of 'to know and to act' becomes self-evident."

His second inspiration has been the Shinpuren Incident: "I had faith that the dark clouds would one day be blown away and that a bright and clear future lay ahead for Japan. Wait as I might, however, that day did not come. The longer I waited, the darker the clouds became . . . Who was to carry word to heaven? Who, mounting to heaven through death, was to take upon himself the vital function of messenger? . . . To join heaven and earth, some decisive deed of purity is necessary. To accomplish so resolute an action, you have to stake your life, giving no thought to personal gain or loss. You have to turn into a dragon and stir up a whirlwind . . ." He concludes: "Loyalty, I think, is nothing else but to throw down one's life in reverence for the Imperial Will [the Emperor]. It is to tear asunder the dark clouds, climb to heaven, and plunge into the sun, plunge into the midst of the Imperial Mind. This, then, is what my comrades and I pledged within our hearts."

Shortly afterward, the judge lets Isao go free. Following his release, he hears a report that Kurahara, the business leader who finances his father, has committed an impiety at the Ise Shrine—the shrine of the sun goddess. Ten days before Isao's release, Kurahara had been in the Kansai, attending a meeting of bankers; he had visited Matsuzaka, a famous place for beef, and eaten an inordinate amount of meat (meat eating is a custom introduced to Japan from the West). On the following day he had visited the Ise Shrine, accompanied by the governor of Mie prefecture, as an honored guest of the shrine. While listening to the recital of norito, of prayers, Kurahara had put down on his chair his sprig of tamagushi (a sacred leaf), to have a hand free to scratch his back; then he had sat down on the tamagushi by mistake, failing to realize what he had done. The right-wing press make much of this incident. Kurahara had unknowingly profaned the most holy shrine in the country.

Isao is unimpressed by the story when he first hears it.

Later, however, when drinking with his father and Honda, he learns the secret of his father's tie with Kurahara and is told that his father had informed on him. He weeps. "I've lived for the sake of an illusion. I've patterned my life upon an illusion. And this punishment has come on me because of this illusion . . . Maybe I ought to be reborn a woman. If I were a woman, I could live without chasing after illusions."

Honda helps the boy to bed and watches over him as he sleeps. He hears him say as he dreams: "Far to the south. Very hot . . . in the rose sunshine of a southern land." Two days later Isao evades his father's assistant, buys a short sword and a knife in the Ginza, and takes a train to Atami, where Kurahara is reported to be.

He reaches the cottage where Kurahara is staying at about ten at night. Crossing an orchard, he looks into a lighted room, furnished in Western style, in which a fat, stern-looking old man is sitting on a sofa. Isao waits until a maid has left the room, then he dashes in with his sword. Kurahara stands up but does not cry out.

"Who are you? What are you doing here?"

"Take the punishment you deserve for profaning the Grand Shrine of Ise," Isao says calmly.

"What?" Kurahara exclaims, unable to remember anything.

The old man looks very frightened. He makes a movement of his body and Isao jumps at him. Holding the businessman to him, he thrusts the sword through his heart. Kurahara's eyes open wide and his false teeth fall out. Isao pulls out his sword and dashes from the room, brushing the maid aside.

He heads for the sea close by, looking for a cliff. At last he finds the high cliff he seeks. Making his way toward its top, he pauses to pluck a mikan, a tangerine. He eats the fruit and rests, getting his breath back. He has run and is out of training after months in prison. Isao takes off his jacket and gets out his knife. He has lost the sword. A cold wind blows from the sea.

"The sun will not rise for some time," he thinks, "and

I can't afford to wait. There is no shining disk climbing upward. There is no noble pine to shelter me. Nor is there a sparkling sea."

He takes off his shirt and unbuttons his trousers. Far away there are voices: "The ocean. He must have got away in a boat."

Runaway Horses concludes: "Isao drew in a deep breath and shut his eyes as he ran his left hand caressingly over his stomach. Grasping the knife with his right hand, he pressed its point against his body, and guided it to the correct place with the fingertips of his left hand. Then, with a powerful thrust of his arm, he plunged the knife into his stomach. The instant that the blade tore open his flesh, the bright disk of the sun soared up and exploded behind his eyelids."

The book contains a brilliant picture of the manner in which right-wing terrorism functioned in Japan in the 1930's; it is a unique portrayal of the mechanism of the Uyoku (the right) in the days of greatest power of this small minority. The involvement of a member of the Imperial family in Isao's plotting of a coup d'état, although Toin no Miya is not himself a party to the affair, is especially intriguing (the role of the Imperial princes in the numerous fracases of the 1930's is still a mystery). *Runaway Horses*, however, has a kind of coldness about it; the murder by Isao of a man totally unknown to him, with whom he has no personal quarrel, is brilliantly done; but the boy's preoccupation with the act of hara-kiri reflects Mishima's own obsession with the subject, so it seems, rather than appearing as one aspect of a credible terrorist personality. Isao has a woman friend, Makiko; and he faces two possible choices. One is to have an affair with Makiko and be corrupted; the other is to commit hara-kiri—when and where does not seem to matter. Thus, the act of hara-kiri acquires a sexual meaning which rings true to the character of Mishima but not to that of Isao. The author's interest in hara-kiri—about which no other Japanese novelist of repute has written—lends a morbid air to *Runaway Horses.*

At the same time that he completed *Runaway Horses*, Mishima also finished *Sun and Steel*. In the later passages of the essay he confirmed the points he had made in the sections I have analyzed; tragedy remained the core of the work. Of his training with the Jieitai, Mishima wrote: "My life with the army could be finally endorsed only by death." The essay is imbued with a sense of the gradual weakening and aging of his body: "I, however, had already lost the morning face that belongs to youth alone." "My age pursued me, murmuring behind my back 'How long will it last?'" What he is seeking is the "tragedy that I had once let slip." More accurately, "what had eluded me was the tragedy of the group, or tragedy as a member of the group . . . The group was concerned with all those things that could never emerge from words—sweat, and tears, and cries of joy or pain. If one probed deeper still, it was concerned with the blood that words could never cause to flow . . . Only through the group, I realized—through sharing the suffering of the group—could the body reach that height of existence that the individual alone could never attain . . . The group must be open to death—which meant, of course, that it must be a community of warriors . . . We were united in seeking death and glory; it was not merely my personal quest . . . I had a vision where something that, if I were alone, would have resolved back into muscles and words was held fast by the power of the group and led me away to a far land, whence there would be no return." In an epilogue to the essay, in which Mishima described a test flight in an F-104 jet fighter, he fell back on sexual metaphor to describe his attitude to the experience which he felt awaited him. "Erect-angled, the F-104, a sharp silver phallus, pointed into the sky. Solitary, spermatozoon-like, I was installed within. Soon, I should know how the spermatozoon felt at the instant of ejaculation."

Such was the mood in which Mishima created his Tatenokai in the autumn of 1968. That his inspiration was fundamentally personal and aesthetic (and not political) is suggested by *Sun and Steel* and also by the manner in which he described the Tatenokai in an essay written a year after its formation in October 1968 (*Queen* magazine, January 1970): "The words I value are to be found only in the pure realm of fiction. For I support the tradition of yuga in Japanese literature [a type of refined elegance having its origins in courtly aesthetics during the period before the samurai rose to power]. Words used for political action are soiled words. To revive the traditions of the samurai and the way of the warrior (Bushido), which are so vital in Japanese culture, I have chosen a way without words, a way of silence . . . My aim is to revive the soul of the samurai within myself . . . I should like to describe an episode that may typify the soul of the Tatenokai. Last summer I took a group of about thirty members to the foot of Mt. Fuji. It was a mercilessly hot day and under a broiling sun all of us worked hard in combat exercises. After a bath and supper several of the young men gathered in my room. There was the sound of thunder in the distance; from time to time lightning flashed across the deep purple fields; directly outside our window we could hear the first autumn crickets. After a long talk about how to command the attack squad, one of our members, a young man from Kyoto, brought out a flute in a beautiful damask bag. It was the type of flute used for court music ever since the ninth century, and only very few people can play it nowadays. This lad had been studying it for about a year . . . Now he began playing for us. It was a beautiful and moving melody that reminded me of the heavily bedewed autumn fields and of the Shining Prince Genji who had danced to this very music. As I listened in sheer rapture, it crossed my mind that for the first time in the postwar years the two Japanese traditions had come happily together, if only for a fleeting moment—the tradition of elegance and that of the samurai. It was this union that I had sought in the depth of my heart."

By the autumn of 1968 the tone of Mishima's work had changed drastically. In place of the light articles that he had been writing for women's magazines two years before, he had shifted to a different type of short literature. For the magazine *Eiga Geijutsu* he wrote a piece entitled "Samurai"; for the Japanese *Playboy* for serialization there was *Inochi Urimasu* ("I Will Sell My Life"); and for the publisher Pocket Punch Oh a long series entitled *Wakaki Samurai no tame no Seishinkowa* ("A Lecture in Psychology for Young Samurai"). He also wrote an ironical work with the misspelled title *Alle Japanese Are Perverse*, and completed the play *My Friend Hitler*. His chief preoccupation, however, was the third volume of his long novel. *The Temple of Dawn*, as he called the book, is quite unlike its two predecessors, *Runaway Horses* and *Spring Snow;* those two contain lengthy stories full of drama. *The Temple of Dawn* is primarily a description of religion, both Buddhism and Hinduism. In the previous year Mishima, accompanied by his wife, had visited India at the invitation of the government; and he had then carried out research for his book, visiting Calcutta, Benares, and Ajanta (as does Honda in *The Temple of Dawn*)—having bid Yoko goodbye at Bombay airport.

Just after the appearance of the first installment of the book in *Shincho*, Mishima heard that, once again, he was being considered for the Nobel Prize; the previous year the rumor that he might get the prize had also been strong. A friend told me that Mishima was returning from an overseas trip in 1967 and had timed his arrival in Tokyo for the day on which the announcement of the Nobel Prize was made in Stockholm. He had fancied a hero's welcome: "He had taken a VIP room at Haneda. When the plane landed, he was the first out of the first-class compartment, laughing and smiling. But there was no one there to greet him apart from a few of us; the VIP room was empty; there were no reporters. I have never seen him so depressed."

A Guatemalan novelist, Miguel Angel Asturias, had won the prize the previous year, and in 1968 Mishima was once again disappointed. He very nearly was awarded the Nobel Prize, according to Swedish journalists, but at the last moment the committee veered in favor of an older man, on the theory that Mishima would have his turn later. Their choice was Mishima's old friend Kawabata.

Mishima, when he heard the news, rushed to Kamakura to be the first to congratulate Kawabata; photographs were taken of the two men sitting together and smiling. Mishima was disappointed: "If Hammarskjöld had lived, I would have won," he said afterward. The diplomat had been reputed to be an admirer of his work. But this failure to win the Nobel was not a turning point in his life, as some have said. The slow creep of age and his doubts about his writing were the dominant considerations for Mishima. Not for nothing had he remarked in *Sun and Steel* that he feared he was "on the verge of non-communication" as a writer. To all appearances, he remained unchallenged in Japan as the leading novelist of his generation, but, as he well knew, his reputation was declining steadily.

The extent to which Mishima had fallen out of favor with the critics was apparent in early 1969, when *Spring Snow* and *Runaway Horses* came out in book form. The first volume sold 200,000 copies in two months, and rights were bought by television and the theater as a matter of course. *Runaway Horses* sold less well, but this had been predicted because of its grisly subject matter. Mishima had announced that his tetralogy was to be called *The Sea of Fertility*, after a region of the moon (close to the Sea of Tranquility). He had made this choice, he told Keene, for this reason: "The title *The Sea of Fertility* is intended to suggest the arid sea of the moon that belies its name. Or, I might go so far as to say that it superimposes the image of cosmic nihilism with that of the fertile sea." Mishima's novel, however, though its first volumes sold well, and despite its challenging theme—this was the most ambitious literary project so far conceived in Japan in the twentieth century—received scarcely a single notice in the press. Mishima had associated himself with the right in politics since 1966 and had alienated the Bundan, the literary establishment, which is inclined to the left; his work had become taboo. The only man to speak out strongly in favor of *The Sea of Fertility* was Yasunari Kawabata. Kawabata told a foreign interviewer, Philip Shabecoff of *The New York Times:* "A writer of

Mishima's caliber appears only once every two or three hundred years in our history"; *The Sea of Fertility,* he added, was Mishima's masterpiece. With the exception of this lone voice, no one of importance praised the work. Mishima found himself in a peculiarly Japanese situation; he had alienated the Bundan, but there was not one hostile squeak from the critics, just silence—a characteristic Japanese method of criticism.

Mishima had always been at odds with the critics, and at this point he became hysterically hostile toward many of them—rather like a foreign businessman who has been surrounded and outwitted by unseen competitors in Japan. In his preface to the biography of Zenmei Hasuda, he wrote: "When I got close to the age of forty, at which age Hasuda killed himself, I gradually understood the man better. Above all, I recognized the source of his anger; his fury was directed at Japanese intellectuals, the strongest enemy within the nation. It is astonishing how little the character of modern intellectuals in Japan has changed; i.e., their cowardice, sneering, "objectivity," rootlessness, dishonesty, flunkeyism, mock gestures of resistance, self-importance, inactivity, talkativeness, and readiness to eat their words . . . Hasuda's anger has become my own." Personally, he remained on good terms with some of the best-known critics. He also had many friends—fellow writers and theater people—on whom he could have fallen back at this time of crisis in his career and, much more so, in his private life. It required no special powers of observation to realize that Mishima was in grave trouble; his pranks and capers had gradually assumed a more and more grotesque form, culminating in the Tatenokai.

Mishima's difficulty, however, was that he had no truly close friends to warn him of the dangers into which he was running. He had no kokoro no tomo or real intimates; he was too self-controlled a man to have encouraged close friendship. Among those he saw regularly for many years were some sterling individuals full of common sense. One I think of is Kobo Abé; another, in the world of the theater, is

Takeo Matsuura. But Mishima had never trusted others with his innermost thoughts. Neither Abé nor Matsuura nor anyone else near to him fully understood what was on his mind. The odd thing is that they might easily have done so had they read his writing; for example, *Sun and Steel*. But no one—or scarcely anyone—took the essay seriously. Mishima suffered from a peculiar misunderstanding which he had long before described in *Confessions of a Mask:* "What people regarded as a pose on my part was actually an expression of my need to assert my true nature, and . . . what people regarded as my true self was a masquerade." The Tatenokai, while it appeared to be part of Mishima's masquerade, was in fact a reflection of his need "to assert my true nature."

Those who had known Mishima for a long time had become so accustomed to his clowning and his endless talk of death and suicide that they did not take him seriously any more. Mishima's plight was thus ignored by his friends and his contemporaries. His family too was unable to do much for him. His mother was far too uncritical to chide her son for anything he did, and Azusa had had no influence on him for decades. Yoko, in fact, was in a better position than anyone else to chide and tease her husband back to common sense. When I saw them together, I felt that she was doing that all the time; but Mishima was too closed up in himself to respond.

Mishima at this time associated with people whose politics were to the right—a minority of critics and intellectuals in Japan. Among them were Takeshi Muramatsu, a Francophile with right-wing inclinations; Toshiro Mayuzumi, one of the leading composers of the younger generation and another Francophile with right-wing inclinations; Kinemaro Izawa, an education critic and an exact contemporary of Mishima, perhaps the only person who retained Mishima's confidence until the very last—a nationalist of the old school with limited knowledge of the international scene; Fusao Hayashi, a much older man who had been classed as a war criminal under the Occupation, and whose record of opportunistic alternation between extreme left and extreme right speaks for itself; Kei Wakaizumi, an establishment intellectual who was closely associated with Prime Minister Eisaku Sato during Sato's long tenure of office (1964–72) and who acted as an intermediary between the Japanese and United States governments—a man of great ability, but tense and introverted; Seiji Tsutsumi, a poet and businessman with right-wing inclinations, almost the only zaikai member—man of high finance—with whom Mishima had much patience. There were others: Shintaro Ishihara and Wataru Hiraizumi, younger men of the right in the Liberal Democratic Party—the first a brilliant showman, the second a man of aristocratic family and of immense wealth, a member of the upper class to which Mishima aspired, not without success, to belong. The collective influence of these individuals upon Mishima, whom they tended to patronize—with the notable exception of Izawa, a humble man—was not good.

The Temple of Dawn, which Mishima began in the late summer of 1968, took almost two years to complete, and is the most difficult of the four books of *The Sea of Fertility.* In this respect it was unlike anything that Mishima, who favored lucidity and clarity of exposition, had ever written. It is Mishima's extensive treatment of religion that makes *The Temple of Dawn* difficult to read; he incorporated his study of Hinduism and Buddhism in the volume, however, for specific and good reasons. He was afraid that the Buddhist theme running through his long novel—the idea of reincarnation—would fail. Specifically, he thought that if the reader did not believe that he, Mishima, was serious about reincarnation, then he would regard the entire novel as a kind of fairy story. In *The Temple of Dawn* Mishima presents the idea of reincarnation as fundamental, as fact. At the outset Honda, who is now a successful lawyer of forty-seven—a man with a desperately nihilistic outlook but nonchalant outward appearance—pays a visit to Bangkok. The year is 1941 and he has been sent there by a big trading company to take care of a complicated lawsuit. Mishima describes the city of Bangkok, the history of the Thai royal family, and also the Hinayana Buddhism of the country. Honda's companion in the city is Hishikawa, a Japanese who serves as his interpreter—a strange-looking, perpetually exhausted man who has been furnished by the trading company. (In the course of a long monologue, Hishikawa compares art to a gigantic sunset. Art, he says, is like a sunset—in no way fundamental; rather, a purposeless though honest joke.) Honda has brought with him the diary of Kiyoaki, the dream diary, and he tries to see someone connected with the Thai princes, who had studied with him and Kiyoaki at the Gakushuin many years before.

Honda remembers how, before his death, in a dream, Isao had spoken of a place "far to the south. Very hot . . . in the rose sunshine of a southern land . . ." The lawyer steadfastly pursues the notion of the reincarnation of Kiyoaki into Isao and of Isao into a third person; Honda feels intuitively that he may be in this part of the world. With the help of Hishikawa, Honda obtains an audience with a mad, seven-year-old princess, the daughter of one of the two princes he had known at the Gakushuin, a little girl who lives in a Rose Palace. During the meeting the girl suddenly jumps up and flings herself at Honda, insisting that she is a Japanese who had died eight years before (Isao had killed himself in 1933). She answers Honda's questions about the dates of the deaths of Kiyoaki and Isao; and he concludes that in this little princess, Ying Chan ("Moonlight"), he has probably found the reincarnation of Isao—though he is unable to ascertain if Ying Chan has three moles. After a short while Honda is offered a trip to India by his trading-company client and he sets off for the subcontinent, planning to return to Bangkok. In Calcutta he witnesses the Durga Festival and watches the sacrifice of the goats. A headless kid kicks its back legs in the air as if it is having a nightmare; the youth who beheads the kids has a shirt spotted with blood, and Honda reflects that the sublime and the dirty go hand in hand in India (they are poles apart in Japan). Thereafter the lawyer travels to Benares, a city where "holiness and defilement reached an extreme." He walks down a tiny street, passing the booth of a clairvoyant, and goes out onto a stone-paved square facing the river. Lepers crouch there; they have come on pilgrimage from all over the country, to die on the banks of the Ganges. Flies cluster on the wounds of deformed creatures; they glow a golden green.

Honda takes a boat on the Ganges and sails toward the funeral ghats. He observes the burning of corpses. A blackened arm emerges from the fire; a corpse bends over backward, as if the man were turning his back in his sleep. The sound of boiling comes to Honda across the water. At the end, the skulls are left, and a man with a bamboo stick walks about the fire cracking the skulls. His muscles glow in the fire as he works, and the sound of cracking bone echoes off the walls of the temple close by. It is not a sad spectacle, at all. What appears to be heartlessness is joy. Karma is a plain and natural phenomenon like fruit on a tree or rice growing in a paddy. Honda believes that at Benares he has seen the ultimate truths of this world.

From Benares, Honda travels to Ajanta, where he views a beautiful waterfall, two streams cascading over a cliff face. One runs down between rocks, while the second falls like a silver rope; both are narrow, steep falls. Honda watches one of the falls, dropping down toward the Wagola River, slipping over a rock wall of yellow-green, giving an echo from the mountains all around. Behind the fall is a dark, empty, stone cave; otherwise, bright green surrounds it. Trees and vermilion flowers spread about the fall. The water gives off a glowing light in which floats a rainbow. As Honda watches the stream, he sees several yellow butterflies, precisely in a line between him and the fall. And looking farther up, he is astonished by the dazzling height from which the water tumbles. It is so high that a world of a different dimension seems to manifest itself above. The rock wall is green, with dark moss and ferns. At the top a light yellow is visible. The grass above is so bright in color, it seems to be not of this world. A single black kid is feeding on the grass there. High above float clouds and light at a dizzy height in the blue sky. As he watches, Honda remembers the words of Kiyoaki,

which remain like a single drop of water in his mind: "I'll
see you again. I know it. Beneath the falls." This must be
the fall of which Kiyoaki spoke, not the fall under which
Honda had once found Isao, after all.

Returning to Bangkok once again, Honda is forced to
mingle with Japanese businessmen, seekers after gold who
have nothing in common with the beautiful Kiyoaki and the
stern Isao (Mishima's descriptions of the Japanese business
community might be translated to the present day without a
line being changed). One day Honda comes across a little
book of poems written by an unsuccessful revolutionary in
Thailand in 1932. He takes comfort in the poetry, which
would, he believes, console the spirit of Isao: he gives the
book to Ying Chan, believing that Isao has been reborn in
the little girl. India, Honda has concluded, showed him that
his life's work must be the observation of karma. Since his
childhood, he has firmly believed that history cannot be al-
tered by human will, but he acknowledges that the core of
human will is precisely a ceaseless endeavor to influence
history. He pays a last visit to Ying Chan and has to tear
himself away: she clings to him, weeping desperately and
asking to be taken back to Japan, as she is really Japanese.
After his return home, war breaks out, and Honda spends
most of his spare time in the study of karma.

Here Mishima explains in great detail the various ancient theories of karma, of Greece, Rome, India, and Thailand. There is a long discourse on Mahayana Buddhism: at
the core of karma is arayashiki, the raison d'être of existence
itself; everything in this world is to be attributed to arayashiki, and this is mysteriously connected with reincarnation.
The first part of *The Temple of Dawn* concludes with a description of an air raid in Tokyo during the war.

In the second half of the book the mood changes. There
is a sense of collapse and of failure; this is seen in Honda,
who has undergone a decline. It is 1952 and Honda, fifty-
eight years old, has built a country villa for himself at Gotemba; he is rich and visits the place on weekends. Between
the study and a guest bedroom next door Honda has had a

secret peephole constructed, so that he can peer into the bedroom at his leisure. Honda has turned into a Peeping Tom; he is no longer the observer of karma. In the house next door lives an aging lesbian, Keiko Hisamatsu, a former countess who has become the mistress of a U.S. Army colonel. Ying Chan, who is eighteen, is studying in Japan. One evening Honda invites her to a party at his house; Keiko is invited as well. Honda conceives a desire to see Ying Chan naked; he arranges for a playboy nephew of Keiko to seduce Ying Chan in the bedroom next to Honda's study. Watching through the peephole, Honda observes Ying Chan's body. Suddenly the girl leaps up and pushes the young Japanese aside. She flees from the room and takes refuge in Keiko's house next door, declining to see Honda, whom she has identified as the author of the unsuccessful plan to seduce her. Honda is desperate to confirm that Ying Chan has the three moles on her body and decides to build a swimming pool at his home and give a swimming party. But at the party Honda is unable to see whether Ying Chan really has the moles. He puts her and Keiko in the guest room that evening and takes up watch at his spy hole; through the hole he sees the two women embracing and making love.

"At that moment Ying Chan, perhaps jealous that Keiko's thigh had freedom of movement, raised her left arm high and grasped it as though to claim it as her own. She placed it firmly over her head as if she could do without breathing. The imposing white thigh completely covered her face. "Ying Chan's whole side was exposed. To the left of her bare breast, an area her arm had previously concealed, three extremely small moles appeared distinctly, like the Pleiades in the dusky sky of her brown skin that resembled the dying evening glow."

That night a fire breaks out in Honda's home and the house is burned to the ground. *The Temple of Dawn* ends with a short meeting between Honda and the twin sister of Ying Chan in 1967, almost fifteen years after the fire at Honda's home. From the sister Honda learns that Ying Chan died at twenty in Thailand, from the bite of a cobra. (Isao had had a dream of being bitten to death by a "green snake," much, we assume, as Ying Chan was killed.)

A judgment of *The Temple of Dawn* must rest on the passages in the first part of the book in which Mishima describes Honda's study of karma and reincarnation. This, however, is a telling criticism of the book. For the great majority of Japanese and Western readers, certainly, the religious passages are hard going. (Finding a translator for the book proved a headache to the U.S. publisher, largely on account of the section on Buddhism.) By and large, Mishima must be deemed to have failed in his effort to convince the reader that he takes reincarnation seriously.

The letdown at the end of *The Temple of Dawn*, however, is a prelude of what is to come in *The Decay of the Angel,* the fourth and final volume of *The Sea of Fertility*—a much more striking book, which Mishima wrote in its entirety after his decision to kill himself and which was published after his death.

3
The River of Theater

Once the theater was like a jolly party I enjoyed attending after a hard day's work. There I could find another world—a world of glittering lights and colors, where the characters of my own creation, clad in alluring costumes, stood in front of a handsome set, laughed, screamed, wept, and danced. And to think that I, as a playwright, governed and manipulated all these theatrical worlds from behind the scenes!

Yet such delights gradually turned bitter. The magic of the theater—to give people the illusion of life's noblest moments and the apparition of beauty on earth—began to corrupt my heart. Or was it that I grudged being an alienated playwright? Theater, where a false blood runs in the floodlights, can perhaps move and enrich people with much more forceful and profound experiences than anything in real life. As in music and architecture, I find the beauty of the theater in its abstract and theoretical structure, and this particular beauty never ceases to be the very image of what I have always held in the depth of my heart as Ideal in Art.

Yukio Mishima, Catalogue to the Tobu Exhibition

The modern theater had a slow start in Japan. Whereas Japanese writers were attracted to the Western novel in the decades that followed the Meiji Restoration of 1868, and the first "modern" novels were written in Japan in the late nineteenth century, Western-style theater did not become established until after the Pacific War. Valiant attempts were made by small groups of actors and actresses to create a modern theater long before the war; the beginning of Shingeki is customarily traced to 1906, when a society for the promotion of the arts, the Bungei Kyokai, which specialized in drama, was founded. But the theater suffered cruelly from official censorship and, after a brief flowering in the 1920's, succumbed to government control. There were always small, politically radical groups ready to brave the authorities' disapproval—but scarcely any permanent achievements were made before the onset of the Pacific War. (An exception is the establishment of the Bungakuza— Literary Theater—in 1938. It survived the war, taking as its slogan "Art for art's sake.") In addition to all this, modern theater had strong competition from both the traditional Japanese theater, the Kabuki, a form established in the seventeenth and eighteenth centuries, and the successful lowbrow theater known as Shinpa, which had none of the intellectual appeal of Shingeki and drew large audiences, catering to a popular taste for Western-style, sentimental drama.

After the war, Shingeki benefited from a relaxation of censorship. The radical character of modern theater in Japan was apparent in the choice of plays made by the leading theatrical groups: works by Ibsen, Gogol, Tolstoy, Chekhov, and a number of Japanese writers who drew on the Russian tradition. The prestige of Western writers was great. Among the most popular Shingeki productions in the 1950's were

Tennessee Williams's *A Streetcar Named Desire* and John Osborne's *Look Back in Anger*. The Western classical reper- toire was also drawn upon; in 1955 the Bungakuza played *Hamlet* with great success. For the first time, good transla- tions of the plays of Shakespeare were available and Shake- speare was for a time the height of fashion; veteran Kabuki actors vied for the honor of playing Hamlet. Few Japanese writers of the older generation rose to the challenge of the Shingeki in the late 1940's. It was left to the young men— among them Yukio Mishima and Kobo Abé—to respond. Abé did so in a manner consonant with the tradition of Shingeki, in which radical, proletarian protest had played so large a part before the war. In one of his early plays, *Dorei Gari* ("Slave Hunt," 1952), he satirized the business world in Japan—describing a particularly bizarre form of postwar commerce (a trade in the remains of the war dead). Mishima, by contrast, showed no taste for ideology; his forte was style. These two young playwrights, the most successful newcomers to Shingeki after the war, were far apart in politics, which was equally apparent in their novels and in the translations of their works (Abé was taken up by the Soviet literary world; Mishima was translated exclu- sively in the West). Mishima showed a taste for the West- ern classical tradition—he was to write plays modeled on works by Racine and Euripides; Abé had a taste for Brecht.

Mishima's first work for the Shingeki was the one-act play *Kataku* ("Fire House," 1949). This was performed by the Haiyuza, one of the two leading Shingeki groups, and he was gratified to hear well-known actors and actresses speak- ing his lines. His first major success came the following year, in a genre which he made his own, the modern No play. Since its establishment in the fifteenth century as the theatrical form of the feudal aristocracy and the Imperial Court, No has attracted many writers, even in modern times. According to Keene's preface to *Five Modern Nō Plays*, published by Alfred A. Knopf: "Some have fashioned pastiches on the traditional themes, others have tried to fit modern conceptions into the old forms. The hysteria of wartime propaganda even led to the composition of a *Nō* play about life on a submarine. Some modern works have enjoyed temporary popularity, but they were essentially curiosities, having neither the beauty of language and mood of the old plays, nor the complexity of character delineation we expect of a modern work. The first genuinely successful modern *Nō* plays have been those by Yukio Mishima." As an example of Mishima's success, Keene takes *Kantan*, the first of his modern No plays, written in 1950; he compares the classical original with Mishima's work. In the classical No, "a traveler naps on a magic pillow, and during the brief time that it takes his hostess at the inn to cook a bowl of gruel, he dreams of a glorious life as Emperor of China. He awakens to the realization that life is but a dream. In Mishima's play, instead of a traveler, we have a spoiled young man of today who sleeps on the magic pillow while his old nurse prepares the breakfast. His dreams are not of ancient China but of riches and power as a financial tycoon and a dictator."

Mishima wrote many modern No plays. The second book of his to be translated was a collection of these plays, which had a great success overseas. They were performed in many European countries and in Australia and Mexico as well as in North America, eventually being staged Off-Broadway late in 1960; that production ran for two months and had good notices. It was partly through these short plays—all are one-act dramas—that Mishima first acquired a measure of fame in the West; the dialogue is taut and the playwright retains sufficient of the ghostly quality of the classical No to give his works a unique character. Their appeal was considerable in Japan itself. The plays were produced by Shingeki companies and also appeared on the classical No stage. One play, *The Lady Aoi*, was sung as a Western-style opera. Translations of the classical No plays were long ago done by Arthur Waley, but they can scarcely be performed without the settings of the genuine No—the uniquely shaped stage, the gorgeous costumes and masks, and the musicians and chorus—often compared to classical Greek drama. Mishima's modern No plays gave the West a

taste for No some time before it was possible for No companies to travel to foreign cities to perform the superb reper-
toire of the classical Japanese theater.

Some insight into Mishima's character is afforded by his
attitude toward the classical No. While he was in Tokyo he
would go "once a month without fail" to see a No play. But
his attitude toward the No was peculiar; I do not believe
that he really enjoyed No performances—during which he
often fell asleep. A month before his suicide, he sent me a
copy of an article on the No published in *This Is Japan* for
1971: "There [at the No] one may see in its original form a
classical stage art that dates back to the fifteenth century, an
art that, complete and perfect in itself, admits of no med-
dling by contemporary man . . . The No theater is a temple
of beauty, the place above all wherein is realized the supreme union of religious solemnity and sensuous beauty. In
no other theatrical tradition has such an exquisite refine-
ment been achieved . . . True beauty is something that attacks, overpowers, robs, and finally destroys. It was because
he knew this violent quality of beauty that Thomas Mann
wrote *Death in Venice* . . . The No cannot begin until after
the drama is ended and beauty lies in ruins. One might
liken this . . . 'necrophilous' aesthetic of the No to that of
works by Edgar Allan Poe, such as *Ligeia* or *Berenice* . . .
In No lies the only type of beauty that has the power to
wrest 'my' time away from the 'exterior' Japan of today . . .
and to impose on it another regime . . . And beneath its
mask that beauty must conceal death, for some day, just as
surely, it will finally lead me away to destruction and to
silence."

Mishima also wrote plays for the Kabuki theater in the
early 1950's—before he had established himself as a
Shingeki playwright. He had a unique advantage over his contemporaries: he alone had mastered classical Japanese and
knew sufficient of the difficult language used in Kabuki to
write plays in this genre. A photograph taken in 1953 shows
him seated with Mantaro Kubota, a grand old man of the
Japanese theater with a special affection for Kabuki. Mi-

shima is going over a draft of a play, perspicaciously racing through the script. Kubota looks over one shoulder with a perplexed expression of admiration on his face, while an acolyte of the old man regards the youthful prodigy between them from the other side. Mishima loved the Kabuki; the baroque bloodletting and fierce swordplay appealed to his instincts. So, too, did the theme of many a Kabuki play—that true love may end in a shinju, or double suicide. His attitude toward the No was reverent and a little constricted, even ridiculous; his admiration for Kabuki was unrestrained. Many of the great actors of the day were his friends and he spent long hours backstage conversing with them (his friendship with Utaemon has already been described). Mishima's Kabuki plays are of no great importance; during his life, however, they attracted much attention. In some ways the most successful was his last work for the theater, *Chinsetsu Yumiharizuki* (whose title is untranslatable). He wrote it in 1969 and himself produced it at the National Theater. Mishima was a good mimic and an able Kabuki actor. After this production, he made a record of the play in which he took all forty parts.

Mishima defined his approach to Shingeki, for which he wrote most of his forty plays, in his essay "The Play and I" (1951): "The modern play is far, far removed from the chaotic world of the novel, as I see it. It must look like a paper cathedral floating in the sky. No matter how naturalistic a play may be, the theme which makes for dramatic tension is such that it never suits the novel form. Strong emotion bears down upon the details and marches forward, treading the details underfoot."

His first successful long play was *Shiro Ari no Su* ("The Nest of the White Ant," 1955), set on a Brazilian coffee plantation where an aristocratic Japanese couple have taken refuge with two servants—a chauffeur and his wife—after the war. The structure of the play, a tale of adultery and suicide attempts, is excellent, and *Shiro Ari no Su*—the hollow nest of a white-ant colony is the symbol of the empty

lives of the Japanese émigrés—established Mishima's reputation as a Shingeki dramatist. Not long after completing this
work, for which he won a dramatic award, Mishima declared: "My ideal life would be to write one long novel a
year and no short stories at all. Or, if I have to, then nothing
longer than twenty pages. Otherwise, I would devote my
time to plays." And on the relationship between his novels
and his plays he commented: "Plays awaken a different part
of my desire, that part which is unsatisfied by writing novels. Now, when I write a novel, I want to write a play next.
Plays occupy one of the two magnetic poles of my work."

Mishima never achieved his ideal. He continued to
write two or three novels a year, and some of his most striking works—for example, "Patriotism," the tale of hara-kiri—
were to be longish short stories. For the remainder of his
life, however, with the exception of the last year, he alter-
nated continually between writing plays and novels. In
1956, for instance, he wrote *The Temple of the Golden Pavilion* in the early part of the year and followed it with a
play, which he completed in time for the autumn season—
Rokumeikan. This drama, the most frequently performed
of Mishima's plays, is not an interesting play, in my opinion.

Toka no Kiku ("Tenth-Day Chrysanthemums," 1961)
was the great triumph of Mishima's career as a dramatist.
September 9 is a day of festival in Japan, on which exhibitions of chrysanthemums are staged. Tenth-day flowers
would be too late for the show—they would be wasted.
The chrysanthemum is a symbol of loyalty in Japan (the
Imperial crest is composed of a thirty-two-petaled chrysanthemum). Thus, Mishima's play has as its theme wasted loyalty.

The principal character is a politician, a former Finance
Minister named Mori, who had once, before the war, in the
1930's, been the target of an assassination attempt by right-
wing terrorists. Mori's attitude toward the incident is
brought out during a visit paid him by Kiku, the faithful

maidservant who saved his life sixteen years before, who has not seen him since the assassination attempt (described in the play as if it were a minor detail in one of the numerous unsuccessful coups d'état of the 1930's). The old man states that the most honorable day of his life—which he prizes more highly than the day on which he was appointed Finance Minister, his highest office—was the day on which patriotic youths tried to kill him. The most fortunate accident that can befall a statesman, Mori implies, is to be struck down by the hand of an assassin. Death in the service of the nation and the Emperor is to be preferred to life, if that life has no meaning. Mori spends his days pursuing a lonely hobby, the growing of cacti; his activities as a cactus fancier are much dwelt upon in Mishima's play. The old man is depicted as one who, like the cactus, has no blood; his existence is without meaning, The political background to the play is the murderous struggle which took place in the 1930's between those whose prime objective was order—politicians, men of business, and civil servants—and those who put a premium on honor. Mori has belatedly realized that he belongs, at heart, to the latter camp. In Mishima's play, Kiku gives Mori short shrift at their meeting. *Toka no Kiku* may be read as an assault upon sentimental conservatism; the dramatic action favors such an interpretation. The playwright himself, however, had a streak of sympathy for Mori's attitudes; the play was based on the Ni Ni Roku Incident of February 26, 1936, carried out by rebel army officers with whom Mishima later claimed he had much in common.

Not that *Toka no Kiku* is a political play. The dramatic interest lies in the relationship between Kiku and her former master and employer, Mori. The part of Kiku was taken by Haruko Sugimura in the production given by the Bungakuza in November 1961, on the occasion of the twenty-fifth anniversary of the foundation of the theatrical group, and this was one of the most distinguished performances by an actress generally regarded as the finest of Shingeki players. How far the Bungakuza, whose dominant personality was Miss Sugimura, was from regarding *Toka no Kiku* as an ideological drama was made apparent two years later when the group rejected a fairly mild play of Mishima's on ideological grounds, precipitating a furious quarrel between the Bungakuza and Mishima that ended in his resignation from the group with which he had worked, almost exclusively, for nearly a decade. Had *Toka no Kiku* been sympathetic to the right in the eyes of the Bungakuza, it would scarcely have been selected by them for performance at an anniversary.

The play which caused a rupture between Mishima and the Bungakuza was *Yorokobi no Koto* ("The Harp of Joy," 1963), and it is not one of Mishima's important works. It is set in postwar Japan and is based on the Matsukawa Incident—the derailment of a train in 1949 by saboteurs whose identity was never established, although the authorities believed for a time that they were from the left. The principal character is a senior police officer, Matsumura, a veteran who is popular with his subordinates, one of whom, Katagiri, he instructs to investigate the derailment of a train (the Matsukawa Incident is not identified as such in the play). The zealous Katagiri arrests several men and is astonished by their immediate release, when it has been ascertained that they are rightists. There are frequent left-wing demonstrations in the streets, the object of which is to show popular discontent with a government which is trying to pin the blame for the train derailment on the left, without any proof. A strange incident then occurs at the police station where Katagiri and his men work. A young policeman says he has heard the sound of a koto (a classical musical instrument) while on duty. The others laugh at him—how, in the midst of noisy demonstrations, could he have heard such a thing? Shortly afterward the investigation of the sabotage takes a totally unexpected turn. Matsumura, the man who is carrying out the police inquiry, is himself accused of having organized the sabotage; the police chief is said to have been an undercover Communist agent. The faithful Katagiri is shattered by this. Later the charges against Matsumura are shown to have been fabricated by the right; nonetheless, the younger man loses his faith in his superior. One day, when Katagiri is on duty in the streets, with demonstrators surging about him, he hears the beautiful sound of a koto. A man who had placed his faith in absolute authority, in the immutable system of the law, seeks refuge in fantasy after the collapse of his belief in order.

The turning point in the play comes when Katagiri realizes that Matsumura, his revered leader, has exploited him for his own ends—though these are not political. The Bungakuza, after starting rehearsals of *Yorokobi no Koto* in mid-November 1963, and following the return of Haruko Sugimura from travels in China, suddenly suspended rehearsal and informed Mishima that the production was off. Some of the actors, it was explained to Mishima by a succession of delegations which visited him at his home to give reasons for the suspension of rehearsals, objected to the right-wing lines spoken by the policemen in the play. Mishima was incensed. His angry rebuttal of the Bungakuza was printed as an open letter to the group; it appeared in the *Asahi Shimbun* a few days later, following his resignation from the Bungakuza. It read in part: "Certainly *Yorokobi no Koto* is quite different from my other works and includes an element of danger. But what have you been thinking about me all this while that you should be astonished by a work such as this? Have you been making a fool of me, saying that Mishima is a playwright . . . who writes harmless dramas which gather large audiences? You set up such safe criteria as 'Art' and conceal within yourselves a vague political inclination [to the left], dropping the phrase 'art for art's sake' from time to time . . . Isn't this just hypocrisy and commercialism? I would like you to understand this: there is always a needle in art; there is also poison; you can't suck honey without the poison too." The break was complete. Shortly afterward, Mishima joined another theatrical group, the NLT (New Literature Theater). It was a sad moment. Mishima never again found a group as effective to work with as the Bungakuza and the Bungakuza lost their best playwright.

The quarrel is a puzzling one. Within three years Mishima was to profess political beliefs which would have fully justified the Bungakuza in breaking with him. He was to assert that *Toka no Kiku* was in fact a play about the Ni Ni Roku Incident. He was also to state that he shared the patriotic attitude of the fanatically imperialist young officers who staged the Ni Ni Roku Incident. But his imperialism did not surface clearly in his writing until the summer of 1966, when he wrote *Eirei no Koe* ("The Voices of the Heroic Dead"). Nevertheless, there was a surprising violence to the quarrel. Mishima had very few squabbles with people or with organizations during his life. There were disagreements, but Mishima avoided public hostility on almost all occasions. Like many Japanese—and however un-Japanese he may have been in many respects—he abhorred public fracas.

Madame de Sade, the next play, again showed Mishima to be far more interested in problems of structure than in political matters. He wrote it after becoming intrigued with the problem of why the Marquise de Sade, who was absolutely faithful to her husband during his many years in prison, left him the moment he was free. The play was an attempt to provide a solution to the problem; it was "Sade seen through women's eyes." All six characters are women and the action is controlled exclusively through dialogue. Mishima intended that visual appeal would be provided by the rococo costumes of the women; the five characters must form a precise, mathematical system around Madame de Sade. Keene has described the debt owed by Mishima to Racine: "Mishima's classicism . . . is given its most extreme expression in the play *Madame de Sade* . . . Here he adopted most of the conventions of the Racinian stage—a single setting, a reliance on the *tirade* for the relation of events and emotions, a limited number of characters each of whom represents a specific kind of woman, and an absence of overt action on the stage."

Madame de Sade was a considerable success in Tokyo, although the subject matter was a little too recherché. After its translation into English, Mishima hoped that it would be produced on Broadway and pressed his agent in New York, Audrey Wood, to find a theater for it. *Madame de Sade*, however, proved to have no appeal to American actresses; the absence of overt action on the stage was the major problem. Quite possibly, none of Mishima's long plays will ever be performed on the Western stage. Certainly, it is unlikely that Mishima's subsequent major plays, *Suzaku Ke no Metsubo* ("The Fall of the House of Suzaku," 1967)—a play based on Euripides—and *Wagatomo Hitler* ("My Friend Hitler," 1969), would have great appeal to Western audiences. The latter is set in Germany in 1934; in it Mishima describes the events before and after the Night of the Long Knives. It makes the point that Hitler steered a "neutral" course between the Brownshirts and the conservative forces—the regular army and big business—on that occasion. Mishima neither praises nor criticizes Hitler; nor does he develop the character of the dictator in the play. Mishima treats the Night of the Long Knives as an incident in a struggle for power, a technical operation. The title of the play refers to Roehm, the head of the Brownshirts, one of Hitler's victims on the Night. In the play Roehm believes the Führer is "my friend"—until it is too late. At the première, held in Tokyo on January 19, 1969, Mishima distributed a note to the audience: "The dangerous ideologue, Mishima, dedicates an evil ode to the dangerous hero, Hitler." His intention was to mock the critics and the vaguely leftist neutralism of Japanese intellectuals. Neutralism, the play said, can lead anywhere.

Mishima's last play for the modern theater was *Raio no Terrasu* ("The Terrace of the Leper King," 1969). He invited me to the première and I remember how he looked that evening—he was wearing all-white evening attire and was accompanied by Yoko. Tennessee Williams was supposed to put in an appearance and there was an empty seat next to Mishima where he should have been. The performance itself went well enough. *Raio no Terrasu* is an untranslated play about the Khmer king Jayavarman III, the builder of the temple of Bayon at Angkor Wat. The monarch suffered from leprosy; Bayon is his monument. Mishima used the tale to make the point that the material triumphs over the immaterial, the Body over the Spirit—Bayon alone remains. He was especially proud of the last scene, an exchange on the steps of the newly constructed Bayon between the Body—the youthful image of the king—and the Spirit, represented by the voice of the dying, leprous king (a sepulchral, tape-recorded voice in the Teigeki production we saw).

BODY: King, dying king. Can you see me?

SPIRIT: Who is calling me? I remember the voice. That brilliant voice.

B: It's me. Do you see?

S: No. Of course not. I'm blind.

B: Why should the Spirit need eyes? It has been your source of pride that you see things without using your eyes!

S: Such harsh words. Who are you?

B: I'm the king.

S: Absurd! That's me.

B: We share the same name. King, I am your Body.

S: Who am I then?

B: You are my Spirit. The Spirit that resolved to build this Bayon. What is dying is not the Body of the king.

S: My Body was rotten and has vanished. You cannot be my Body, speaking so proudly and boldly.

The actor who played the part of the Body was heavily suntanned and wore a short tunic with straps across his bare chest. As he spoke his lines, he strode about the terrace of the temple, flourishing his arms. Behind him was a giant face made of foot-high blocks of stone, one of many such faces at the temple of Bayon. The actor, Kinya Kiyaoji, was slightly overweight; his voice boomed out cheerfully, while the groaning Spirit endeavored to reply:

B: It's not true. Your Body was never rotten. Your Body is here, shining with youth, full of vigor, like an immortal golden statue. The cursed illness is an illusion of the Spirit. How could such a triumphant king as I be affected by illness?

S: But what could the Body achieve? What imperishable things can he construct? It is not stones that planned and constructed this imperishable Bayon. Stones are nothing but materials. It's the Spirit that made this.

B (*laughing aloud with pride*): The Spirit cannot see Bayon any more, because even the Spirit depended on the Body.

S: No. I don't need to see it. The finished Bayon shines in my spirit.

B: Shining? It's only a small streak of light, which is about to be put out. Think, if it is enough to be shining in the Spirit, why was it necessary to construct Bayon with such an enormous quantity of stones?

S: The Spirit always longs for a shape.

B: That's because you are shapeless. Shape always takes its model from a beautiful body like me. Did you use as a model of this temple the rotten body of a leper?

S: Rubbish! The body of a leper is nothing.

B: Nothing? You suffered for so long.

S: No, nothing. The Spirit is everything.

B: What are they, the rotten, the shapeless, and the blind? They are the shape the Spirit takes. It's not you that suffered from leprosy. Your very existence is leprous. You are a born leper.

S: Sharpness, clarity, and the power to see through to the bottom of this world constructed Bayon. The Body cannot have such power. You are only a slave captured by the Body.

B: You say that you are more free than me? Are you? More free because you cannot run, cannot jump, sing, laugh, or fight?

s: I run through one hundred years. You run only in space.

B: There is light in space. Flowers bloom, bees hum. A beautiful summer afternoon stretches ahead. But what you call time is a damp and dark underground tunnel.

s: Oh, Bayon, my love.

B: Why do you leave it here? Bayon is the present. The forever-shining present. Love? Were you ever so beautiful as to be loved?

s: I'm dying. Each breath is agony. Oh, my Bayon.

B: Die! Perish! . . . You planned and constructed. That was your illness. My breast, like a bow, shines in the sun. Water flows, sparkles, and is still. You didn't follow me. That was your illness.

s: My Bayon . . .

B: The Spirit perishes, as a kingdom perishes.

s: It's the Body that perishes. The Spirit is imperishable.

B: You are dying . . .

s: Bayon . . .

B: You're dying.

s: . . .

B: What has happened?

s: . . .

B: No answer. Are you dead?

s: . . .

B: You are dead.

(*The sound of bird song*)

Look. The Spirit has died. A bright blue sky! Beautiful birds, trees, and Bayon protected by all these! I will reign over this country again. Youth is immortal. The Body is imperishable. I won. It is I that am Bayon.

Early in 1970, Mishima surprised his friends by announcing that he would write no more plays. The drama had been such an important part of his life for so many years that his decision was incomprehensible: some put it down as a foible; others believed that he was tired by his struggle with *The Sea of Fertility* and had decided to concentrate all his strength on that single novel.

Not long before he killed himself, Mishima arranged a shelf of objects in his upstairs sitting room at home in Magome. These were a Greek vase, a small bronze nude of himself, a collection of translations of his books, and a stage model for the last scene of *Raio no Terrasu*. One evening he showed this display to some friends. "How do you like it?" he asked them in an ironic tone. "This really sums up my life, don't you think?" And he burst into laughter.

4
The River of Body

This is a young River that suddenly began flowing at the midpoint of my life. I had been dissatisfied for quite some time by the fact that my invisible spirit alone could create tangible visions of beauty. Why could not I myself be something visibly beautiful and worthy of being looked at? For this purpose I had to make my body beautiful.

When at last I came to own such a body, I wanted to display it to everyone, to show it off and to let it move in front of every eye, just like a child with a new toy. My body became for me like a fashionable sports car for its proud owner. In it I drove on many highways to new places. Views I had never seen before opened up for me and enriched my experience.

But the body is doomed to decay, just like the complicated motor of a car. I for one do not, will not, accept such a doom. This means that I do not accept the course of Nature. I know I am going against Nature; I know I have forced my body onto the most destructive path of all.

Yukio Mishima, Catalogue to the Tobu Exhibition

Mishima was physically a small man. He was 5' 4½", somewhat below the average for Japanese men of his generation, though the Japanese as a race are physically smaller than other Asian peoples. He was slim. Even after he had taken up body building—at the age of thirty—he did not spread out very much. In a suit, he looked a man of average build for one of his height. His shoulders did not seem large, nor did his chest bulge out. He held himself straight, in the manner of a professional soldier. He had, however, a fine, well-proportioned, strong body. Shoulders, arms, and legs were heavily muscled, and the muscles lay well on his small-boned frame. His waist was slim, the stomach perfectly flat and strong, and his chest—showing the signs of training with weights—was well developed and powerful. Unusual for a Japanese, he had a lot of black hair on his body, mainly on his chest—for which he was teased by other Japanese. His body had one defect: the legs were much too short in relation to the trunk—a not uncommon feature among Japanese men and women. This was one subject on which Mishima, who often mocked himself, was never known to make jokes. He considered himself to be beautiful, and when he stated, in an introduction written for a book containing pictures of young Japanese body builders— *Young Samurai*—that he was the ugly duckling among them (he also appeared in the volume), he was in fact trying to say the opposite, that he was the finest-looking of them all. Actually, he was right. Professional body builders, with their masses of bulbous muscles, are not beautiful. By comparison, the amateur Mishima was sleek and trim.

In his book *Sun and Steel*, Mishima gave the genesis of his decision to take up physical training. He warned his readers that his explanation would be hard to follow. "Thanks to the sun and the steel, I was to learn the language of the flesh, much as one might learn a foreign language. It was my second language, an aspect of my spiritual development. My purpose now is to talk of that development. As a personal history, it will, I suspect, be unlike anything seen before, and as such exceedingly difficult to follow."

In essence, what Mishima had to say was this: early in his life he felt a loathing for his body; he put all his emphasis on words, on the pursuit of literature; words tended to corrode his being—as if white ants were eating into his person—and he sought a second language, "the language of the flesh." It was the sun that opened his eyes to this possibility. During the war he had "longed for Novalis's night and Yeatsian Irish twilights" and rejected a sun which he associated with destruction: "It was the way it gleamed so encouragingly on the wings of planes leaving on missions, on forests of bayonets, on the badges of military caps, on the embroidery of military banners; but still more, far more, it was the way it glistened on the blood flowing ceaselessly from the flesh, and on the silver bodies of flies clustering on wounds. Holding sway over corruption, leading youth in droves to its death in tropical seas and countrysides, the sun lorded it over that vast rusty-red ruin that stretched away to the distant horizon." Not long after the war, he had learned to see the sun differently: "It was in 1952, on the deck of the ship on which I made my first journey abroad, that I exchanged a reconciliatory handshake with the sun. From that day on, I have found myself unable to part company with it. The sun became associated with the main highway of my life. And little by little, it tanned my skin brown, branding me as a member of the other race."

Mishima's discovery of the sun led to his decision to take up body building three years later: "The sun was enticing, almost dragging, my thoughts away from their night of visceral sensations, away to the swelling of muscles encased in sunlit skin. And it was commanding me to construct a new and sturdy dwelling in which my mind, as it rose little by little to the surface, could live in security. That dwelling was a tanned, lustrous skin and powerful, sensitively rippling muscles . . . It was thus that I found myself confronted with those lumps of steel: heavy, forbidding, cold as though the essence of night had in them been still further condensed."

Mishima started intensive physical training in 1955—according to an article he wrote for *Sports Illustrated* (December 1970). During a trip to America he had heard about body building and one day in the summer of 1955 he came across a picture in a Waseda University magazine which carried the caption: YOU TOO CAN HAVE A BODY LIKE THIS. He got in touch with Hitoshi Tamari, the coach at Waseda, and when they met, in a hotel lobby in downtown Tokyo, the coach was "able to astound me by the feat of so rippling his chest muscles that their activity was apparent even beneath his shirt." When Tamari insisted that "you yourself will be able to do the same thing someday," Mishima put himself under the guidance of the coach. Tamari came to his house three times a week and Mishima bought some barbells and an exercise bench and thus began "to provide cartoonists with material for years to come." The start was painful. His tonsils became chronically swollen and he worried that he had ruined his body. He had X-rays taken, and there was nothing wrong with him; he had to persist. Day by day he grew in strength, and the realization that his muscles were increasing in size strengthened his resolve to carry on. After a year he realized one day that the stomach pains which had bothered him for many years had ceased. At the end of the first year Mishima found a second coach, Tomo Suzuki; and he made Suzuki's slogan of "exercises for everyday life" his own. Suzuki was a colorful character, and amused Mishima greatly. "See, Mr. Mishima," he said one day, pointing to an exemplary trainer under his command, "in a sound body you'll find a sound spirit. Look at the perfect suppleness of his body, the dexterity of his movements. There's a real human person for you." Somewhat later the model youth absconded with Suzuki's earnings from the gym. "Even now," Mishima wrote, "I have to smile every time I recall Suzuki's sour expression when I joked with him afterward about a sound body ensuring a sound mind."

In addition to training at the gym, Mishima engaged in a number of other physical activities. In the summer of 1956 he joined a team of local youths in the district of Jiyugaoka, the outlying part of Tokyo where the Hiraoka family lived. The function of these young men was to carry about the heavy omikoshi, the portable shrine, on the occasion of the summer festival. Escorted by a Shinto priest and attended by crowds of children with their own little omikoshi, the procession went up and down the narrow streets of Jiyugaoka, with Mishima jostling and struggling amid the youths who carried the shrine. For the occasion he wore a hachimaki around his head and a light tunic; a photograph shows Mishima with an expression of childlike glee on his face. The ambition to carry an omikoshi on a summer's day had been with him since childhood when he had first seen such a spectacle and had been fascinated by the raw, sweaty men who had stampeded in and out of Natsuko's front garden in the house at Yotsuya where Mishima was born (the scene described at length in *Confessions of a Mask*): "Now the shrine itself came into view, and there was a venomous state of dead calm, like the air of the tropics, which clung solely about the shrine. It seemed a malevolent sluggishness, trembling hotly above the naked shoulders of the young men carrying the *omikoshi*. And within the thick scarlet-and-white ropes, within the guardrails of black lacquer and gold, behind those fast-shut doors of gold leaf, there was a four-foot cube of pitch-blackness." Mishima's exploit at the summer festival was reported in the gossip magazines in Tokyo. It was the start of a stream of publicity given to his non-literary exploits, a stream which became a torrent in later years.

Mishima also began to make stage appearances. He appeared briefly as a gardener in a production of *Rokumeikan;* and in a production of Racine's *Brittanicus*, the translation of which he had supervised, Mishima played another small part—that of a soldier carrying a spear. A photograph was taken of him in the second role, standing together with two fellow soldiers on stage. Mishima is in front of the other two and has a set expression on his face. Behind him are two taller men, professional actors with a softness about the jowls. The picture is intriguing. It is among the first of many group photos of Mishima in which he appears to be the same stature as tall men with him. In fact, he would arrange that the photographer shoot from a low angle—or use some other device to give the impression that Mishima was the same height as his companions. One of the best ways he devised for the purpose was to wear an extraordinarily tall pair of geta, wooden shoes. Geta, which are wooden platforms on two parallel, rectangular sections of wood—one under the heel, the other under the ball of the foot—can easily be made taller. On one occasion Mishima appeared in a duel scene with Shintaro Ishihara—a tall, graceful figure—treading on geta five inches high, and waving his sword vigorously.

Mishima's great ambition was to become an athlete, and in the autumn of 1956 he took up boxing at a gym run by Nippon University. There he had a third coach, an austere trainer named Tomo Kojima. Mishima loved the gym itself: "We were housed in an old and dirty building. The odor of the lavatory encroached upon the shower room. Trunks and sweat shirts were draped over the ring ropes. Torn punching bags hung from the ceiling. Of such stuff, I reflected, were sports epics made. All these props symbolized a kind of barbaric elegance I had not previously experienced." But boxing was too hard for him. During a sparring session a novelist friend, Shintaro Ishihara, appeared with an 8-mm. movie camera and recorded Mishima's performance on film. "Sometime later, when the literary crowd gathered at my house, he showed his film to a mambo accompaniment (the mambo was in fashion at the time), to the hilarity of all. And, indeed, my on-screen figure making its desperate evasive actions to the Latin rhythm seemed like something out of a cartoon." In the end he gave up boxing.

Mishima was witty enough about his misfortunes in the boxing ring—this willingness to make himself a butt of humor was an attractive feature of the man. I used to think, when I met him years after these experiences, that this ironical Mishima was real. I believed that his physical training was an aspect of his physical exuberance and that he did not take this part of his life seriously. His narcissism sometimes got out of hand; I put this down as a quirk of character. Many others must have had a similar attitude. He was obviously a little ill; he suffered from romanticism. It was hard to believe, however, that so intelligent a man could regard himself—his body—as a temple of beauty for more than a few seconds a day.

Had one read his books more carefully, had one believed that he meant what he wrote, the mistake would have been avoided. In *Sun and Steel* he described his attitude toward body building quite clearly. With reference to his reasons for pressing on with bodei-biru, he remarked, first, that it was part of an educational process. *Mens sana in corpore sano*, was his argument; and he expounded the merits of classical education like an earnest English public-school boy. Second, he said he needed a "classical" body to achieve his aim in life, which he described thus in *Sun and Steel:* "Beyond the educative process there also lurked another, romantic design. The romantic impulse that had formed an undercurrent in me from boyhood on, and that made sense only as the *destruction* of classical perfection, lay waiting within me. Like a theme in an operatic overture that is later destined to occur throughout the whole work, it laid down a definitive pattern for me before I had achieved anything in practice. Specifically, I cherished a romantic impulse toward death, yet at the same time I required a strictly classical body as its vehicle; a peculiar sense of destiny made me believe that the reason why my romantic impulse toward death remained unfulfilled in reality was the immensely simple fact that I lacked the necessary physical qualifications. A powerful, tragic frame and sculpturesque muscles were indispensable, in a romantically noble death. Any confrontation between weak, flabby flesh and death seemed to me absurdly inappropriate. Longing at eighteen for an early demise, I felt myself unfitted for it. I lacked, in short, the muscles suitable for a dramatic death. And it deeply offended my romantic pride that it should be this unsuitability that had permitted me to survive the war."

Here is the most probable explanation of Mishima's faking of his army medical in 1945, though this is a matter to which Mishima apparently never alluded later in life. A straightforward reading of *Sun and Steel* leads one to the conclusion that Mishima, while he mocked his wretched performance as a sportsman, took his body for a work of art: "The steel taught me many different things. It gave me an utterly new kind of knowledge, a knowledge that neither books nor worldly experience can impart. Muscles, I found, were strength as well as form, and each complex of muscles was subtly responsible for the direction in which its own strength was exerted, much as though they were rays of light given the form of flesh. Nothing could have accorded better with the definition of a work of art that I had long cherished than this concept of form enfolding strength, coupled with the idea that a work should be organic, radiating rays of light in all directions. The muscles that I thus created were at one and the same time simple existence and works of art; they even, paradoxically, possessed a certain abstract nature. Their one fatal flaw was that they were too closely involved with the life process, which decreed that they should decline and perish with the decline of life itself."

Mishima had found an alternative to literature—what he called a "true antithesis of words." And he governed the last years of his life according to his Bunburyodo, the dual way of Art and Action, which ended with his suicide. How did he arrive at such a system as his Bunburyodo, one might ask. How did he make the move from the River of Body to the River of Action? The clue may be found in the passage above. His muscles had one fatal flaw: he was bound to get old. In order to achieve his romantic apotheosis he had to die while his body was still beautiful, while he was still comparatively young. Such is the argument of *Sun and Steel*.

Does one take it seriously—as a description of what went on in Mishima's mind in the mid-1960's? I think so. One test is that of intellectual coherence. The essay is consistent throughout—unlike Mishima's "political" writing in the late 1960's. A second criterion is a personal one. *Sun and Steel* has, for me, a passion that is—in retrospect —sincere, however unpleasing it may be. Talking with Mishima about the book, I discovered that he cared a great

deal for what I had taken to be a mere diversion; this was
not a discovery on which I acted during his life—I did not
look up *Sun and Steel*. It was hard, while he was alive, to
read more than a few pages of his romantic thoughts without
falling asleep, hard to take seriously a tome full of dire
threats when its author—so "intrepid, dispassionate, and robust," in his own words—seemed a living refutation of his
romanticism.

After his disappointment with the novel *Kyoko no Ie*,
he plunged into a whirl of activity. Early in 1960 he took the
lead part in a gangster film, *Karakkaze Yaro* ("A Dry Fellow"), in which he appeared, at the start of the film, exercis-
ing, stripped to the waist, in a prison yard. The film ended
with the murder of the black-jacketed thug played by Mishima. (He also wrote and recorded the theme song of the
film.) He appeared to be indulging his narcissism a little, no
more. For the most part he led a highly controlled, hard-
working life and poured most of his energy into his writing
and the relentless training in gyms and kendo halls.

Three years later he posed for an album of photographs
by the fashionable photographer, Eiko Hosoe. In these magnificent pictures he appears in a number of extraordinary
poses—lying on his back in his garden against a baroque ornament, stripped naked, with a white rose in his mouth, or
lying upon his hairy chest. The album, *Barakei* ("Torture by
Roses"), gave Mishima a bad reputation in some quarters.
Critics and other writers who disliked him said he was
going off his head at last. And the nude pictures encouraged
a class of correspondents for whom Mishima was not prepared—anonymous "friends" who wrote passionate notes to
him requesting still bolder nude portraits. Yet these pictures
were generally felt to reflect only one part, and not a very
vital part, of the man; his narcissism seemed, to most people, to be irrelevant to his literary work. Besides, it was said,
he was doing such things in jest, seeking to irritate the
critics whom he so despised, not only for their scrawny
chests, but more on account of their flabby intellectual attitudes. Other Japanese got used to Mishima's exhibitionism,

and not a great deal of attention was paid to the startling photographs which appeared in cheap weekly magazines.

Not even the famous portrait of Mishima as St. Sebastian aroused more than a flicker of interest. This was a photo taken in 1966 by Kishin Shinoyama, the leading young Japanese photographer. It showed Mishima in the pose selected by Guido Reni for the painting of St. Sebastian which—as Mishima had described in *Confessions of a Mask*—had inspired his first ejaculation. He is standing against a thick tree trunk, the lower foliage of which is visible, acting as a canopy over the man below. In the background is a hazy, Titian-like view of dappled sunlight and leaves. Mishima is shown bound at the wrists by a rope suspended from the tree above, which holds his arms high above his head. He gazes upward, with his head turned slightly to one side. He is clad only in a light, white cloth, folded about his thighs and revealing his chest, which he inflated fully for the picture. In it are implanted three arrows—one in his left armpit. The wounds are bleeding a little; a trickle of blood dribbles from each arrow.

By the time this picture appeared in Japan, the public was inured to Mishima's buffoonery. The other photographs taken by Shinoyama at this time—one of them portraying Mishima in boots, black jockstrap, and sailor cap, leaning against a massive motorcycle—did not create a lasting impression either. This reaction, which may now appear obtuse in the West, where Mishima's portraits are well known, is understandable. Most of the time, Mishima was engaged in serious pursuits; above all, his writing. He was regarded as the leading writer of his generation; no one paid much attention to his foibles. "What trick will he think up next?" was the most common reaction. Not long after the Shinoyama pictures, he appeared in the cabaret act with Akihiro Maruyama, singing his song "The Sailor Who Was Killed by Paper Roses," at the end of which the two men, Mishima and Maruyama, exchanged a kiss. "Mishima has done it again," was the reaction of the weekly magazines, and the little incident was quickly forgotten.

One who underestimated Mishima's energy might think he spent all his time posing for photographers. Also in 1966 there was a picture of Mishima squatting on a tatami floor in a white fundoshi, bearing a long samurai sword—the weapon with which his head was to be cut off four years later. His bronzed torso and the light sweat on his body added flavor to the photos, which were shot in the house of Meredith Weatherby in Tokyo. In fact, Mishima was engaged in a thousand other activities and would rush off a series of pictures with a skilled photographer in a matter of minutes. They amused him, but he was not prepared to waste a great deal of time over them. My own reaction to these exploits—I received a batch of Mishima's latest photographs one day in 1969—was probably typical; I was shocked and then grew bored. The sheaf of pictures he sent me for publication in *The Times* of London included a portrait of Mishima dressed in a suit and standing with a No actor wearing the mask used for the play *Hagoromo*. The mask is a beautiful one, and Mishima has an absentminded, sad expression on his face which made this one of the most attractive portraits I had seen of him. A second picture was as repulsive as the first was sympathetic. It shows Mishima, naked to the waist, upper lip curled, with a hachimaki around his forehead on which is written the slogan *Shichisho Hokoku* ("Serve the Nation for Seven Lives"). In his hands he is holding his Seki no Magoroku sword, over which he glowers at the camera.

As he neared forty, Mishima began to worry about his age, yet he was still extremely fit five years later, showing little sign of slowing down physically. His figure was almost as good as it had been fifteen years earlier, though his shoulder muscles had a slight tendency to sag and he did not look so impressive when he inflated his chest in the style of a body-building fanatic. According to his father, Mishima's wrist was stiff and he had frequent massages to enable him to do kendo. There were other signs of encroaching middle age. During the training at Camp Fuji he could not keep up with the Tatenokai youths; he would join them only in those exercises at which he was best; push-ups, for example. On the whole, however, he was still in extraordinarily good condition for a man of forty-five. Two months before his death, he posed for a last series of photographs by Shinoyama. These, he said, should be published in a volume to be entitled *Otoko no Shi* ("Death of a Man"). Among the poses Mishima struck for this volume (still unpublished) were a number in which he committed hara-kiri. He also posed as a traffic-accident victim, covered in blood. This was his last journey down the River of Body.

<h2 style="text-align:center">5</h2>

<h1 style="text-align:center">The River of Action</h1>

The River of Body naturally flowed into the River of Action. It was inevitable. With a woman's body this would not have happened. A man's body, with its inherent nature and function, forces him toward the River of Action, the most dangerous river in the jungle. Alligators and piranhas abound in its waters. Poisoned arrows dart from enemy camps. This river confronts the River of Writing. I've often heard the glib motto, "The Pen and the Sword Join in a Single Path." But in truth they can join only at the moment of death.

This River of Action gives me the tears, the blood, the sweat that I never begin to find in the River of Writing. In this new river I have encounters of soul with soul without having to bother about words. This is also the most destructive of all rivers, and I can well understand why few people approach it. This River has no generosity for the farmer; it brings no wealth nor peace, it gives no rest. Only let me say this: I, born a man and alive as a man, cannot overcome the temptation to follow the course of this River.

Yukio Mishima, Catalogue to the Tobu Exhibition

PART ONE
"PATRIOTISM"

A most mysterious aspect—perhaps the most impenetrable feature—of the Japanese tradition is the Imperial system. This was crucial to Mishima's River of Action.

The role of the Emperor has been a varied one in Japanese history. Throughout feudal times the Emperors lived in Kyoto, the ancient capital, and their temporal powers were minute. The Emperor was respected as a religious and cultural symbol of state. As such, he had an important part to play in Japanese society; he was a mysterious, unseen presence. However, the actual rulers of Japan, the so-called Shogun, or Tycoon—the English word has a Japanese derivation—allowed the Emperors very little part in government. The weakness of the Imperial Court in Kyoto was ensured by successive Shoguns who limited the Imperial revenues to such an extent that one Emperor was obliged to resort to the sale of samples of his calligraphy in order to pay for his modest establishment—scrolls written by him were lowered over the wall at the end of his garden in a basket. Only after 1868, when the Imperial Court was moved to Tokyo and a young Emperor installed on the Chrysanthemum Throne—the Emperor Meiji (1868–1912) —was the Japanese sovereign accorded the trappings of power. Even then, he remained largely in the hands of his senior officials, his advisers. Meiji is not known definitely to have been responsible for a single major policy decision during his long reign. Taisho, his son, who reigned from 1912 to 1926, and who was mentally deficient, also remained aloof from policy matters. The present Emperor— known in the West as Hirohito—who succeeded Taisho after a period as Regent, made only two decisions during his reign, but they were important ones. He stamped out the revolt known to the Japanese as the Ni Ni Roku Incident—the rebellion of February 1936—and he made the decision to end the Pacific War in 1945.

To this day, the role of the Emperor in Japan is a mystery. According to the law—the postwar Constitution drafted by General MacArthur and his advisers in 1946 and ratified the following year—the Emperor has no temporal authority. He is the symbolic head of state; and his functions are limited to opening sessions of parliament and to making occasional public appearances. His powers were drastically cut back under the Allied Occupation of 1945–52—first, by the declaration called the ningen sengen, in which he formally disclaimed the cardinal beliefs of twentieth-century Japanese imperialism; and second—implicitly—by the treatment accorded him by the U.S. authorities. The Emperor was not consulted by the occupying administration on matters of state, nor was he treated as a figure with anything more than nominal power. His children, also, were subject to unprecedented treatment; his eldest son, the Crown Prince, had an American governess. This was all in accordance with the United States understanding of demokurashi in Japan. The marriage of the Crown Prince to a commoner in 1959—this was the first occasion on which a future Emperor or even an Imperial prince had married outside the traditional aristocracy—seemed to mark Japanese acceptance of the system of government introduced to the nation during the Occupation. There has in fact been a considerable change in the position of the Emperor from pre-World War II to postwar Japan. The postwar Emperor has been a popular figure rather than a divine symbol of authority. The prewar practice of keeping the Emperor hidden within his palace except for rare occasions on which he emerged as a man on a white horse has been abandoned. The change might be compared to that which took place in the seventeenth century in England between the reigns of Charles I and Charles II; the Emperor of Japan still has a very special atmosphere about him, but he is no longer a figure of ultimate authority armed with divine right.

The change, however, has not been a complete one. Many aspects of the Imperial system are still not open to the public; for example, the Emperor's position cannot be discussed in the press. Mishima's attitude toward this taboo was aggressive. He was in fact more outspoken on the subject of the Emperor than any other Japanese since the end of the Pacific War. Sometimes he lauded the Imperial system; sometimes he castigated the incumbent, Hirohito. At times he appeared to be an out-and-out nationalist; on other occasions he seemed to deliver a deadly assault on the Emperor. My impression is that Mishima's imperialism —contradictory as it was—had its roots both in a genuinely felt worship of the Emperor system and in his personal aesthetic. His aesthetic, I believe, was the strongest influence on Mishima, and the wellsprings of his decision to commit hara-kiri—traditionally, an action undertaken by a samurai wishing to demonstrate his loyalty to his lord (who could be the Emperor)—were individual and were connected to his long-held aesthetic: "My heart's longing for Death and Night and Blood." Mishima was an imperialist, of course, but he was a great deal more than that—a cold and self-obsessed creature given to fits of passion; a novelist, a playwright, a sportsman. He was a man with many sides to his character, and his imperialism cannot be regarded as central; Emperor-worship was only one facet of Yukio Mishima.

The River of Body, Mishima remarked, flowed into the River of Action. The best illustration of what he meant by this is to be found in his practice of the martial art of kendo, fencing with a blunt Japanese lance, a shinai. He took up kendo in 1959, and this sport, he asserted in an article published in *Sports Illustrated* in December 1970, just after his death, "makes me what I am." As a child at the Gakushuin school he had hated kendo, which had been compulsory. He had been embarrassed by the "rude, barbaric, threatening cries" which the combatants emit, yelling at the tops of their voices, as they circle one another, clad in medieval armor. "Now, thirty years later," he wrote, "I feel quite otherwise." The kendo cries had become pleasant to him; he had fallen in love with them. "This sound is the cry of Nippon itself buried deep within me . . . a cry that present-day Nippon is ashamed of and desperately tries to suppress, but it breaks out, shattering all presence. It is something bound up with memories that are dark, something that recalls the flow of new-shed blood." The cries of kendo men, Mishima said, called up "the ghost of Nippon Past," which had been long confined in chains. (His support of the martial art earned

him the gratitude of the experts in Japan, and he was duly
awarded a very high rank in kendo. His fifth dan was be-
stowed on him in August 1968, much as an eminent statesman receives a doctorate and tasseled hat from an ancient
university—his kendo form was not good, he insisted.)

Mishima's nostalgia for Nippon Past—a romantic
ideal—was catalyzed by the political events of the year
1960. His father, Azusa Hiraoka, said after Mishima's death
that the riots and disorders of the summer of 1960 played a
part in turning Mishima's mind toward romantic imperialism. The evidence is impressive. Mishima took a keen interest in political events for the first time in the postwar
years after the onset of the Anpo (U.S.–Japan Security Treaty)
demonstrations in the spring of 1960—the worst civil disturbances in postwar Japan; up to this time he had shown no
response to political developments in Japan the country, not
even to the spectacular changes of the early 1950's when the
Occupation ended and the Japanese Communist Party made
an abortive effort to prepare the way for violent revolution.
During the Anpo riots, Mishima went out into the streets,
observed at first hand, and reported for the national press.
Commenting on the position of Nobusuke Kishi, the un-
popular right-wing Prime Minister who was thrown out of
office as a result of the Anpo disturbances, he recounted in
the *Mainichi Shimbun* how he had spent an entire night on
a balcony of the building next to the Prime Minister's office
looking down on the place while crowds surged about it. He
thought of "the thin, lonely old man [Mr. Kishi] who must
have been sitting in the darkness of the official residence,
all windows of which were shrouded by night. Kishi is a
tiny, tiny nihilist whom people instinctively dislike because
they can identify themselves with such a person . . . How
easily the psychology that 'somehow I don't like Kishi'
could be transformed into the psychology that 'I like somebody somehow.' While one hates a tiny nihilist, one may accept a nihilist on the grand scale such as Hitler."

Shortly after the Anpo disturbances ended, Mishima
wrote the short story "Patriotism." Mishima was an ex-

cellent critic and a fair judge of his own writing. He remarked of "Patriotism" that it contained "both the best and
the worst features of my writing"; it may also be regarded
as representative of his entire oeuvre. "Patriotism," which
Mishima wrote in the early autumn of 1960, is the story of
a young Imperial Army lieutenant at the time of the Ni Ni
Roku Incident of February 1936. The two principal factions
in the Japanese Armed Forces at the time were both ex-
pansionist, wanting Japan to pursue a policy of foreign con-
quest. The Kodo-ha, the Imperial Way faction, favored a
strike north against the Soviet Union; and the Tosei-ha, the
Control faction, favored a strike south against Britain and
other European colonial powers. The conflict came to a
head with the Ni Ni Roku Incident, which was triggered by
Kodo-ha officers seeking to forestall seizure of power by
their Tosei-ha rivals. The action was spurred on by a plan
for the dispatch of the First Division, many of whose officers
were Kodo-ha members, to Manchuria—this would have
greatly reduced the strength of the Kodo-ha in Tokyo. The
Kodo-ha adherents, led by a few young officers—Takatsugu
Muranaka, Asaichi Isobe, Teruzo Ando, Yasuhide Kurihara,
and others—decided to strike against the authorities before
that happened. Early on the morning of February 26, with
the capital under a fresh fall of snow, the officers mobilized
1,400 men and seized control of the center of Tokyo after as-
sassinating three leading members of the government. The
action, they declared, was carried out on behalf of the Emperor and was aimed at his evil advisers. After a brief hesita-
tion Hirohito himself ordered them to surrender. The revolt
collapsed in four days.

The protagonist of Mishima's story, Lieutenant Takeyama, is an officer in a regiment stationed in Tokyo. He is
a friend of the rebel officers and sympathizes with their aims,
but he is left out of the plans because he is newly married.
After the outbreak of the Ni Ni Roku, he is ordered to lead
an attack on the rebels. His way out of the moral dilemma
created for him by this order is to commit hara-kiri. His
wife, Reiko, must also kill herself. In "Patriotism" (one of

the short stories collected in *Death in Midsummer and Other Stories,* published by New Directions, with the translation of "Patriotism" by Geoffrey W. Sargent), Mishima described the hara-kiri of the young man in extraordinary detail. This is probably the most elaborate account of the samurai rite in the whole of Japanese literature, and it is all the more striking in that the author appears to endorse the ideology of Lieutenant Takeyama and his associates. The hara-kiri, subtly idealized by Mishima in the story, appears as a grisly act justified by a high ideal:

"By the time the lieutenant had at last drawn the sword across tò the right side of his stomach, the blade was already cutting shallow and had revealed its naked tip, slippery with blood and grease. But, suddenly stricken by a fit of vomiting, the lieutenant cried out hoarsely. The vomiting made the fierce pain fiercer still, and the stomach, which had thus far remained firm and compact, now abruptly heaved, opening wide its wound, and the entrails burst through, as if the wound too were vomiting. Seemingly ignorant of their master's suffering, the entrails gave an impression of robust health and almost disagreeable vitality as they slipped smoothly out and spilled over into the crotch. The lieutenant's head drooped, his shoulders heaved, his eyes opened to narrow slits, and a thin trickle of saliva dribbled from his mouth. The gold markings on his epaulettes caught the light and glinted.

"Blood was scattered everywhere. The lieutenant was soaked in it to his knees, and he sat now in a crumpled and listless posture, one hand on the floor. A raw smell filled the room. The lieutenant, his head drooping, retched repeatedly, and the movement showed repeatedly in his shoulders. The blade of the sword, now pushed back by the entrails and exposed to its tip, was still in the lieutenant's right hand.

"It would be difficult to imagine a more heroic sight than that of the lieutenant at this moment, as he mustered his strength and flung back his head."

One other remarkable feature of the story is that Lieutenant Takeyama kills himself first, leaving Reiko to follow him in death afterward. She stabs herself in the throat with a knife, having firmly secured her skirts so that she shall not be found dead in an indecorous posture. The reason given for the husband taking precedence instead of the wife dying first, as would have been normal, is that "it was vital for the lieutenant, whatever else might happen, that there should be no irregularity in his death." The point is not easy to follow. What is clear is that the officer wants to be *watched* as he performs hara-kiri. "Patriotism" emerges, from this detail alone, as a work by an abnormal man.

Mishima wrote twice more about the Ni Ni Roku affair. In his play *Toka no Kiku*, and in his unclassifiable work *Eirei no Koe* ("The Voices of the Heroic Dead," 1966), an elegy for the war dead, and also an assault upon Emperor Hirohito for deserting the souls of the departed by intervening in the Ni Ni Roku Incident and by announcing his *ningen sengen* in 1946, Mishima endorsed the ideology of the rebel officers of 1936. He put the three works—"Patriotism," *Toka no Kiku*, and *Eirei no Koe*—together in one volume, which he called his Ni Ni Roku trilogy. In a postscript to the trilogy he described his conclusion, which I condense a little here:

> I wrote "Patriotism" from the point of view of the young officer who could not help choosing suicide because he could not take part in the Ni Ni Roku Incident. This is neither a comedy nor a tragedy but simply a story of happiness . . . If they [husband and wife] had waited one more night, the attack on the Imperial Army [the rebels] would have been called off and the need for their deaths would have decreased, although the legal authorities would have caught up with him [Takeyama]. To choose the place where one dies is also the greatest joy in life. And such a night as the couple had was their happiest. Moreover, there was no shadow of a lost battle over them; the love of these two reaches to an extremity of purity, and the painful suicide of the soldier is equiv-

alent to an honorable death on the field of battle. Somewhere I obtained the conviction that if one misses one's
night one will never have another opportunity to
achieve a peak of happiness in life. Instrumental in this
conviction were my experiences during the war, my
reading of Nietzsche during the war, and my fellow
feeling for the philosopher Georges Bataille, the
"Nietzsche of eroticism . . ."

Surely some great God died when the Ni Ni Roku
Incident failed. I was only eleven at the time and felt
little of it. But when the war ended, when I was twenty,
a most sensitive age, I felt something of the terrible cruelty of the death of that God, and this was somehow
linked with my intuition of what had happened when I
was eleven. For a long time I was unable to understand
the connection, but when I wrote *Toka no Kiku* and
"Patriotism" there appeared a dark shadow in my consciousness as I wrote—and then it disappeared again
without taking definite shape. This was a "negative"
picture of the Ni Ni Roku Incident; the positive picture
was my boyhood impression of the heroism of the rebel
officers. Their purity, bravery, youth, and death qualified them as mythical heroes; and their failures and
deaths made them true heroes in this world . . .

In the meantime, the melancholy within me became enlarged and I was astonished by the realization
that the endless fatigue, which I used to take as a condition of "collapse" common to the young, metamor-
phosed into something the reverse of the corrupt—
something which urged me on. I fell in love with
kendo, and found true significance only in the clear
echo of bamboo sword on sword and the fierce, fanatic
shouts. After that I wrote my short story "Ken"
["Sword"]. How can I explain my mental condition?
Am I rotten or in a state of exaltation? Slowly, a purposeless sorrow and anger pile up within me; sooner or
later these had to combine with the intense cry of the
young officers of the Ni Ni Roku Incident. This incident

has been with me for the past thirty years, going back and forth between my conscious and my subconscious . . . The desire to console the spirits of the true heroes who had influenced me for so long, to restore their reputation and to reinstate them, was always deep within me. But whenever I consider the matter further, I am at a loss how to treat the Emperor's ningen sengen. The history of the Showa period [the reign of Hirohito] is divided in two by the defeat in war, and one like me who lived through both parts [of the Showa era] continuously cannot help desiring to find a real continuity and a basis for theoretical consistency. This seems perfectly natural for a man, whether he is a writer or not. The ningen sengen declaration by the Emperor himself was more important than the new Constitution which provides that the Emperor be a symbol. I was forced to the point where I could not help but describe the shadow of the Ni Ni Roku Incident; thus I started *Eirei no Koe*. It may seem strange if I use the word "aesthetics" in this context. But I came to realize that there is a hard, huge rock at the very foundation of my aesthetic—the Emperor system.

Whatever one may feel about Mishima's imperialism, there is no denying his passion. It was a turning point in his life when in 1966 he shut himself up for three days in a hotel in Tokyo and poured out his feelings in *Eirei no Koe*, a work of eighty pages in length. It was after writing *Eirei no Koe*, he told me three years later, that he decided to create the Tatenokai. His frame of mind in early 1966 was vividly illuminated by *Eirei no Koe*, the refrain of which runs: "Nadote Sumerogi wa hito to naritamaishi" ("Why did the Emperor have to become a human being?"). The work, most Japanese critics agree, is not a fine piece of literature, and the book was quickly forgotten, once the scandal of its publication died down. It is important, however, to know more about Mishima's attitudes at this time. He expressed himself forcibly in an interview about *Eirei no Koe* headed "Theory of the Emperor," which he granted the *Sunday Mainichi* magazine early in March 1966:

MISHIMA: This is a theme I wanted to write about some-day. Of course, there is a great possibility that I would be counterattacked from many sides because the work itself has a dual aspect. I was quite prepared for this.

Q.: What do you think about the Ni Ni Roku Incident?

MISHIMA: This incident occurred when I was eleven and had a big spiritual influence on me. My hero worship and feeling of collapse, which I experience now, are both derived from the incident.

Needless to say, I support the young officers, the so-called traitors. Therefore, I was beside myself with rage with those authors who have denounced them in their works as men who betrayed the army.

The action of the young officers could have brought about the Showa Ishin, the Showa Restoration, and was based on a belief in national salvation. But they were called traitors because the cowardly, sniveling, timid old vassals who surrounded the Emperor plotted against them. Consequently, the Emperor has responsibility; he accepted it. The Emperor should send an Imperial messenger [to the graves of the dead] as soon as possible, to end the dishonor of those who were bereaved.

Q.: What was your intention in writing?

MISHIMA: I wrote *Toka no Kiku* from the point of view of the vassals, and "Patriotism" was a story about a single young officer who was left out of the rising.

This time [in *Eirei no Koe*] I wrestled with the spirit of the incident head on.

There is a tendency now for journalists to avoid discussing the chrysanthemum [the Imperial family], America, and the Soka Gakkai [a militant Buddhist sect], letting these subjects be taboos. Authors do the same. The best kind of self-discipline for writers and journalists is introspection.

That the Communist Party has also ceased to criticize the Emperor system is also cowardly.

I can say that my frustration with the modern trend lay behind my decision to write and to complete this story [*Eirei no Koe*] in a short space of time.

Q.: Do you think the prewar Emperor system is the only one for the nation?

MISHIMA: Yes. The kokutai, the national system, has collapsed since the Emperor made his ningen sengen. All the moral confusion of the postwar period stems from that. Why should the Emperor be a human being? Why must he be a God, at least for us Japanese? If I explain this matter, it all boils down to a question of "love" in the end. In modern times nations have moved forward from the physiocratic to the capitalist system. This is unavoidable. Feudalism collapses, the nation industrializes and then cannot but become a modern welfare state—the most desperate of conditions. In the meantime, the more a nation modernizes, the less meaningful, the cooler, become personal relationships. For people who live in such a modern society love is impossible. For example, if A believes that he loves B, there is no means for him to be sure of it, and vice versa. Therefore, love cannot exist in a modern society—if it is merely a mutual relationship. If there is no image of a third man whom the two lovers have in common—the apex of the triangle—love ends with eternal skepticism. This is what [D. H.] Lawrence calls agnosticism. From ancient times the Japanese have had an image of the apex of the triangle (God), which was a God in a physiocratic system; and everyone had a theory of love, so that he should not be isolated.

The Emperor was the absolute for us Japanese.

That is why I always say that [Shinto] festivals are necessary.

Q.: What about the Imperial family today?

MISHIMA: I am of course an imperialist. And I think one who says what he wants to say is a patriot.

The present situation of the Imperial family is chaotic.

For example, treating Princess Michiko [consort of the Crown Prince] as a film star is nonsense. They [the media] simply boost her popularity. I think they should underline Michiko's worship at the Grand Shrine of Ise [the main Shinto shrine] following Prince Akihito; after all, she graduated from a Catholic university. The Crown Prince should also visit the Jieitai Staff College and should offer cigarettes with the stamp of the chrysanthemum upon them to those who are bursting with patriotism.

One cigarette may be worth 100 million yen in the future. These are the people on whom the Imperial family can rely, ultimately.

The unfortunate thing for His Majesty is that there were no able advisers around him. The vassals closest to him were all educated in England, and those Japanese educated there all became opportunists and such weak characters, determined only to maintain the status quo.

One exception was Shigeru Yoshida [the most famous of postwar Prime Ministers], who was a symbolic figure, the first Japanese to resist the British and U.S. system during the Occupation by a skillful "English" counterattack.

Secondly, His Majesty did not have the chance to contact young men.

At the time of the Ni Ni Roku Incident, His Majesty was filled with deep hatred. If he were a human being, he should naturally have been enraged by the assassination of his own men. But His Majesty as a God should not be. If he had had contact with the young officers, he could have understood what lay behind the incident and would not have trampled on the faith of young patriots.

Q.: What do you think should be the future of Japan, including the Imperial household?

MISHIMA: Since I am an author, I wish to look at the

human situation, so the actual system must be the concern of politicians, I think. Although the present lot of politicians are corrupt . . .

After the publication of *Eirei no Koe,* Mishima became a favorite of the Uyoku, the violent right, and also the right wing of the Liberal Democratic Party, the ruling conservative party. He did not associate with the former, which has criminal elements. He did, however, become friendly with many conservative leaders, including Prime Minister Sato and his sharp-witted wife. But his imperialism was unique; it had the same narcissistic quality which characterized all Mishima's thoughts and actions—as is clear in these selected quotations from a long dialogue which took place in 1966 between Mishima and the right-wing bigot, Fusao Hayashi:

[The leaders of the Meiji Restoration] succeeded in Westernizing Japan ninety-nine percent. The remaining one percent was the definition of the Emperor as sacred and untouchable—this was the fort against Westernization.

The Emperor is infallible. He is the most mysterious existence in the world.

To me, the Emperor, works of art, and Shinpuren are symbols of purity. I want to identify my own literary work with God.

The two first statements are orthodox enough. The last is true to Mishima. I think that he sometimes confused himself with God or with the Emperor. He remarked to me once: "There is no one I can respect in Japan today, the situation is hopeless, there is no one to take account of . . ." There followed a long pause. A strange expression flitted across his face. "Except perhaps the Emperor . . ."

In other writings he revealed a masochistic side to his character. This matters, for it showed that hara-kiri was not simply an act of loyalty toward the Emperor, an act of kanshi (the suicide of remonstration); Mishima also wanted to hurt himself. So much is apparent from the autobiographical essay I have often gone back to for insights, *Sun and Steel:* "Pain, I came to feel, might well prove to be the sole proof of the persistence of consciousness within the flesh, the sole physical expression of consciousness. As my body acquired muscle, and in turn strength, there was gradually born within me a tendency toward the positive acceptance of pain, and my interest in physical suffering deepened. Even so, I would not have it believed that this development was a result of the workings of my imagination. My discovery was made directly, with my body, thanks to the sun and the steel." In his use of imagery, Mishima was fairly specific about the instrument which should cause pain—a knife: "The subtle contradiction between self-awareness and existence began to trouble me. I reasoned that if one wants to identify seeing and existing, the nature of the self-awareness should be made as centripetal as possible. If only one can direct the eye of self-awareness so intently toward the interior and the self that self-awareness forgets the outer forms of existence, then one can 'exist' as surely as the 'I' in Amiel's *Diary* . . . Let us picture a single, healthy apple . . . The apple certainly exists, but to the core this existence as yet seems inadequate; if words cannot endorse it, then the only way to endorse it is with the eyes. Indeed, for the core the only sure mode of existence is to exist and to see at the same time. There is only one method of solving this contradiction. It is for a knife to be plunged deep into the apple so that it is split open and the core is exposed to light."

Mishima classified various of his writings—"Patriotism," *Eirei no Koe,* and *Sun and Steel* among them—under the heading of his River of Action. They outlined his reasons for committing himself to action. The commitment itself came in the latter part of 1966, when he applied to train at Jieitai camps after his completion of *Spring Snow.* The second stage of his commitment began in the early summer of 1967 when he began to look around for young men to join his private army or militia—he preferred the second term.

This was a time when the left-wing student Zengakuren had begun their campaign against the government in earnest, and right-wing student bodies, though few in number, had organized themselves against the ultra-left. Mishima had, therefore, a number of places to look for potential recruits. He settled on two groups: a small contingent of students who published a little-known, right-wing magazine, the *Ronso Journal*, whose leader was a student named Kuramochi; and a group of students at Waseda University, the Tokyo university at which the ultra-left was most active. Among those was a twenty-one-year-old from Yokkaichi, a coastal town near Nagoya, whose name was Masakatsu Morita. Mishima kept in touch with both sets of students during 1967, and though of the two he had preferred the Waseda group—perhaps because they were cohesive and well defined—he was forced to settle for the support of the *Ronso Journal* youths, as the former would have nothing to do with Mishima at first, taking him for an exhibitionist, an odd fellow.

Mishima launched his activities with the *Ronso Journal* youths—these activities were at first confined to meetings and long conversations—at a session held in the offices of the magazine. One of those present described the scene to Azusa Hiraoka, and we are indebted to Mishima's father for this description of a scene which might have come straight from a morbid passage in *Confessions of a Mask*. There were about a dozen people present, gathered around a table in the seedy office of the building in Kami-Itabashi where the *Ronso Journal* had its headquarters. "On a piece of paper he [Mishima] wrote in sumi [Chinese ink]: 'We hereby swear to be the foundation of *Kokoku Nippon* [Imperial Japan].' Then he cut his little finger with a penknife and asked everyone else to follow his example. They dripped blood from their fingers into a cup, all standing, until it was full to the brim; then each signed his name on the piece of paper, dipping a *mohitsu* [brush] into the cup and signing in blood . . . Some of the people felt faint and one had to rush out to vomit. Mishima then suggested that they should drink the blood . . . He picked up the glass and asked: 'Is anyone here ill? None of you have VD?' All seemed well. He called for a saltcellar and flavored the cup; then he drank from it. The others followed his example. 'What a fine lot of Draculas,' said Mishima, looking around at the youths with their red mouths and teeth, laughing his raucous laugh." Afterward the students placed the cup, with whatever blood was left, in the safe of the *Ronso Journal*. Then Mishima called for coffee and cakes and they sat down to eat.

From the beginning, this little organization, which was to become the Tatenokai, was a personal vehicle for Mishima. In the early spring of 1968, Mishima, who was organizing his first party to train at Camp Fuji with the Jieitai, appealed to the Waseda students to send a dozen of their number as members of his party. A number of his own men had dropped out—youths who had enjoyed associating with a famous man but whose desire to participate in any form of action was minimal; some had been put off by the requirement that they cut their hair. The Waseda students were reluctant to follow Mishima and only at the last moment did half a dozen students join him in the party which trained at Camp Fuji in March 1968. Morita, who had broken his leg a month before in an accident, joined the group last of all. Mishima took an immediate liking to him and singled him out for praise in front of the others, commending him for his willingness to train despite the fact that his leg was in a cast. In a letter written to a friend from Camp Fuji, Morita referred to Mishima by the honorific term "sensei" ("teacher"), a clear sign that he acknowledged him as leader. The two men became friends.

Morita is the key to subsequent events. He was born the youngest child in the family of a poor secondary-school headmaster two weeks before the end of the war. His first name, Masakatsu, which is "Victory by All Means" in a literal rendering of the characters, reflected his father's patriotic belief that Japan would win the war. The boy was orphaned at the age of two. He was looked after by his older brother, Osamu, and sent to a Catholic missionary school at Yokkaichi, where he proved himself to be a leader. He was made head of his class in the senior school, although his academic work was no better than average. Morita preferred judo, a Japanese sport, to baseball, a popular game in Japan; and his ambition was to become a conservative politician, an extraordinary aim in one so young. Most young Japanese of his age were radical or non-pori, unpolitical, in their attitudes. Morita, advised by a younger brother of Ichiro Kono, the leading independent conservative politician of the day, to attend the university before taking part in politics, entered Waseda at his third attempt, in the spring of 1966, at a time when left-wing students had overrun the university. Waseda, the place of Morita's dreams, was the center of ultra-left student activity in the nation. He reacted against the Zengakuren by joining a new, right-wing student club in the university, the Nichigakudo (Japan Students Movement), a tiny organization.

Morita and Mishima came together, originally, because their political views were similar. Both were among the few Japanese who held that the Zengakuren must be opposed by force. Both wanted to lead groups to do battle with the left-wing students; both were zealous imperialists and wrote pamphlets—independently—calling for Japan to have the H-bomb. People of such character were bound to drift into association with one another, as they were so few; and Mishima and Morita, realizing how much they had in common, cooperated with each other after the spring of 1968. Mishima attended rightist student meetings at which Morita took the chair; and Morita ensured that the Waseda students stayed with Mishima. Kuramochi, the *Ronso Journal* man, was the official student leader of the Tatenokai at its establishment on October 5, 1968, when its principles were laid down:

(i)   Communism is incompatible with Japanese tradition, culture, and history and runs counter to the Emperor system.

   (ii)   The Emperor is the sole symbol of our historical and cultural community and racial identity.

   (iii)   The use of violence is justifiable in view of the threat posed by Communism.

Morita gradually emerged as the effective student leader of the Tatenokai under Mishima. He had unshakable determination, and his slow, steady character appealed to the other students. He was not disturbed by Mishima's flashiness—many of the best recruits left the organization in the summer of 1968 when Mishima showed them the new Tatenokai uniform. He was also untroubled by the infighting that went on between Tatenokai members under Mishima. His stolid temperament and his position as a favorite of Mishima's kept him from becoming embroiled in the bitter disputes between rival factions.

Mishima organized the Tatenokai into eight independent sections, whose leaders were responsible to him alone. Each section had roughly ten members—making a total membership of about eighty. Almost all the recruits were students at universities in the Tokyo region; Mishima would have liked working men as well, but the demands he made on the members' time made it inevitable that most of them be students. Mishima's organization of the Tatenokai into sections, each one of which he controlled independently, was skillful; but his leadership was poor. The private army was nominally imperialist; however, as Mishima's thinking about the Emperor was muddled, he could not give his students the kind of realistic leadership which would have made a reality of the Tatenokai.

In the summer of 1968 he wrote an essay which showed how muddled he was about the Emperor. This essay was "Bunkaboeiron" ("On the Defense of Culture"), which he labored over for nearly a year. It concluded: "Military honors, also, must be awarded by the Emperor, as a cultural concept. As I think it legally feasible under the present Constitution, the Emperor's prerogative to grant honors should be revived in substance. Not only should he receive military salutes, he should award regimental colors in person."

The weakness of "Bunkaboeiron" is that Mishima makes no attempt to connect the main theme of the essay—that the Emperor is a cultural symbol—to the militaristic conclusion, reminiscent of prewar imperialism, when the Emperor was the divine symbol of the nation and also supreme commander of the Armed Forces (and did, in fact, present regimental colors).

Mishima made a chatty and unimpressive defense of the Tatenokai in *Queen* magazine (in January 1970): "My Shield Society (SS) [the literal translation of "Tatenokai" is "Shield Society"] has only one hundred members: it is the smallest army in the world, and I do not intend to enlarge it. My men receive no pay, but twice a year they are given a new uniform, cap, and boots. The uniform, especially designed for the SS, is so striking that passers-by stop on the street in amazement. I designed the flag, which shows two ancient Japanese helmets in red against a white silk background; this simple design also appears on our caps and on the buttons of our uniforms.

"Members of the SS are usually college undergraduates . . .

"The SS is a stand-by army. There is no way of knowing when our day will come. Perhaps it will never come; on the other hand, it may come tomorrow. Until then, the SS will remain calmly at the ready. No street demonstrations for us, no placards, no Molotov cocktails, no lectures, no stone throwing. Until the last desperate moment, we shall refuse to commit ourselves to action. For we are the world's least armed, most spiritual army.

"Some people mockingly refer to us as toy soldiers. Let us see. When I am on duty, the bugle call gets me out of bed at the crack of dawn . . ."

Mishima's attitude toward the Tatenokai is reflected in the anthem which he composed for it (a translation of which was given to me by Ivan Morris):

In the summer the lightning,
In the winter the frost—
To the foot of Mt. Fuji
We have come in good trim.
Here we stand, we young warriors,
Here we stand, fully armed.
Old Yamato's pure spirit
Is the weapon we bear.
On our swords finely tempered
Gleams the hue of the sky.
Let us boldly go forward
With our shield to the fore!

We must hide our great sorrow
And conceal our great dream—
In our land so low fallen
We all frown with dismay.
For what son of Yamato
Can just idly stand by
While the enemy rages
And pollutes our dear land?
The true soul of Yamato
Is the blood of our youth
Who so bravely step forward
With our shield to the fore!

The proud crest on our helmets
Is the shield that we bear—
To protect our loved Emperor
From the storms of the night.
The red glimmer of daybreak
On our warriors' fresh cheeks
Is the color that glitters
On our Flag of Great Truth.
From the night's dark corruption
We bright youths have leapt up
To march gallantly onward
With our shield to the fore!

PART TWO
PICNIC ON MT. FUJI

Early in March 1969, Mishima invited me to watch the Tatenokai in training at a Jieitai (Self-Defense Forces) camp on
Mt. Fuji. So far as I know, I was the first, and last, journalist
to see the Tatenokai in the field. After my visit to Camp Fuji
and the publication in *The Times* of an article describing
the Tatenokai, the training program was closed to journalists.

I remember being in a reluctant frame of mind as I
made my way through the crowds at Shinjuku Station in
Tokyo en route to Mt. Fuji. I was to observe an all-night exercise of the Tatenokai; and my worry, the source of my
reluctance, was the weather. On the previous night, eighteen inches of snow had fallen on Tokyo, and heaven only
knew how much snow had fallen on Mt. Fuji. The snow
hung heavily from the trees in my garden in central Tokyo,
and around midday had begun to drip; but on Mt. Fuji it
would be much colder, and really bitter at night—these
were not ideal conditions for an all-night exercise. I was
reluctant, too, because I was not sure that the excursion
would yield anything of great use to me as a journalist. I
could see Mishima virtually any time in Tokyo; it was not
necessary for me to go all the way up to Mt. Fuji to meet
him. The only argument for going had been to see the Tatenokai in training, but was it worth it in such weather?

At that time, like almost everyone else in Japan, I knew
very little about this recently created organization, beyond
what Mishima had told me in a short conversation or two.
"Tatenokai" he had translated as Shield Society from *tate*,
meaning "shield," and *kai*, "society." He had named the
Tatenokai after a short poem taken from the eighth-century
classical Japanese anthology, the *Manyoshu*—a poem in
which a warrior pledges his life to shield his lord and master, the Emperor, from the enemy. It was a poem which had
been popular with soldiers during the war.

Today I depart
Without a care for my life,
A shield to the Emperor.

The Tatenokai was to shield the person of the Emperor from
the threat of Communism.

I knew that the Tatenokai had been established by Mishima not long before, and was largely financed by him; that
the membership was small; and that the Jieitai were training members of the group. It was that fact which intrigued
me. From what Mishima had said, the training program was
unique—but why should the Jieitai be training such an organization as the Tatenokai, "the world's smallest and most
spiritual army," as he had described it? By doing so, the
Jieitai appeared to be breaking the basic rule which had
governed relations between the Armed Forces and civilians
since the end of the war: that the Jieitai should have no political role of any kind. However one looked at it, the Tatenokai had the odor of a right-wing organization. Although
Mishima was not connected with the traditional right in
Japan, who tend to be not much more than highly refined
gangsters, he had established a reputation for holding right-
wing political views, and it was he who had founded the Tatenokai. The Jieitai was in fact giving training facilities to a
group organized by a writer whose views on politics in
Japan, if accurately expressed by his writings, were in many
respects virtually indistinguishable from those held by the
Japanese military before and during the war.

I was aware that a political view of the Tatenokai was
not the only one possible, and that many people doubted
the seriousness of Mishima's politics. In Tokyo the Tatenokai tended to be dismissed as a wild joke. One view was
that the organization had been created by Mishima on a personal whim, and was nothing more than the colorful toy of
one much given to exhibitionism. A second theory, retailed
by Japanese journalists, was that the Tatenokai was simply
a homosexual club. Accustomed as I was, however, to allowing for the playful extremes to which Mishima would go

in his non-literary enterprises, I could not quite imagine that he had created the Tatenokai to meet beautiful boys; it would have been altogether too roundabout an exercise. That he had homosexual tendencies had long before been suggested by his novels *Confessions of a Mask* and *Forbidden Colors* with its "gloomy evocations of the sodomite underground of Tokyo"—as Donald Keene puts it. But I knew no more about this aspect of his private life, and I was certainly not about to write for *The Times* on the subject. As a journalist, my question was whether the Tatenokai was a right-wing organization or merely the writer's plaything. I had in fact almost made up my mind on a hunch, more or less deciding on the former; but it hardly seemed necessary for me to participate in an all-night exercise on Mt. Fuji to check my conclusion. There was no hurry; even the Japanese press was completely ignoring the Tatenokai, and *I* had got interested only because I knew Mishima personally.

Mishima, however, had anticipated my reluctance to see to a conclusion the eccentric idea of midnight reporting on Mt. Fuji. Regarding me as unpunctual and unreliable, which I certainly was by his rigid standards, he had made arrangements which made escape difficult. At the beginning of the week he had phoned to double-check that I would be making an appearance at Camp Fuji, the Jieitai establishment, on Thursday, March 13; he had said that I would be the only journalist taking part. Having lured me with this bait, and having then confirmed my intention to participate in the exercise, he had sprung the trap. In five years of reporting in Japan I had not been given such detailed instructions, a multitude of arrangements and safety checks. I was to catch the 3:10 p.m. train from Shinjuku, arriving at Gotemba station, on the south side of Mt. Fuji, at 4:46. I was to be put on the train by two young assistants of his, Maeda and Nakatsuji, whom I had once met in a karate gym with Mishima and knew vaguely; and at Gotemba I was to leave the platform by the exit on the Mt. Fuji side of the station, where I would be met by a Jieitai sergeant called Imai, who would escort me to Camp Fuji. In case these arrangements failed, Mishima gave me the phone number of the inn at Gotemba, the Fujimotoya, the Inn at the Foot of Mt. Fuji, where he had booked me a room, and suggested that I should ring there in the event of trouble. Even the Soka Gakkai, the very active and efficient Buddhist movement, did not give one instructions as elaborate as these.

Thus, hope of a last-minute withdrawal abandoned, I had come to Shinjuku that afternoon. I found my way through the unfamiliar maze of department stores, underground passages and platforms, all connected to one another, and finally arrived at the Odakyu Line. The platform from which the 3:10 train for Gotemba was to leave was crowded. People had formed lines at the painted white marks on the platform, waiting to board the train the instant the doors were opened; and others were dashing about, trying to get seat tickets. It was a scene peculiar to Japan, one of disciplined frenzy. Amid the crowds I spotted three athletic-looking youths in dark suits and ties, two of whom had familiar faces. Their eyes were darting about and at that moment met mine. They were journalists from a small right-wing magazine with which Mishima was associated, the *Ronso Journal*. We exchanged bows, and they told me that it would soon be time to board the train, an express with a scenic observation car. This was the Romance Car, so named by the Odakyu Line in honor of the weekend lovers and honeymoon couples whom it hoped to attract as customers. As the automatic doors opened, my guides gestured me to go aboard and showed me to my seat. To my surprise, they too sat down: it was clear that they were going to accompany me all the way to Gotemba, as they had three sets of tickets. The third member of the party stayed on the platform, peering in at us from time to time; he was to phone Gotemba to confirm that we were on our way.

Mishima had left nothing to chance. Honored as I was by the extreme care being taken to ensure my arrival at Gotemba, I wondered why he was going to so much trouble. The explanation must be that he greatly desired publicity for the Tatenokai and regarded *The Times* of London as a suitable vehicle. Having failed to have the Tatenokai taken very seriously in Japan, he hoped to have a little attention overseas. (Mishima's love of self-advertisement reminded me of Norman Mailer, as did the erotic quality of his writing; but the two men had little else in common, unless it was an interest in boxing.)

The train pulled out of Shinjuku at 3:10 precisely. Our departure was followed by loudspeaker announcements about our journey in the disturbing singsong accent adopted by Japanese women speaking to the general public. Then we were brought hand towels, timetables, and menus for tea by uniformed girls. Before the tea arrived, my companions showed me a copy of the *Ronso Journal*, issue No. 27. I had never seen the magazine before, and my interest was aroused, as I wondered if this could be a guide to the political beliefs of members of the Tatenokai, to which these two belonged. But if I had expected this to be a fanatical right-wing publication, I was disappointed. On the cover was the beaming face of Prime Minister Sato, the least charismatic right-wing figure imaginable, a friendly ally of big business. An article on the left-wing Zengakuren, the mass student movement, caught my attention: it included a recent breakdown of the strengths of the Zengakuren factions, or inner groups, one which looked like police information. Two weeks before, I had gone to Sugamo Prison to pay a visit to a leader of the largest of these factions, and one question on my mind at the time was whether the Tatenokai represented a reaction, if a belated one, to the activities of these left-wing students, whose movements had by this time been thoroughly broken by the police, and whose leaders had been locked up. I chatted about this with my two companions, but because of the language barrier we made little progress.

My interest reverted to the weather. We had been traveling for forty-five minutes and were already close to the foothills of Mt. Fuji; and as I looked out of the windows at the snow lying deep in the villages and at the slow-moving traffic on the roads, I wondered how the clothing I had brought would stand up to the night ahead. In contrast to the two youths, who wore suits, I had dressed in ski clothing, ready for the night to come; I had brought heavy sweaters and a black anorak to go on top. I had also armed myself with my secret weapon against the cold, a Japanese haragake, a woolen hoop which goes around the stomach. Boots had been the biggest problem, as I had had a choice between heavy Henke ski boots with flip buckles and a pair of U.S. Vietnam boots with canvas sides; I had taken the Henke, huge as they were. It was just as well. All we could see from the windows were yellow clouds, promising a bitter night. I had never been as close as this to Mt. Fuji, but we could see nothing except snow-laden clouds.

At Gotemba station we leaped out onto a snowy platform and were greeted by a man in a gray-blue uniform who had been given our seat numbers and had thus identified us. He saluted and announced that he was Sergeant Imai. We hurried through the ticket gate. In front of the station, parked so that it would not block traffic, stood a small American-type Willys Jeep, left-hand drive. The seat beside the driver was covered with white cloth, and I was given this seat of honor, in front of which there had been placed a plastic yellow Hong Kong flower in a holder. My companions sat in the rear of the jeep, and we were whisked along the snowy main street of the small town of Gotemba, past a row of shops, and out along a straight road in the direction of Mt. Fuji, the forests of which we could see through the gloom. After a minute or two the jeep slowed down and we turned sharp right through the gates of a military compound, attracting brisk salutes from the sentries. Right on time, at a quarter to five, we arrived at regimental headquarters, a long, nondescript building, into which we were quickly led, the two men from the *Ronso Journal* turning one way at the door, while I was led in the opposite direction, the sergeant carrying my weekend bag with the sweaters.

Once inside the building, I was led along a corridor to a door on which my escort knocked loudly. We entered a small office with a large desk. On the walls were a regimental standard and some plaques, one of which commended Chiimu-waaku in the large katakana letters which I had learned to read: "Teamwork." On one side of me was a big tank full of goldfish, and on the other an empty chair, placed in front of the desk. It was a comfortable military man's office. A man in uniform, whom I took to be the regimental commander, rose to meet me with a smile. As we shook hands he simultaneously produced from his breast pocket a small white meishi, the name card without which one is naked and a nobody in Japan. I played my meishi with my left hand, having also learned to do this trick some years before, and we examined one another's credentials. He was Hiroshi Fukamizu, the colonel in command of the infantry regiment based at Camp Fuji, and he was responsible for the Fuji military school. With the manner of a Japanese well accustomed to meeting foreigners, he gestured toward the empty chair at my side, and instructed the sergeant to leave my bag with me.

The third man in the room was Mishima. No matter how many times I met him, I was surprised by his small stature. He came up to above my shoulders, but he always seemed shy about his height, as if feeling dwarfed. That well-known head, with its heavy black brows, large staring eyes, and ears sticking out a fraction, seemed for a moment to sit ill upon his shoulders. He drew himself in, and we shook hands. I quickly accepted the colonel's invitation to be seated, and watched Mishima relax as he also took his chair and reached for a cigarette from a tin of Peace which he carried with him. He smiled as he surveyed my ski clothes and my boots. For my part, I was seeing him in the role of military man for the first time, clad in denims and brown polo-neck jersey, with his hair cut even shorter than usual; only short black bristles remained on his large skull.

The colonel, the greetings over, expressed doubts about my Henke boots. How far did I expect such objects to carry me in bad conditions, in deep snow? It was a question of getting used to them, I replied; I had bought them six years before, and I knew how heavy they were. Fukamizu smiled, not reassured, and diplomatically turned the conversation to the subject of the boots of his own men. The Jieitai budget was insufficient to cover necessary supplies, he said, and they were even short of boots at Camp Fuji. I could believe him: the gray-blue uniforms adopted almost twenty years before, the peeling paint on the outside of the build-ings, and the Willys Jeep all told the same story—lack of funds. If one compared the Japanese military budget with European defense budgets, it was small, at that time; but the real contrast was with the Americans, as their forces were on Japanese soil. It would take time to put things right, and get proper boots for his men, said Fukamizu, and Mi-shima agreed, puffing on his Peace cigarette.

At this point a bugle was sounded, and the commander rose from his seat behind the desk. It was 5 p.m., and time for the evening meal, Mishima explained. We trooped out behind the commanding officer, who led the way to a mess close by, where we were joined by half a dozen officers. The meal was one of fried prawns, with a delicious salad and hot soup. It was a special supper in my honor, I suspected—I was accumulating moral obligations, yet I was not Japanese and could spare myself the nice calculations which a Japa-nese must make under such circumstances (a familiar inter-nal dialogue for the foreigner in Japan). The talk at table was of local politics, but I listened to Mishima's translation with only one ear as I stoked myself up for the long night ahead; it might be our last hot meal for many hours. The officers talked about the situation in Gotemba, where a con-servative mayor had just been elected, and about the prob-lem of iriaiken, the rights of entry of farmers and foresters in-to land in use for military purposes around Mt. Fuji. On the northern side of the mountain there had been trouble at an artillery range where the farmers had interrupted firing practice. The farmers were being supported by the opposi-tion political parties in Tokyo and also by the national press. Here was the problem of the Jieitai in Japan in microcosm; the armed forces had no accepted place in postwar society.

It was to my great relief that I heard, finally, the news that the Tatenokai all-night exercise had been canceled because of the bad weather and the deep snow. Mishima's plans had for once been thwarted. It was the first time in our acquaintance that he had been forced to change his plans completely, but he took the reverse in his stride. In a loud voice he discussed the training program of the Tatenokai at the camp, equating Camp Fuji to Fort Benning in the United States. The comparison between the two leading military training establishments in the two countries was somewhat farfetched, as the latter is very much bigger, but Mishima, as usual, wanted everything to be larger than life, in accordance with his romantic view of the world. The Tatenokai training was going very well, he said. There were two parties at the camp, one of two dozen men doing a refresher course of one week, and a second which would be in the camp with him for an entire month. Mishima would boast how they ran a mile a day and marched twenty-eight miles a day, but they would not be doing so under these conditions. We were all being given a break, thanks to the weather.

I had escaped the all-night exercise after all, but Mishima had in store for me an experience which, if different, was quite as severe as scrambling about the forests of Mt. Fuji at night. After the evening meal he suggested that we pay a visit to the Tatenokai billeted nearby. We left the regimental headquarters and trudged through the snow. Lights were shining in a barracks close at hand, and Mishima led the way there, and along a corridor in the building. He stopped at a door, opened it briskly, and led us into the room beyond. It was full of young Japanese men in denims. Some sat at a long table close to us, and others were lying on their bunks, double-decker beds which occupied much of the room, where they were reading manga (comics) or chatting. This was an hour of relaxation, and there was none of the activity which I associated with a barracks, no polishing of boots or pressing of uniforms. One or two of the young men came forward and joined Mishima and me as we took our seats at the table by the door, and others moved into the background. This was no doubt by prearrangement; Mishima did not leave such things to chance.

I asked Mishima if I could put questions to the Tatenokai members, and he introduced me to the few who sat with us as Stokes-san of *The* (London) *Times*, taking a cigarette from his tin as he did so; he was going to translate for me. Most of the Tatenokai members were university students. This was the first fact which I established, talking to a twenty-two-year-old from Waseda University in Tokyo. I asked this youth, Ikebe, why he had joined the Tatenokai. His reply was that he had been attracted by what he described as Mishima's jintoku, a word which the writer translated as "personality." I should understand, he added, that the Tatenokai was not a code organization, by which I took him to mean that it was not secret, and in no way dangerous; Mishima's English was usually excellent, but on this occasion we were having translation problems. There was, I suspected, a second barrier to communication. I had the feeling that Mishima had briefed the students what to tell me, and that he had told them to say that the Tatenokai was not dangerous. Mishima, if this was so, had correctly anticipated that I had come to Camp Fuji with the idea that the Tatenokai was an extremist group; I did not like the movement, as I thought, simply, that it was right-wing.

The next student to whom I spoke took, however, a recognizably independent line of his own, and my reservations about the way the meeting was going disappeared. Mishima had introduced him as Morita; he was a twenty-three-year-old student from Waseda. Morita's appearance was not unusual in any way, and he made no impression on me at all; later I could not even remember what he looked like. He was serious and at first sight dull, and I put him down simply as a conscientious student who was playing a leading role in the Tatenokai. (When I looked at photographs of Morita later, after his suicide with Mishima, I could recall his features: the heavy jowls which one finds in a few Japanese faces, big lower jaws, thickening toward the ears and suggestive of strength of character. He was not good-looking; there was no trace of sensitivity about his heavy face, or any mark of intelligence on his brow. But there was no doubt about his strong personality; he was a born leader.)

Morita chatted about himself, giving a long explanation of his reasons for having joined the Tatenokai, in reply to my question. Too few people in Japan cared about the national interest, he said. At Waseda he had been shocked to find how active the Zengakuren students were, and how destructive their demonstrations at the university. He had also felt it wrong that they should be taken by the general public in Japan to be representative of students as a whole at Waseda. He had joined anti-Zengakuren student groups at the university, and had become the leader of one of these small organizations, the Counter-Protecting Club, as Mishima translated its name from the Japanese. This move had not given him satisfaction, as such student groups actually did very little; and he had read the works of Japanese nationalist writers to enhance his understanding of the situation. Once again his efforts had been frustrated, however. He had not been able to develop himself as a man, and he had turned, eventually, to the Tatenokai to study military techniques. He concluded by saying, via Mishima, who used the third person in translating: "In his way he wants to follow Mishima . . . Mishima is related to the Emperor."

I asked Morita what he meant by these words, and in particular what was the meaning of the expression "related to the Emperor." In what way was his leader linked with the Emperor, in his view? Morita appeared troubled and confused when Mishima translated my questions back to him. He looked about him as if at a loss for a reply, and for a while it seemed that he was going to say nothing. When his answer came, it may have been meaningless; the phrases which Mishima translated were, in any case, disconnected. Morita talked of "Japanese culture" and "his own emotions"; it was through these that he could grasp "the relation between the Emperor and Mishima's mentality." Books had been of no assistance in this process; he had "never tried to catch through book reading" what he understood by feeling. As for Mishima, Morita praised him because "he keeps a sense of tradition," "not through politics" but by his own "personal approach."

Hard as it was to understand Morita, I thought I could grasp his two main points. The first was the importance of the concept of the Emperor to the Tatenokai; the second, his strong personal feeling toward Mishima. It was the first point which interested me. If Emperor-worship was central to the Tatenokai, then the organization *had* to be taken seriously, and was not a toy of Mishima's. (As a matter of course, those who exalt the Emperor in postwar Japan are assumed by most Japanese to be heirs to the tradition of the militarists of the 1930's.)

My feeling was that if the Emperor was the central value of the Tatenokai, as Mishima's choice of the name of the organization had suggested in the first place, and as Morita was asserting, then the organization *was* a dangerous one. Emperor-worship had once before in this century led Japan along the path of war, and it was hardly desirable that militarism should be revived. Worship of the Emperor had supplied both a motive and a justification for the most grave actions: the annexation of Korea in 1910; the invasion of Manchuria in 1931 and the creation of the independent republic of Manchukuo; the invasion of northern China in 1937; and finally the attacks against the Allies in December 1941, which had precipitated the Pacific War. Behind these acts of aggression had lain a form of Emperor-worship which had poisoned men's minds. If the Tatenokai was imbued with the wartime spirit, then my suspicions had been amply confirmed. And yet I felt that it could not be as simple as that, not in 1969, and with Mishima involved.

Morita's second point had been his strong feeling for Mishima as an individual. I could not easily understand at the time, however, what he was saying, or, beyond that, what could be Mishima's role as leader of the Tatenokai. It was natural that much younger men should look up to Mi-

shima. He was twenty years older than the oldest of the Tatenokai students; he had been educated before and during
the war; and he shared their presumably nationalistic views,
unlike most of his contemporaries. It was not surprising that
they should admire one of the best-known men in Japan.
What was puzzling was the relation which Morita had insisted on, between the Emperor and Yukio Mishima. The
student leader was a prosaic-seeming person in his way, and
Mishima a careful translator; there could be no doubt that
Morita had twice spoken of such a relation. Mishima was the
only person, I reasoned, who could have put such an idea
into the heads of the Tatenokai members; *he* must have told
the students this, persuading them that in some mysterious
way he was connected with the Emperor. The question was
how one of Mishima's great intelligence had put this point
to the students. However he had done it, I had the feeling
that it was in this manner that he had secured the affections
of such a stolid student as Morita, and those of other
members of the Tatenokai, who had been willing to follow
Mishima to Camp Fuji.

After the talk with Morita and a few others, Mishima
suggested that we pay a visit to the second group of Tatenokai members, those who had come to Camp Fuji for an
entire month, and were comparative newcomers to the
group. Mishima took me along to them then. We found the
students in a long room similar to the one we had just left;
there was the same high ceiling, rows of bunks, and young
Japanese in denims sitting on the beds talking to one another. I decided not to ask questions this time, and Mishima
started to tell me about some of the students in the room
with us. They were, I noticed, paying attention to our conversation, and listening to what Mishima said; unusual for
Japanese students, some of them could follow English. One
student, said Mishima, had waited for two nights outside the
Imperial Palace to be the first of 200,000 to sign the Emperor's book at the New Year. The students around us listened carefully, and I felt that they were a much more lively
and intelligent group than those with whom we had just

been talking. One of them asked me: "Do you think that war must come every twenty years? Quite recently more and more students have wanted to fight, just look at the streets of Tokyo . . . What do you think about it?" Giving a brief answer, I asked the student his opinion of the Zengakuren, hoping to provoke my questioner.

"They are very childish," one of the students said in a loud voice. There was a little burst of applause. "We have guns," said another, "and all they have are gewabo"; he referred to the Gewalt sticks carried by the left-wing students during their street battles with the police. Mishima at once qualified what he had said, adding that, although the Tatenokai might carry rifles in the camp, they were not permitted to fire them, under Jieitai regulations. The students were chattering loudly, and the room became distinctly noisy; some unfriendly faces looked down on me from the bunks, and other students laughed and joked as they looked across at us, sitting at a table. Mishima introduced me to the student who had waited outside the Imperial Palace for two nights, Tanaka from Asia University. "Why did you wait for two days and nights outside the palace?" I asked him. Mishima almost had to shout so I would hear the reply: "Because he respects and loves the Emperor from his heart." Others were shouting, too. "Don't compare us to the Sampa," said a tall student in English—Fukuda from Waseda University—referring to the most militant of the Zengakuren factions, the Sampa Zengakuren. My answer should have been that Mishima himself had made such a comparison when talking about the spirit of the Tatenokai; but for a moment I was lost for a reply. "What do *you* think of the Tatenokai?" the tall student shouted. "Are you terrified of us?" "Yes, I am scared to death," I replied, wondering if I did not mean what I said. There was something odd about this tense questioning, an atmosphere of sexual excitement amid all the shouting.

I had been in Japan for almost five years, but I had not encountered a reception like this before. It was usually hard to get much of a response from a group of Japanese at a first meeting; the first Tatenokai contingent had been typical in this respect: slow and stodgy and hard. The second group could not have been more different. "Are you a gaijin spy?" shouted one, using the word for "foreigner," gaijin, which has either a familiar or a pejorative meaning, when used by an adult. There was more laughter and chattering among the Tatenokai students, and also one or two distinctly sour faces. "Gaijin spy! Gaijin spy!" Some were treating it as a joke, and others definitely not.

It was a hard experience to analyze, but at the back of my mind there lay the question: What was the meaning of the Emperor to this second group of Tatenokai? It was as if Mishima read my thoughts. Sitting close to me at the table, he said: "In the Tatenokai, A relates to B, and B relates to me, and I to the Emperor." It was precisely what he must have told the Tatenokai members. And he added: "The whole thing is built on personal relationships." I did not have the wit at that moment to ask Mishima how his personal relationship with the Emperor had been established. I felt fuddled and ill at ease. "You all scare me to death," I tried to joke once more, and I half meant it. "That boy," said Mishima, pointing to a student, "has been arrested eight times by the police for attacking Sampa barricades."

Before I left the barracks that night, I talked to Mishima about the organization of the Tatenokai. He told me then that the finances were entirely borne by him. The students bought their train tickets and paid for travel; and the Jieitai gave them free accommodations at the barracks, and also paid for such items as petrol for the armored personnel carriers which they used at Camp Fuji. Apart from this, the entire burden fell on Mishima. For this reason, he said, the organization would have to remain small; the membership would go no higher than a hundred. He also told me about the recruiting of the Tatenokai. Almost all the members were students, as students, unlike working men, had time to train with the Jieitai for a month at a time. The first-year members were found through advertisements in the *Ronso Journal* and through Mochimaru, the student leader of the

Tatenokai. The requirements were stiff, he stated; only five out of 150 applicants were admitted the first year. The second-year members were brought in through personal introduction, though Mishima had also put a notice on the board at Waseda University. That was after the Tatenokai became publicly known, in the autumn of 1968, when it was formally inaugurated and the first report about it appeared in a Tokyo magazine.

Shortly after eight I left the barracks, driven by jeep to the Fujimotoya, which turned out to be very near the gates of the camp. In two minutes I was back in what I thought of as the real world. After being greeted by an elderly maid in the hall, I took my shoes off and was led along the ice-cold corridors which one expects in a Japanese ryokan (inn) in winter to my room. There I quickly changed into a yukata gown, with the maid assisting me, folding up my ski clothes. With an effort I managed to conceal the fat haragake about my waist; I was not anxious to be the laughingstock of the village, the funny foreigner with the haragake. Was the Fujimotoya busy at this time of year, I asked. "Botsu botsu," replied the old woman—"Not very"—and hurried me down the icy corridors once more to the bath. I slipped off my yukata, all set for a long soak, and taking note of the inscription in English that read: DO NOT SOAP IN THE BATH. I was surrounded in that inn by the tiny problems raised by the foreigner in Japan: normal problems, real people. When I returned to my room, I found that the mattress on the tatami floor had been made up with a small brown blanket obstinately tucked between the sheets, Japanese-style; I removed the blanket, and got into bed. Thank goodness I was not on Mt. Fuji at that hour.

When I arrived back at the camp the next morning just before seven, I found that a full-day exercise had been planned. It had been decided that Mishima and I would play the parts of local collaborators, or spies. We would lead a column of Tatenokai guerrillas through enemy territory, and finally make an attack on an enemy camp. I summoned up memories of military training at an English public school fifteen years before; essentially, this was to be an exercise in map reading, moving across ground, and attack. I would observe from the perspective of my training in the Winchester College Cadet Corps. Images of flank attacks and smoke-bomb charges flitted through my mind, and a recollection of my last field exercise, at the age of eighteen, lying in a wood in East Anglia, being tormented by flies.

The weather was extraordinary. Instead of the murky skies of the day before, they were a brilliant blue, not a trace of a cloud anywhere. The air was dry and cold, and the snow sparkled everywhere. Above the camp there was a great sheet of snow stretching up to the forests a mile or two away; and beyond the trees was Mt. Fuji, looking very high, inaccessible, and sacred; it formed a pointed white triangle against the blue. This was as close as I had ever been to the mountain, a more or less extinct volcano which had not erupted since the eighteenth century. Could anything be more magnificent? What I longed to do was climb Mt. Fuji on skis, wearing a fine pair of sealskins, and then ski slowly down in what would surely be superb powder, but it might be lost in a day. There was no prospect of any such thing, and I was afraid we would get no farther up the mountain that day than the tree line, which at six thousand feet was halfway up Mt. Fuji. On skis it could easily have been done, but without them the going would be slow.

I had found Mishima in his little room at the barracks, and after coffee and a chat about the novel *Spring Snow*, which had just been published, he led me outside, where we waited for a jeep to pick us up. Mishima had dressed for the role of spy with a good deal more care than I had anticipated. He wore a pair of blue jeans with a fashionable fade, and gaiters to keep the snow out of his plain army boots. He had also put on a black leather jacket, a double-breasted, belted garment of the kind he had once worn to play the lead in a gangster film, *Karakkaze Yaro*. His chief ornament on this occasion, however, was a big khaki-brown hat. It was round, the shape of the head, and lined with white fur. Two heavy flaps of white fur hung down over the ears, and he was letting these fly in the air as he exercised in the brilliant morning sun to keep warm. The flaps jumped and swung as he leaped into the front seat of the jeep, telling me to get into the back with a sergeant. We left the compound and went east, traveling along a narrow road that had been cleared of snow, with Mt. Fuji on our left.

Soon we arrived at our rendezvous point. There we would meet the Tatenokai column which had set out from the barracks before us, on foot. We were then to take over as guides, according to the exercise plan. We had some time to wait, and the sergeant, who carried a poacher's sack, took dry wood from it and busied himself with a fire. Mishima chatted to me about the nationalist leader, Masaharu Kageyama, as we warmed our backs against the fire. As I listened to the curious tale of how the supporters of this person had committed hara-kiri to the last man at the end of the Pacific War, and how Kageyama had refrained from following them, the Tatenokai came in sight, walking slowly up the road toward us. They were well equipped for their roles as guerrillas, I had to admit. Some had walkie-talkie sets, a model known as a P-6, which had a long, waving aerial. Everyone in the group, a dozen or more men, carried the 1964-type Japanese army rifle, a good weapon; and on their heads they wore American-style fiber helmets. Mishima and I swung in line in front of the Tatenokai, and the sergeant, who was the one among us who knew the ground, led the way. We began to trudge up the narrow road, straight toward Mt. Fuji. The students were at first spread out; but as the road dwindled to a narrow path and the snow got deeper, we began to plunge in up to our waists, and the students started to follow one after another in the holes made by the energetic sergeant. Even so it was slow, and it took us more than two hours to reach the forest ahead, where we stopped in the first trees, a scattering of silver birches. We were going no farther than this up Mt. Fuji.

It was time for lunch, and I noticed that an army vehicle had managed to come up behind us with supplies; there must have been an easy road. From the lorry a number of officers descended, clad in white anoraks, to distinguish them from the rest of us; they were the referees of our little war game. The officers did not join Mishima and me at lunch, but went over to the Tatenokai, who had settled down in the woods nearby, leaving us to have an honorable picnic on our own, served by the sergeant. The latter cleared the ground and spread blankets for us on the snow. He then placed in front of us large tin trays with a great deal of food. It was a nourishing Japanese meal, mainly sekihan, glutinous rice with little red beans, a special dish. Bottles of soy sauce were brought out, and stuck in the snow by us, and the feast began. Mishima was a fast eater and swallowed the rice in mouthfuls at a time; it went straight down in mighty gobs. But the rice would not go down my throat; draughts of hot green tea would not send it on its way either. When Mishima finished his bowl of sekihan, I was still only one tenth of the way through mine: how did the design of his throat differ from mine? Swallowing more green tea brought by the sergeant, I got down about a third of the sekihan, but it was out of the question to do more. I got up from my blanket and, with an apology, scooped a hole in the snow and disposed of my sekihan, burying the feast.

Mishima glanced over his shoulder at me and said nothing, but there was no doubt, from the sour expression on his face, that I had made a blunder. There is a difference in kind between the English and the Japanese idea of a picnic, of which I had not been aware. Mishima was untypically quiet, suspending his chatter about Yomeigaku, a neo-Confucian school of philosophy, and the sins of Professor Masao Maruyama, the political scientist, whom he had been accusing of having failed to study Yomei. I felt like a dog who has offended his master, and who must wait mutely for pardon to be granted. The time would come when we would move away from the spot I had polluted, and in the meantime I would be made to suffer. Shortly afterward, to my relief, everyone began to move around and prepare for departure. Marching through the deep snow brought warmth back to our bodies, and Mishima seemed to regain his former good spirits. He trudged in front, visible only from the knees up, and casting his eyes about him. The weather was still perfect, the snow flat, level, and undisturbed, as if there were little animal life around us. There was an occasional rumble of artillery from the range on the other side of Mt. Fuji, and from time to time helicopters would pass overhead on their way to one of the Japanese or American bases close to us. But for most of the time we were undisturbed, and could enjoy the walk.

Mishima looked up toward Mt. Fuji, around which one or two clouds had begun to form at a high altitude, increasing the beauty of the mountain. There was no sound but that of our feet crunching through the snow, and an occasional swoosh as someone knocked snow off the branch of a tree. We were small black and brown figures in a vast expanse of white; in this deep snow we seemed to swim and then to fall back rather than to make progress. Mishima swung his head around and began to shout across the snow at me: "It's a good excuse to walk in this beautiful snow. If you go alone, you feel crazy." As he turned back, and bounced forward in his stride again, the earpieces of his hat spun in the air, jumping and banging against the sides of his close-shaven head. The sun caught the white fur, as if he had two great dandelion clocks dancing over his shoulders.

We were coming close to our target, the enemy camp, but the entire party seemed careless of this fact, infected by good spirits. The Tatenokai members trudged along in a line in the open; making no effort to spread out or to conceal themselves, they were in fact all bunched together close to the edge of the forest. Vague memories of the Meads at Winchester and of schoolmasters shouting "Spread out" came to my mind. Did one not spread out, in case we all were machine-gunned at once? Was this not one of the most basic rules? It occurred to me that in fact we *were* just going for a walk; it *was* "a good excuse to walk in this beautiful snow." Even the army officers who were with us seemed to take it all in a most lighthearted way. They waded along in the snow parallel to us, in their white anoraks and dark glasses, chatting and laughing; they might have been ski instructors. I recalled the conversation I had had with Mishima that morning over coffee; he had compared the Tatenokai to the Zengakuren and had asserted that the former had more "spirit" and were closer to the "samurai spirit." Yet it had to be admitted that the Zengakuren fought, while the Tatenokai only trained; and the standard of training, even, was low. It seemed that the Tatenokai had little to do with the traditional samurai, except in the romantic ideals of their leader; he wanted to be a kind of Japanese Lord Byron. Indeed, that morning he had talked with envy of Byron, how the poet had been able to afford to gather three hundred men in his service and repair ships.

We had been following the lower edge of the forests for about two hours, when an order came via the army instructors that Mishima and I were to detach ourselves from the guerrilla column and make our way to the enemy camp. From there we would view the final assault by the Tatenokai on the enemy position. When we arrived at this point, well in advance of the students, we found that the army NCOs who occupied the camp had built a couple of rough igloos and a snow wall, keeping themselves warm in the process; it was a snug place. For a long time we waited; sometimes there were shouts, and we would catch sight of an army instructor. It was late afternoon when the attack finally came. Streaming down a nearby hill, the students came on at us in twos and threes, while smoke bombs fizzed in the snow. They had all been "dead men" at a range of two hundred yards, the way they had come over the skyline, but on they advanced, making no attempt to keep low, exposed to "fire" in the form of thunderflashes hurled from our igloos. When they eventually struggled through the snow, already tired, they were set upon by the NCOs, who wrestled them to the ground and ripped off their boots in a flash, trussing them up tightly, one to another. Mishima joined in the skirmish, and rolled over in the snow, shrieking with laughter as he grappled with the sergeant. It was all over in ten minutes.

After our long walk through the snow, we were ready for baths, and I returned to the inn to rest until the evening meal. I passed the time making notes and phoning Tokyo; shortly before five, I left the inn and walked up to the camp. Our meal was to be a farewell party for the senior Tatenokai members, who had completed their refresher course. At the camp gate I was directed to the NCOs' mess, where the feast was to take place. I arrived there first and found a room full of tables and chairs with places already set and food put out. There were nests of beer bottles and soft drinks and a quantity of sandwiches. In one corner of the room was a jukebox and on the wall a calendar with a picture of a buxomy blonde. Wishing to be as inconspicuous as possible, I seated myself at a table in the corner of the room and waited for the Tatenokai to arrive. We would be a large party, fifty in all.

One by one the Tatenokai students came clattering in, and at five exactly Mishima followed them, dancing into the room in denims. The meal began, beer was passed around and chased with saké or Japanese whisky, and before long there were red faces everywhere. As the students shouted and gesticulated, the jukebox was drowned out. One after another the students rose to sing songs, all joining in the chorus. There were ballads of cherry blossoms, kamikaze pilots, gangsters, and Yamato Damashii, the spirit of old Japan. Mishima stood in the center of the room, while the others remained in their chairs. He rose and led the choruses, passing the stubs of his cigarettes to his acolytes to be put in the ashtrays. There was obviously a good deal of hero worship here. Everyone was a little tipsy; and my neighbor, an intellectual student with glasses who had arrived late, speared pink cocktail sausages with his chopsticks with vicious swipes. Song followed song, and finally at seven o'clock Mishima declared an end to the party, calling for three banzai for the Tatenokai. Everyone got to their feet, my neighbor and I with them, and the national anthem was sung. At the close my companion turned toward me and seized my hand, pumped it hard, and said: "I love England," a sentence which he twice repeated.

When I woke the next day, I felt far from lively. The weather had changed again; it was a close, muggy day with clouds, a lot warmer than the day before. I had to breakfast quickly, and leave the inn before I was properly awake, to be at the barracks by 7:30. Though this was the last day at the camp, I had not thought out the questions I must put to Mishima before we parted. It was too early in the morning for that, and we still had time; Mishima and I were not to leave the camp until midday, when we would return to Tokyo by train together.

I had been summoned to the camp at this early hour to witness a Tatenokai ceremonial parade. It was to take place in a large building close to the entrance of the camp. Normally, it would have been staged on the regimental parade ground in the open air, but the snow was too slushy for that. I walked into the building and found there a number of Tatenokai members forming up in their yellow-brown uniforms; there were also army NCOs and one or two officers. Mishima came up to me; he was also dressed in the Tatenokai uniform with its large cap and badge composed of ancient kabuto (samurai helmets). We discussed briefly—he was short of time—where I should stand to observe the proceedings. I favored an inconspicuous position to the side; but Mishima wanted me in the front, on the extreme left, where I would see the whole parade, the rostrum from which the colonel would speak, and also the brass band which was just then forming up. The NCOs then held a short rehearsal, with Mishima standing by; he did not give orders, it seemed, either on exercises or on parade at Camp Fuji. The twenty-five men on parade were kept at attention for only a couple of minutes, but, to my surprise, two of them keeled over, and had to be carried away. The atmosphere was too close; I felt uncomfortable myself.

At eight o'clock precisely the Tatenokai were brought to attention once more, and Colonel Fukamizu made his entrance from the far side of the hut, accompanied by officers. An order was given, and the entire parade faced in my direction. As the national anthem was played—and it seemed to last for an interminable time—twenty-five pairs of Tatenokai eyes looked through me. I realized what was going on. The students had faced toward Tokyo; that was where the Emperor lived. It was just unfortunate that I, clad in ski clothes, none the more elegant for three days of continuous wear, happened to be in the line of fire. Should I also have made a gesture, by turning in the direction of the Imperial presence? I contemplated the idea for a second, but it was too late . . . I cursed Mishima for having overlooked what would happen. At last the anthem came to an end, and the parade again faced the front. This time the colonel took the salute, and as instructed by Mishima at the outset of the proceedings, I bowed twice in his direction, wondering whether this was really necessary. The colonel then inspected the parade (what *did* he make of those uniforms?), and took his place on the rostrum, from which he gave a short speech on riidashippu, on leadership. A few minutes later we were all trotting out of the hut into the open.

My visit to Camp Fuji was at an end. I waited for Mishima to tell me about our travel arrangements, watching him and the Tatenokai members in uniform line up outside the hut for the last time, to have their photographs taken. Mishima quickly arranged the men, putting the short ones in the middle, and ranging them so that the tallest students were at either end. Then he took his place in the center, and with Mt. Fuji showing through the clouds behind them, the picture was taken. Mishima was in a hurry, but we talked for a moment and he told me that there had been an incident the night before. At the end of the party they had held, a student had poured a bucket of water on the head of the sergeant. There had been tears and apologies, and the offender had been made to do fifty push-ups, with Mishima leading. It was this student and one other who had fainted that morning. Mishima then told me that he had changed the travel plans and had hired a taxi to take us back to Tokyo at midday; he would pick me up at the Fujimotoya.

I was grateful for this extravagant arrangement, which meant that I would have the opportunity to prepare my questions in advance, and would also be able to talk to Mishima without fear of interruption. I had seen two sides of the Tatenokai. In the evening, two days before, I had been exposed to all manner of wild ideological talk, centering on the Emperor and suggesting that the Tatenokai was an alarming organization, right-wing and nationalistic. The following day, when we had exercised in the snow, I had seen a completely different side of the organization. Essentially, the students were untrained, and unlikely to be effective as a force. My question, at the start of the proceedings, and before I had set foot in Camp Fuji, had been whether the Tatenokai was a right-wing group or simply a plaything; I had been inclined toward the former. Seeing the men in the field, however, had made me doubt my conclusion. My questions to Mishima must revolve around the problem— the nature of the Tatenokai: Fascist club or writer's toy? (Not that I thought the problem was to be easily resolved by questions, one way or the other. Nor did I think it was a matter of fundamental importance to Mishima himself, whose chief activity was writing.)

Just after midday Mishima arrived at the inn by car, and I piled into the back seat beside him. It was an expensive way of returning to Tokyo. We could have taken a train, which would also have been quicker—but that method of traveling evidently did not suit him that day. He was simply *sui generis.* For the occasion, he had dressed in the manner of one returning to the capital after a weekend in the country with friends: a beautiful tweed suit cut from English cloth, matching tie, and imported brown walking shoes. But to which capital did he think he was returning? What country were we in? Could there have been any other intellectual in Japan who would have gone to the trouble of so fitting himself out? Leaving aside the Tatenokai exercise, it was a culminating touch which only Mishima could have devised. His heavy baggage must have been left at the camp, for he had nothing but a small case with him; I had seen into the trunk of the car. Here was effortless superiority à la Mishima. What on earth was the point of questioning a man for whom style was obviously so much more important than anything else?

The interest of our drive back to Tokyo was the scenery. From the hills around Hakone we had our best view of Mt. Fuji; we had really been too close to the mountain at Gotemba to get the proportions right. As the Toyota taxi began to drop down toward Odawara, however, we were both in more of a mood to talk. And so I asked Mishima why he had created the Tatenokai. The Tatenokai, he replied, as our car began to run into heavy traffic above Odawara, was "the first example of a National Guard"; he was reaching for a phrase to express the essence of the organization—it was a show. He wanted to "inspire people with a sense of national pride," he said, as if imagining the sound of brass bands and cheering multitudes of onlookers. When talking to me, I realized, Mishima was inclined to stress that aspect of the Tatenokai which was personal to him, non-ideological and romantic, no more. I tried to press him on the right-wing nature of the organization, by asking him to confirm that it had unique training privileges with the Jieitai. Yes, this was true; the Tatenokai alone could exercise with guns. Tens of thousands of civilians passed through Jieitai camps, but they mostly stayed only a few days, under a holiday program designed for Jieitai public relations. They were not allowed to touch rifles. How had the exceptional arrangements been made for the Tatenokai, I asked. It had been very difficult, Mishima replied. He had had to see a great number of people in the Jieitai, senior generals, but in the end it had been arranged with the help of the civilian head of the Defense Agency, Kaneshichi Masuda—and, I suspected, the Prime Minister.

And what did the Tatenokai amount to, in practical terms? I put the question while we were stuck in slow-moving traffic. Mishima was trying to bully the driver into taking a short cut, and the man firmly replied that the expressway which Mishima wanted to take had not yet been opened to the public. Mishima fell back into his seat, shrugging his shoulders. Well, he wanted to increase the Tatenokai to a hundred members in all; and then each of his men might take charge of twenty, making a force large enough to take effective action. To stage a coup? I might have asked. But I did not put the question. I did not believe in such dreams. Talking to Mishima about the Tatenokai, one felt the conversation bordering on his dreams, and I again sensed that with me he would prefer to stress the personal aspect of the organization, not the ideological. It was hard to pin down a suitable question for Mishima. I adopted a different approach, and asked Mishima when he had decided to create the Tatenokai. It was after completing his book *Eirei no Koe* ("The Voices of the Heroic Dead"), he replied, "three or four years ago" (in June 1966). I had not read the work. As we passed on down the increasingly steep road, swinging around hairpin curves and under the boughs of great trees, Mishima began to talk instead of Goethe and his essay on suicide: "If literature is not a responsible activity, then action is the only course," he paraphrased.

As we left Odawara and reached the coastal expressway beyond, the car passed the first of the succession of big industrial plants which we would see on our return to the capital, still an hour away at least. There was no beach below us, only a dreary series of massive reinforced-concrete tetrapods, intended to break the force of the sea as it hit the mighty wall below us. "I believe in culture as form and not as spirit," said Mishima, referring to the theme of a drama on which he was then working, the story of the leprous Khmer monarch Jayavarman III and his building of one of the temples of Angkor Wat, Bayon. He seemed very tired as he talked. "I want to keep the Japanese spirit alive," he added, as if unaware that he was contradicting himself. His voice drifted on. The Emperor, he said, was "the supreme cultural form"; his "physical body" was *the* form of culture. In the unique Japanese Imperial institution, with its long tradition of poetry, he found the ultimate value. And he added: "I do not believe in the non-material, only in the actual." A few minutes later, he cradled his head in his left arm, leaning back in his seat, and fell fast asleep. The car sped swiftly on toward Tokyo, which we would reach in another half hour. I felt that I was worlds away from understanding this extraordinary person; and I, too, tried to sleep. From time to time I caught sight of buildings, new factories, other expressways. As we passed Chigasaki, there was an occasional pine tree to be seen by the road, still standing on what had once been the historic Old Tokaido Road to Osaka, three hundred miles to the west. That was all that was left of old Japan, perhaps—a few pine trees.

PART THREE
SAUNA BATHS AND SECRECY

A man of action is destined to endure a long period of strain and concentration until the last moment when he completes his life by his final action: death—either by natural causes or by hara-kiri.

Yukio Mishima
Essay on Hagakure, 1967

A month after his return from training with the Tatenokai at Camp Fuji, Mishima was invited to take part in an open debate with ultra-left-wing students at his old university, Todai. Mishima went to the hall where the debate was held—in the Komaba grounds of Todai—wearing a black shirt with a string front; outside the hall he found a large cartoon on a billboard depicting him as a gorilla. Both he and his student hosts were in an aggressive mood and the two and a half hour debate between them was a success, as entertainment. The Todai students, prompted by Mishima, showed a remarkable interest in the subject of the Emperor:

STUDENT: Mishima writes a great deal about the Emperor. The reason for this is that the Emperor does not exist. His non-existence constitutes absolute beauty for Mishima. Why, then, does he play the fool all the time? He should stick to aesthetics. Instead, he starts fooling around and the beauty which the Emperor embodies is thus destroyed.

MISHIMA: I am touched by your patriotic remarks. You want to keep your beautiful image of the Emperor and for that purpose wish me to remain in my study . . . (*Laughter*)

ANOTHER STUDENT: I want to ask you about the Emperor. If he happens to fall in love with a woman other than the Empress, what should he do? He must be restricted in so many ways. One must feel sympathy for him.

MISHIMA: But I really think the Emperor had better keep mistresses . . . (*Laughter*)

(Taken from a verbatim record published by Shinchōsha in 1969)

Mishima had a moment of paranoia when he approached the hall at Komaba, fearing that the students would seize and murder him on the spot. Afterward he remarked: "I was as nervous as if I was going into a lions' den, but I enjoyed it very much after all. I found we have much in common—a rigorous ideology and a taste for physical violence, for example. Both they and I represent new species in Japan today. I felt friendship for them. We are friends between whom there is a barbed-wire fence. We smile at one another but we can't kiss." He also commented: "What the Zengakuren students and I stand for is almost identical. We have the same cards on the table, but I have a joker—the Emperor."

I had numerous discussions with Mishima about events in Japan at this time, and in midsummer I asked him if he would write a short article for me, summing up his thoughts. I proposed to send this to *The Times* in London. In the middle of August he told me that the piece was ready and invited me down to Shimoda, where he was staying with his family for the summer holidays. I was there for a couple of days, swimming with the Mishimas on the beach, and returned to Tokyo with his contribution for *The Times*.

The article, which was published on September 24,

1969, was a crystallization of our conversations and one of the clearest summaries Mishima ever made of his "political" views:

Not long ago, in early August, a young Japanese tried to attack the American Secretary of State, Mr. William Rogers, with a knife, at Tokyo airport. The reaction of the Japanese press was to heap abuse on this individual and totally to condemn his action.

The man explained that he had intended to injure an American representative by way of retaliation; Japanese who took part in the anti-American [military] base campaign on Okinawa had been wounded by American bayonets, he claimed. He had held no personal grudge against Rogers, he said. Nor had he belonged to any right-wing organization.

I do not myself support terrorism; nor do I support the spirit of this young man's action. However, the fact that every Japanese newspaper heaped abuse on him, all displaying the same hysterical reaction, interests me a great deal. Whatever the political persuasion of the paper—left, neutral, right-wing—the reaction was the same. Such hysteria is displayed only by people who have something to hide. Just what is the Japanese press trying to hide under all this anger and abuse?

Let us look back a little. For the past one hundred years the Japanese have been making enormous efforts to make their country a paradigm of Western civilization. This unnatural posture has betrayed itself many times; the cloven hoof has been all too visible! After the Second World War, people thought that Japan's biggest defect had been exposed. Thereafter, Japan came to rank among the leading industrial nations and need no longer fear self-betrayal. All that is felt to be necessary is for our diplomats to advertise Japanese culture as peace-loving—symbolized by the tea ceremony and by ikebana, flower arrangement.

In 1960 when Inejiro Asanuma, chairman of the Socialist Party, was assassinated in Tokyo, I was in Paris. Asanuma was stabbed to death by a seventeen-year-old right-winger, Otoya Yamaguchi; the boy killed himself almost immediately afterward in jail. At that time the Moulin Rouge in Paris was showing a Revue japonaise which included a sword-fight scene. The Japanese Embassy in Paris hurriedly proposed to the Moulin Rouge that the scene should be cut from the revue, in order that "misunderstanding" be avoided. Fear of misunderstanding is sometimes fear of disclosure.

I always recall the Shinpuren Incident of 1877 —that incident which retains today among Japanese intellectuals the reputation of having displayed Japanese fanaticism and irrationality; a shaming thing, indeed, which should not be known to foreigners. The incident occurred during a revolt led by about one hundred stubborn, conservative, chauvinistic former samurai. They hated all things Western, and regarded the new Meiji government with hostility as an example of the Westernization of Japan. They even held white fans over their heads when they had to pass beneath electric lines, saying that the magic of the West was soiling them.

These samurai resisted all forms of Westernization. When the new government enacted a law abolishing swords, collecting up these very symbols of samurai spirit, one hundred rebels attacked a Westernized Japanese army barracks with nothing but their swords and spears. Many were shot down by rifles—imported from the West; and all the survivors committed hara-kiri.

Arnold Toynbee wrote in *A Study of History* that nineteenth-century Asia had only these alternatives: to accept the West and to survive after complete surrender to Westernization; or to resist and perish. This theory is correct, without exception.

Japan, in fact, built a modern and united nation by accepting Westernization and modernization. During this process the most striking pure act of resistance was

that of the Shinpuren revolt. Other resistance movements were more political, lacking the ideological purity and cultural element of Shinpuren.

Thus Japanese ability to modernize and to in-
novate, sometimes in an almost cunning way, came to
be highly praised—while other Asian peoples could be
looked down on for their laziness. Yet people in the
West understood little of the sacrifices that the Japanese
were obliged to make.

Rather than attempting to learn about this reality,
the West prefers to stick to the idea of the yellow peril,
sensing intuitively something dark and ominous in the
Asian soul. What is most exquisite in a national culture
is tied closely to what may also be most disagreeable—just as in Elizabethan tragedy.

Japan has tried to show only one side of herself,
one side of a moon, to the West, while pushing on bus-
ily with modernization. In no era of our history have
there been such great sacrifices of the totality of culture—which must embrace lightness and darkness
equally.

In the first twenty years of my life, national culture
was controlled by the unnatural Puritanism of the militarists. For the past twenty years, pacifism has been sitting heavily on the samurai spirit, a burden on the easily
stimulated "Spanish" soul of the Japanese. The hypocrisy of the authorities has permeated the minds of the
people, who can find no way out. Wherever national
culture seeks to regain its totality, almost insane incidents occur. Such phenomena are interpreted as the
undercurrent of Japanese nationalism, intermittently
bursting out like lava through cracks in a volcano.

Conspicuous radical action of the kind taken recently by the youth at Tokyo airport may be explained
in such terms. Yet few people notice that both the right
and the left wing in Japan are exploiting nationalism
under all kinds of international masks. The anti-Viet-
nam War movement in Japan was predominantly left-

wing, and yet appealed strongly to nationalism—a strange kind of nationalism by proxy. Until the war began, few Japanese would even have known where Vietnam was.

Nationalism is used one way or another for political purposes, and thus people often lose sight of the fact that nationalism is basically a problem of culture. On the other hand, the hundred samurai who attacked a modern army barracks with swords alone recognized this fact. Their reckless action and inevitable defeat were necessary to show the existence of a certain essential spirit. Their ideology was a difficult one; it was the first radical prophecy of the danger inherent in Japanese modernization, which must damage the totality of culture. The painful condition of Japanese culture, which we feel today, is the fruit of what could only be vaguely apprehended by Japanese at the time of the Shinpuren Incident.

What was Mishima to do with his Tatenokai? On November 3 he invited a few foreign correspondents, including me, to witness the only public parade ever staged by his private army. It was held on the roof of the National Theater on a cold, blustery day. A striped tent had been put up on the roof of the building and chairs had been placed there for the VIP's who were to attend. One by one the dignitaries arrived. There was a scattering of senior officers from the Jieitai, among them a retired general who took the salute. Then the Tatenokai members streamed onto the roof in their yellow-brown uniforms. While Mishima watched from the side of the parade ground—a slim, short figure in his tight-fitting uniform—Morita gave the orders. For several minutes the men marched back and forth across the roof; they were inspected by the general. At the end of the parade, all faced east across the moat of the Imperial Palace, which runs below the National Theater, and gave a salute to His Majesty. Thereafter, everyone came downstairs into the theater, where a reception was held. While his audience nibbled at sandwiches, Mishima gave two short speeches, one in Japanese and a second, identical one in English, from which I took notes:

> My reason for creating the Tatenokai is simple. Ruth Benedict once wrote a famous book, *The Chrysanthemum and the Sword*. Such are the characteristics of Japanese history: the chrysanthemum and the sword. After the war the balance between these two was lost. The sword has been ignored since 1945. My ideal is to restore the balance. To revive the tradition of the samurai, through my literature and my action. Therefore, I asked the Jieitai to give my men basic training, one month at a time.
>
> The Jieitai is composed of volunteers. A quarter of a million men is insufficient to defend this country. Therefore, some civilian cooperation is necessary. This is needed because twentieth-century war is fought by guerrillas; this is a new type of warfare, conducted by irregulars . . . My ideal is to give Japan a system like the Swiss system of military service.

Early in December 1969, Mishima set off for South Korea. The purpose of his journey was to see the South Korean Army in action. On his return he wrote to me that he was irritated by the calm situation he found in Korea. He said he had been to the east coast to see the place where guerrillas had landed from the north, the training of anti-guerrilla forces, and the coast-guard militia. The YS-II plane which had taken him back to Seoul was hijacked to North Korea the following day. If only, he said, he had been kidnapped to North Korea, he wouldn't be so bored. This letter gave a misleading impression of his actual state of mind. He was, in fact, secretly keying himself up to take the plunge, to organize the miniature coup d'état and his hara-kiri. So much is clear from a remark made in a discussion in December 1969 with a friend, Ichiro Murakami, which appeared in 1970 in a volume entitled *Shobu no Kokoro* ("The Soul of the Warrior"). Mishima said—his words were hardly ambiguous: "One has to take responsibility for what one says once one has said it. The same is true of the written word. If one writes: 'I will die in November,' then one has to die. If you make light of words once, you will go on doing so."

Early in April 1970, Mishima secretly formed the group of students within the Tatenokai who assisted him in his twentieth-century version of the Shinpuren Incident. The members of this group were—in addition to Morita— Masayoshi Koga and Masahiro Ogawa, both twenty-one and students at universities in Tokyo. Chibi-Koga, as he was known to other members of the Tatenokai (the nickname served to distinguish him from another Koga in the Tatenokai), was the only son of a tangerine farmer from Arita in Wakayama prefecture; his father died in 1953 and his mother brought him up alone. She introduced the boy at twelve to a religious organization with a strong nationalist creed, the Seicho no Ie, and he developed right-wing views. He met Mishima in August 1968 and became a member of the Tatenokai after completing a month's training at Camp Fuji; he was made a section leader in April 1969. Chibi-Koga was tiny but energetic; he was devoted to the Tatenokai and completely trusted by Mishima and Morita. Masahiro Ogawa was a different kind of youth, the son of an office employee, who lived at Chiba, close to Tokyo. He was Morita's closest friend and Morita introduced him to Mishima; he was made a section leader of the Tatenokai in April 1970. Tall and pale, with a toothbrush moustache, Ogawa was the standard-bearer of the Tatenokai; but although he made a conspicuous figure on parade, he was physically weak. This group of four—Mishima, Morita, Koga, and Ogawa—met in secret, frequently changing their rendezvous to avoid arousing the slightest suspicion. And they began to lay their plans.

The chief planners were Mishima and Morita. At the beginning of April, Mishima met Chibi-Koga at a coffee shop in the Imperial Hotel and asked him if he was willing to commit himself "to the very end"—without explaining what he was talking about. Chibi-Koga immediately agreed.

A week later Mishima put the same question to Ogawa at his home in the suburbs of Tokyo; Ogawa hesitated and then agreed. In the middle of May, in the course of another meeting at his home, Mishima proposed to the three students that the Tatenokai, as a whole, should stage an uprising with the help of the Jieitai and occupy parliament; then they would call for revision of the Constitution. Mishima, however, was vague and seemed to have no precise plan of action. About three weeks later, on June 13, Mishima again met the three students—this time in room 821 at the Hotel Okura. He explained that they would have to carry out their plan by themselves, they could not rely on the Jieitai (presumably he had made soundings within the Jieitai, with discouraging results). Mishima then proposed a 180-degree change in course; instead of acting with the army, they would attack the army. He was still very much at sea as to their plans, however, and came up with a number of proposals. One idea was to attack a Jieitai arsenal. Another suggestion was to take an army general hostage—he proposed that their target might be a very senior general who had his HQ at a place of historical importance to the Imperial Army of prewar days, General Kanetoshi Mashita, commander of the Eastern Army at Ichigaya in central Tokyo. Mishima was trying to find a means of forcing a Jieitai command to assemble an audience of young soldiers. His ultimate aim was to make a speech to these soldiers—he had confidence in young soldiers and officers—and induce them to stage an uprising with him and his Tatenokai students.

I assume that Mishima had forced himself into a state of mind in which he could believe in this incredible scenario; at the same time there must have been some cold and logical element within him quietly asserting that he was talking rubbish. One can only make sense of Mishima's determination to ignore this contradiction if one assumes that his ultimate purpose was to die, and that the means by which he achieved this aim, provided that they had a theatrical quality, were not all that important. In any event, at this meeting Mishima and the students agreed that they would take hostage General Kanetoshi Mashita; they would do this at the second anniversary parade of the Tatenokai, to be held in November. And they would create the opportunity to seize the general by inviting him to review the parade.

The next meeting was held at another Western-style hotel in central Tokyo. This time Mishima chose a writers' hotel, the Yamanoue (Hill Top) Hotel. He summoned the group eight days after the meeting at the Okura. And his first move was to inform the students that he had got permission for the Tatenokai to hold an exercise on a heli-pad at the Ichigaya military base. He also said that they would change their target from General Mashita to the commander of the infantry regiment stationed at Ichigaya (which was under Mashita's ultimate authority), a Colonel Miyata, whose office was closer to the heli-pad than that of Mashita (this was an altogether more modest target). He also proposed that they use Japanese swords as their arms and asked Chibi-Koga to buy a car for their use, in which the swords would be carried into the base. Everyone agreed.

What really was Mishima's goal? The three students with him believed him to be an ardent patriot, but he was much more complicated than that. Mishima was on the verge of his final decision to commit hara-kiri. The timing of his decision can be exactly specified—for at the meeting at the Yamanoue he had proposed that the weapons they would use at Ichigaya would be swords. What he appreciated, I presume, is that there was no guarantee that he would die if he simply staged an attack within a Jieitai base (even if he used firearms); he realized that the army would not shoot him down or his men (since the war, the army has not been allowed to fire on civilians under any circumstances). Thus, he was brought to the decision to use swords in the attack at Ichigaya. Whatever happened there, with a sword in his hand and a dagger within reach, he could be virtually certain that he would die—by his own hand.

While all this was going on, I met Mishima, but I saw no sign of it. I met a different Mishima—the usual cordial and outgoing host. I saw him during his summer holidays at

Shimoda. Showing no particular sign of tension, he relaxed by the swimming pool, his body turned a dark brown by the sun; and he went to the beach with his family in the afternoon. One day there was a phone call from Shigeru Hori, the right-hand man to the Prime Minister, proposing a meeting with Mr. Sato. Another day Yasuhiro Nakasone, the head of the Defense Agency (which controls the Jieitai), telephoned to ask Mishima to address a group of his supporters—his faction within the ruling conservative party. I was surprised by these signs of Mishima's popularity with conservative politicians. Mishima was caustic about them. He denounced Nakasone as a fraud and said that he had no intention of going to see them. There was an element of shibai (theater) in all this.

His boisterous talk of suicide also seemed to be an act. As he lay by the pool, basking in the sun, confidently predicting the suicides of other writers (e.g., Truman Capote) and speculating about the mysterious deaths of writers (Saint-Exupéry, who he insisted had flown his plane straight out into the Atlantic until he crashed), it was unimaginable that he was serious. One night I accompanied the Mishimas to a yakuza, gangster, movie and he insisted over coffee afterward, standing up in a snack bar, that the yakuza were the only Japanese who still possessed the samurai spirit. I couldn't help feeling that he was being silly.

Behind this frivolous mask Mishima continued with his plotting. From Shimoda he kept constantly in touch with the three members of the Tatenokai group. He sent them to Hokkaido, the northern island of Japan, paying for their summer holiday. He also asked them to recruit one more member; he knew how small the group was for the task he envisaged. (He decided to take only one more, as he gave first priority to security.) His choice was Hiroyasu Koga, Furu-Koga; he was the son of a primary-school headmaster in Hokkaido, a lecturer at the Seicho no Ie headquarters, who had introduced him to right-wing thinking. He was twenty-three, a year older than Chibi-Koga and Ogawa; and he had just started studying to be a lawyer. On September 9

Mishima met him at a restaurant in the Ginza and told him the whole plan in confidence. Mishima said that it would be impossible to find Jieitai men who would rise with them, that he himself would have to die whatever happened. The date would be November 25.

On September 15 the five had dinner together at Momonjiya in Ryogoku, on their way back from watching a display of ninja-taikai, a feudal martial art performed by men in black garb—their art is to vanish into thin air. And ten days afterward they met at a sauna club in Shinjuku and Mishima said they must make firm arrangements for the monthly meeting in November. Tatenokai members who had relatives in the Jieitai must be excluded from the meeting; and he would personally sign all invitations. A week later they met at a Chinese restaurant in the Ginza, and Mishima described the plan in detail. The monthly meeting would start at 11 a.m. At 12:30 p.m., Mishima and Chibi-Koga would leave the meeting on the excuse that they had to attend a funeral. They would drive off and fetch the swords and also two reporters (friends of Mishima's), who would be waiting for them at the Palace Hotel—but would know nothing of the plan otherwise. They would return to Ichigaya and would park the car at the headquarters of the 32nd Infantry Regiment. The reporters would wait in the car. The group would then take Colonel Miyata hostage. By this time, the rest of the Tatenokai (the reduced contingent which had been invited for that day) would have started the exercise at the heli-pad. On October 9 the group held another meeting, from which Furu-Koga, who was traveling in Hokkaido—saying goodbye to his family—was absent. Ten days later they had a group portrait taken in full uniform at Tojo Hall, where wedding parties are the usual customers (Mishima joked to the others that the Tojo Hall cameramen had the art of making everybody look beautiful).

Mishima's plans entered a final stage in November, when the group met at Misty, a sauna club at Roppongi in central Tokyo. They took their baths in the grotto which is the pride of this club, and adjourned to the lounge at the top of the building, where Mishima gathered them around a table in a room usually reserved for mahjong gamblers, hidden behind smoked-glass screens. He had an announcement to make: "I appreciate your firm resolve to die, all of us together. But I must ask the two Kogas and Ogawa to ensure that the colonel does not also commit suicide following our example, and to hand him over safely to his men." He added: "Morita must do kaishaku, the beheading, at the earliest possible moment. Please don't leave me in agony too long." Thus Mishima reversed the plans for the three youngest members of the party to die; they protested vehemently and Mishima and Morita calmed them down. "It is much harder," Mishima said, "to go on living than to die. What I am asking you to do is to take the hardest course of all." The three students agreed to abide by his instructions. Three days later the group went to Gotemba near Mt. Fuji to say goodbye to other members of the Tatenokai, who were having a course there; the rest of the Tatenokai were not aware that this was a final farewell, when they all met at an inn in the town. Mishima poured toasts of saké for all forty people present, drinking with each student and Jieitai training officer present—and becoming very intoxicated for once in his life. On their return to Tokyo, Morita and the other three visited Ichigaya to check a parking place for the car on November 25, and made a report to Mishima. On November 12, during a meeting at a coffee shop called Parkside, a student hangout near Shinjuku, Morita asked Ogawa to do kaishaku for him. Ogawa agreed. On November 14 the group met again at Misty. Mishima said they would send their pictures and a copy of the gekibun, the last manifesto, to his two reporter friends, the NHK reporter Daté and the *Sunday Mainichi* journalist Tokuoka, on the morning of the twenty-fifth. The group also checked the gekibun. On the following day—meeting at a different sauna club—they discussed the timetable. It would require twenty minutes to take Colonel Miyata hostage and to get the Jieitai garrison to assemble; Mishima's speech would take thirty minutes; each of the other four would speak for five minutes; and the meeting would end with *Tenno Heika Banzai,* "Long Live the Emperor."

At the last moment there was a really major change of plan. On November 21 Morita visited Ichigaya to confirm that Colonel Miyata would be there on the twenty-fifth. He found that in fact the colonel would be away on maneuvers. At a meeting at a Chinese restaurant in the Ginza, Mishima decided that they would take hostage General Mashita (commander of the Eastern Army), after all. He phoned Mashita's office at Ichigaya and made an appointment with the general for 11 a.m. on November 25. That day and the following day, a Sunday, the four students bought supplies (Mishima was busy with his family): rope with which to tie up the general; wire and pincers for the barricades; cotton cloth on which to write their demands, to be hung from the balcony; and brandy and a water bottle. Mishima gave them the money for these purchases. On the evening of the twenty-second, Morita—who had been worrying that he would be unable to behead Mishima properly—asked Furu-Koga to act in his stead if he should fail. Koga, a trained swordsman, agreed.

On November 23 and 24 the group met in room 519 at the Palace Hotel. They held eight complete rehearsals of their plan, which was that Mishima would introduce the four students to the general, explaining that he was going to give them awards; he would then show the general his sword. When Mishima said: "Koga, a handkerchief"— Mishima would need it to wipe the sword before he showed it to the general—Chibi-Koga would step behind the general and pin him down. Furu-Koga and Ogawa would help him. Mishima and Morita would set up barricades at the doors. If the Jieitai officers attempted to enter, they would bar the way. Then they would read their demands to the officers. Once a large crowd of soldiers had gathered in front of the main building, Mishima would make a speech from the balcony, and the four others would also introduce themselves briefly. Thereafter, Mishima and Morita would commit hara-kiri. The others would behead them.

They cut rope into suitable lengths, wrote their de-

mands on the cotton cloth, and also wrote farewell tanka—
31-syllable poems (which were written by soldiers before
going into battle in the Second World War). Mishima rehearsed his speech with the television switched on in the
room so that he could not be heard from outside; and finally
the men packed up their supplies. Among these were wads
of cotton wool. Morita asked Mishima what they would be
used for; the latter smiled and said that the two of them
must pack their anuses with cotton wool, so that they should
not evacuate their bowels when committing hara-kiri. Finally, Mishima phoned his two reporter friends, telling
them to have cameras ready for the morrow, and also arm-
bands; they must be ready by 11 a.m. He told them that he
would call again at ten the following morning to give them
final instructions.

That evening, the twenty-fourth, the group had their
farewell party at a little restaurant called Suegen in the
Shimbashi quarter. Suegen is a traditional restaurant in an
unusual part of central Tokyo. The surrounding bars and
little restaurants face narrow streets and stand two stories
high; yakuza and bar girls inhabit the quarter, where there
is a famous Shinto shrine, the Karasumori Jinja. There is
only one large room at Suegen and the Tatenokai party took
the room for the evening. It has tatami floors and a large
kakeji (calligraphy) done by Ichiro Hatoyama—"Revere the
Gods and Love Mankind," a saying of the nineteenth-century general Takamori Saigo. Mishima ordered the meal: ot-
sumami (small brown beans), tori-arai (raw slices of chicken
with ice slivers), tori-soup-ni (chicken stew with Welsh
onions and Chinese cabbage), and rice and beer.

After the meal, the group drove to Mishima's home. He
left them there and they went on to Morita's lodging in the
Shinjuku district. After dropping Morita, the three younger
men continued to Chibi-Koga's lodging, where they spent
the night.

Mishima then paid a short visit to his parents. Shizue
was out and Mishima found himself alone with his father.
Azusa grumbled about his son's smoking habits—Mishima

was chain-smoking Peace cigarettes—and then Shizue came in. Mother and son talked for a short while and then Shizue saw him out: "I watched him leaving and I couldn't help thinking how tired he looked, how stooped was his back," she said later. In his own house, Mishima sorted through his papers until late. He signed the final installment of *The Decay of the Angel,* dating it November 25, 1970. He also sealed two letters to foreign scholars—Ivan Morris and Donald Keene. And on his desk he put a short note: "Human life is limited, but I would like to live forever."

PART FOUR
THE DECAY OF THE ANGEL

Finishing the long novel [*The Sea of Fertility*] makes me feel as if it is the end of the world.

Yukio Mishima to the author
October 1970

Why Mishima chose November 25 as the day he would die is a matter for speculation. One view is that he chose that day because it was the anniversary of the death of the nineteenth-century hero Shoin Yoshida. During my visit to Shimoda in August 1970 I discussed Yoshida with Mishima, mentioning that there was a large statue of Yoshida in a shrine close to the inn where I was staying—the Mishima shrine (so named after a shrine in the town close to Mt. Fuji from which Mishima had derived his nom de plume almost thirty years before). In conversation, however, Mishima showed little interest in Yoshida, and I doubt whether he was deeply interested in the man.

My guess is that Mishima chose to die on November 25 because that was the day on which he was to hand over the last installment of the fourth book of his long tetralogy, *The Sea of Fertility.* It was the deadline for the manuscript, and Mishima as a rule stuck rigidly to his schedule. He had calculated that at the end of November he would deliver the final section of *The Decay of the Angel,* the fourth book in the tetralogy, to the magazine *Shincho.* The magazine was publishing the work in installments and had been receiving each installment on or about the twenty-fifth of each month. Mishima had in fact completed the final part by August 1970, for another guest at Shimoda, Donald Keene, had seen it at that time. Thus Mishima could plan far ahead so that his death would coincide with the handing over of the conclusion of his last book, and his literature would officially end on the same day as his life. It was typical of Mishima that he controlled his last actions to the last detail. The man who maintained a smiling face throughout his last summer holiday at Shimoda, while secretly planning his bloody end, faithfully kept his literary schedule to the last.

What kind of book was he able to write at the same time that he was planning his death? It might be seen as an attempt at justifying and explaining what he did—a last message to posterity—but that is only one aspect of a very complex book. It certainly reflects his desperate state of mind in the last year of his life: it ends with a "catastrophe," as Mishima put it to the literary critic Takashi Furubayashi on November 18 in the last interview he ever granted. Replying to a question about his use of the theme of reincarnation in *The Sea of Fertility,* Mishima said: "One of the reasons [I used the theme] is technical. I thought the chronological novel outdated. Using [the idea of] reincarnation, it was easy to jump in time and also in space; I found that convenient. But, with the notion of reincarnation, the novel became a fairy tale. That is why I argued the philosophy of reincarnation so strongly in the early part of *The Temple of Dawn.* This was a preparation for the fourth volume. In the last book I wrote episodes only and went straight through to the catastrophe." Mishima had written the book rapidly— once he had made up his mind to die in 1970—and it rounded off not only his view of reincarnation but his view of the course of a human life. And the catastrophe? The whole of *The Decay of the Angel* is the answer to that question.

The action of this last novel (which Knopf published in April 1974 in a translation by Edward Seidensticker) takes place in Japan in the early 1970's, starting in the early summer of 1970 and ending in the late summer of 1975. Honda is once again a main character and is again related to the chief protagonist, another boy of remarkable physical beauty—Toru. The plot is very simple in comparison with the first three volumes of the tetralogy. Honda, the aging lawyer, adopts Toru as his son; Honda is seventy-six and the boy is sixteen. The two live together in Tokyo, where Toru, a highly intelligent youth, passes his entrance examinations for Tokyo University. As Honda becomes older and Toru grows more aggressive, the old man waits for Toru's death at the age of twenty, for the boy has the physical mark on his body to show that he is the reincarnation of Kiyoaki and the others—three moles on the side of his chest. Toru, however, looks forward to inheriting Honda's money. He becomes vicious and finally assaults Honda with a poker, inflicting superficial wounds. Honda can do nothing about the situation—he fears that if he makes a complaint to someone, Toru will have him shut up in a home for the senile. At the end of *The Decay of the Angel*, Toru and Honda both endure misfortune. The boy, tormented by Keiko, Honda's old friend and the ex-countess who in *The Temple of Dawn* was the lover of Ying Chan, tries to kill himself by drinking industrial spirits, but only succeeds in blinding himself, a symbolic incident which takes place just before his twenty-first birthday.

At twenty-one, could he be the true reincarnation? The movements of the heavenly bodies had left Honda aside. "By a small miscalculation, they had led Honda and the reincarnation of Ying Chan into separate parts of the universe. Three reincarnations had occupied Honda's life and, after drawing their paths of light across it (that too had been a most improbable accident), gone off in another burst of light

to an unknown corner of the heavens. Perhaps somewhere, some time, Honda would meet the hundredth, the ten thousandth, the hundred millionth reincarnation. There was no hurry . . ." Toru lives on miserably in his foster father's home. Honda himself is publicly disgraced. He is caught by the police after an incident in a public park where he has been peeping at lovers, and it is reported in the press: "Famous Judge Turned Peeping Tom." He also begins to suffer from pains in the abdomen. "General debilitation and rhythmical attacks of pain brought new powers to think. His aging brain had lost all ability to concentrate, but now it returned, and pain even worked aggressively upon it, to bring certain vital faculties other than the purely rational to bear. At the age of eighty-one Honda attained to a wondrous and mysterious realm that had before been denied him. He knew now that a more comprehensive view of the world was to be had from physical depression than from intelligence, from a dull pain in the entrails than from reason, a loss of appetite than analysis." He had by himself "reached that honing of the senses, achieved by few in this world, to live death from within. When he looked back upon life from its far side other than as a journey over a flat surface, hoping that what had declined would revive, seeking to believe that pain was transient, clinging greedily to happiness as a thing of the moment, thinking that good fortune must be followed by bad, seeing in all the ups and downs and rises and falls the ground for his own prospects—then everything was in place, pulled tight, and the march to the end was in order
. . ."

He makes an appointment at the Cancer Research Institute, and on the day before takes one of his rare looks at television. There is a shot of a swimming pool with young people splashing about in it. "Honda would end his life without having known the feelings of the owner of beautiful flesh. If for a single month he could live in it! He should have had a try . . . When admiration passed the gentle and docile and became lunatic worship, it would become torment for the possessor. In the delirium and the torment were true holiness. What Honda had missed had been the dark, narrow path through the flesh to holiness. To travel it was of course the privilege of few . . ."

After being examined for a week, Honda is told the result. "There seems to be no more than a benign growth on the pancreas." The doctor adds: "All we have to do is cut it away." Honda does not believe him; he fears it is malignant. He asks for "a week's reprieve" before going in the hospital.

He visits Toru. Earlier in the novel, we have been given the five signs of the decay of an angel, the five marks that death has come. According to *The Life of the Buddha*, fifth fascicle: "The flowers in the hair fade, a fetid sweat comes from under the arms, the robes are soiled, the body ceases to give off light, it loses awareness of itself." He seems to discover all these signs in Toru. "There was no smell of flowers"; "the dirt and oil on the kimono had mixed with the sweat into the smell as of a dank canal that young men put out in the summer"; "the smile had left him"; "Toru had abdicated control of the regions above his neck" . . . We see the decay of the angel. And we also see the decay of Honda, but it has taken much longer. ("He who had had no such awareness to begin with lived on. For he was no angel.")

He also decides to fulfill a lifetime's ambition, for there may be little time left—to see again Satoko Ayakura, Kiyoaki's mistress in *Spring Snow*, who has become abbess of the nunnery in which she sought refuge from the world sixty years before. Satoko is now eighty-three. In July 1975 Honda obtains an appointment with her and travels down from Tokyo to Kyoto, where he books into a hotel. The following day he sets off for Gesshuji, the nunnery. It is a fine summer day and Honda is driven by a chauffeur. He refuses the chauffeur's suggestion that he should be taken right up to the front gate of Gesshuji; his intention is to suffer the pains which Kiyoaki experienced sixty years earlier. Countless cicadas are singing in the woods. Honda goes slowly up a long flight of stone steps with his stick, sometimes stoping to fight the pain in his body; finally he reaches the door, covered in sweat. He clearly remembers the scene sixty years before; the years seem no more than a moment. He feels as if he were young once more and Kiyoaki were waiting for him, back at their hotel, with a high temperature and a dangerous fever. At the nunnery he is allowed to enter and is guided to a guest room. He expresses his profound gratitude to the nun who has escorted him and experiences great happiness as he reflects that the scandal about him in Tokyo has proved no obstacle to this meeting. At the same time he thinks to himself that if he did not feel shame and a consciousness of his evil and of death, he would not have come to the nunnery.

An aged nun enters the room, escorted by a younger nun who holds her hand. The old nun wears a white kimono and over this a deep violet robe (a hifu, or mid-length gown). This must be Satoko. For a while Honda cannot look directly at her; he feels tears welling in his eyes. She must really be Satoko, Honda thinks, looking at her face finally— at her nose and the shape of her mouth; she has even kept her beauty. Age has purified Satoko; her eyes are clear. The old abbess has the quality of a precious stone, crystallized in old age.

She admits she has seen his letter. It seemed "almost too earnest." She thought "there must be some holy bond between us."

Honda reminds her that, sixty years before, he had not been allowed to see her. He had been angry. " 'Kiyoaki Matsugae was after all my dearest friend.'

" 'Kiyoaki Matsugae. Who might he have been?' " she replies.

"Honda looked at her in astonishment.

"She might be hard of hearing, but she could not have failed to hear him."

She repeats her question, " 'Who might he have been?' "

Scrupulously polite, he recounts his memories of Kiyoaki's love and its sad conclusion. When he has finished, the abbess says coolly: " 'It has been a most interesting story, but unfortunately I did not know Mr. Matsugae. I fear you have confused me with someone else.'

" 'But I believe that your name is Satoko Ayakura?'

" 'That was my lay name.'

" 'Then you must have known Kiyoaki.' " He is angry. It had to be not forgetfulness but unabashed prevarication.

His persistence "passed a reasonable limit." But she did not seem to resent it. "For all the heat, her purple cloak was cool. Her eyes and her always beautiful voice were serene."

" 'No, Mr. Honda, I have forgotten none of the blessings that were mine in the other world. But I fear I have never heard the name Kiyoaki Matsugae. Don't you suppose, Mr. Honda, that there never was such a person? You seem convinced that there was; but don't you suppose that there was no such person from the beginning, anywhere? I couldn't help thinking so as I listened to you.'

" 'Why then do we know each other? And the Ayakuras and the Matsugaes must still have family registers.'

" 'Yes, such documents might solve problems in the other world. But did you really know a person called Kiyoaki? And can you say definitely that the two of us have met before?'

" 'I came here sixty years ago.'

" 'Memory is like a phantom mirror. It sometimes shows things too distant to be seen, and sometimes it shows them as if they were here.'

" 'But if there was no Kiyoaki from the beginning—' " Honda "was groping through a fog. His meeting here with the abbess seemed half a dream. He spoke loudly, as if to retrieve the self that receded like traces of breath vanishing from a lacquer tray." Honda tells her: " 'If there was no Kiyoaki, then there was no Isao. There was no Ying Chan, and who knows, perhaps there has been no I.' "

For the first time there was strength in her eyes. " 'That too is as it is in each heart.' "

After a long silence, the abbess calls her novice. She wishes to show Honda the south garden. "It was a bright, quiet garden, without striking features. Like a rosary rubbed between the hands, the shrilling of cicadas held sway.

"There was no other sound. The garden was empty. He had came, thought Honda, to a place that had no memories, nothing.

"The noontide sun of summer flowed over the still garden"—that is the last we know of Honda and the last line of *The Sea of Fertility.*

This is presumably the "catastrophe" Mishima referred to. Reincarnation is thrown into doubt; so is Honda's whole life. "Who knows, perhaps there has been no I." The tetralogy has been dependent on the idea of reincarnation exemplified by the lives of Kiyoaki, Isao, Ying Chan, and, finally, Toru. And then, at the close of the 1,400-page novel, Mishima seems to explode the notion that the three successors of the beautiful youth Kiyoaki are reincarnations; the theme which links the four books of *The Sea of Fertility* is questioned with classical irony. Such is my interpretation of the ending and of Mishima's use of the word "catastrophe" in reference to it.

It is an appropriate ending. Mishima himself did not believe in reincarnation and his writing on the subject in *The Sea of Fertility* is lacking in conviction; it was reasonable that he should doubt and even discard the idea at the end of his work. Through his emphasis on reincarnation in the earlier parts of the tetralogy, he works up to a climax in which he questions the entire structure of the story. He leaves his chief character at the very end of his long life doubting that it had any meaning. And yet nothing in the novel is that simple. Honda, it seems, has entered Nirvana, or extinction, in Buddhist terms—a cold and comfortless place "that had no memories," a place akin to the surface of the moon. This is the ironic ending of the ironically titled *The Sea of Fertility,* and no doubt the exact interpretation will long be argued over. How like Yukio Mishima to leave

his last work of literature—and his last comment on life—
this way. One can almost hear his familiar laughter behind
the last pages: Huh-huh-huh.

After Mishima's suicide, events conspired to give me a
privileged view of all that took place in Tokyo. I found myself the only foreign reporter at the press conference held by
the Jieitai at the Ichigaya headquarters some fifteen minutes
after Mishima's death there. On the following day I visited
Mishima's home to leave a note for his widow, and to my
surprise—I had expected the family would not want visitors—I was invited in. The Mishima home was full of white
chrysanthemums and elegant women in black silk kimono,
family or very close friends. I was the only non-Japanese
person there and I stayed only a short time to chat with a
friend of Mishima's. The private funeral service took place
half an hour later, followed by cremation.

In December, in my capacity as a reporter, I attended a
memorial meeting held in a hall at Ikebukuro, not far from
the department store where Mishima's last exhibition had
been staged; and in January I was present at the public funeral at the Tsukiji Honganji temple in Tokyo. The funeral
was attended by over ten thousand people and was the largest of its kind ever held in Japan. Before the general public
was allowed to look into the temple (no one from the public
was admitted inside the building itself), there was a short
service for about three hundred people. The altar was a
beautiful sight—huge spheres made up of small white chrysanthemums, by which flickered tall candles. Members of
the family were seated at the front with Yasunari Kawabata,
who acted as principal mourner; behind them were the Tatenokai, all eighty members, in uniform. After the service,
Kawabata, looking old and frail in his black suit, made a
short, very restrained speech, asking those present to do everything they could to help the widow and children.

I was apparently the only non-Japanese invited to the
funeral (if there were others, they did not come); and I was
also the only Westerner on hand when the trial of the three

survivors of the action at Ichigaya opened in the Tokyo District Court in March 1971. The authorities would not admit more than one foreign reporter to the court, and he had to be someone with a better command of Japanese than I, as he was to take notes for the entire foreign press. (Takeshi Oka of *The New York Times*, a Japanese, accepted this responsibility.) To get into the court, I lined up with about five hundred other people at seven in the morning, taking my chances in the ballot that determined who would be admitted. The odds were ten to one against success, but I was one of those who received a piece of paper with a cross on it: I would be allowed in to the Mishima trial.

The beginning, as it happened, was the only interesting part of the trial, which lasted until April 1972 (and ended with sentences of four years' imprisonment for the Tatenokai students). For the first time, the two Kogas and Ogawa made a public appearance; they wore Western suits and open-neck shirts or polo jerseys and looked neat and alert. What amazed me was their size—they looked so *small*—and their seeming frailty and youth. The two Kogas had fresh, boyish faces and were quite short; Ogawa, the standard-bearer of the Tatenokai, was taller and had a toothbrush moustache that made him appear slightly older; but, beside my memory of Mishima, they all seemed very young and undeveloped. The three were asked to make speeches at the opening session. Furu-Koga, a youth with a sensitive face, proved to be the most eloquent: chauvinism, imperialism, and loyalty to Mishima were his themes. A change had taken place after Mishima's death: the chauvinistic tone of Furu-Koga's speech was in contrast to everything Mishima had stood for as a writer and as a man. I sensed that Mishima's occasional anti-foreign sallies in his novels and in his conversation had been blown up out of all proportion by his self-appointed right-wing allies. As I listened to the evidence in court, it seemed as ironic an ending to the life story of Yukio Mishima as *The Sea of Fertility* had seemed to his writing.

FIVE

Post-mortem

He committed suicide to complete his literary work.

Takeo Okuno, literary critic

He died to defend what he loved.

Shintaro Ishihara, author and right-wing politician

An act motivated by a sense of a phantom crisis.

Daizo Kusayanagi, sociologist

The heightening of his sexuality produced an increasing urge to commit suicide by disembowelment.

Tadasu Iizawa, playwright

A suicide brought about by an explosive self-exhibitionistic desire.

Shigeta Saito, psychiatrist

A gorgeous mosaic of homosexuality, Yomeigaku, and Emperor worship.

A Japanese friend, three months after Mishima's death

1

The image of Mishima's head with the hachimaki headband still secure about it, propped on the blood-soaked carpeted floor of General Mashita's office—the photograph was published by the Japanese press and in *Life* magazine—remains indelibly in my mind. That powerful head had been torn from its shoulders! How had Mishima justified this action to himself?

In *The Decay of the Angel*, Honda, the chief character, regrets that he is the kind of person who is "unable to stop time" and therefore cannot enjoy the "endless physical beauty" which is "the special prerogative of those who cut time short.

"As he grew older, awareness of self became awareness of time. He gradually came to make out the sound of the white ants. Moment by moment, second by second, with what a shallow awareness men slipped through time that would not return! Only with age did one know that there was a richness, an intoxication even, in each drop. The drops of beautiful time, like the drops of a rich, rare wine. And time dripped away like blood. Old men dried up and died. In payment for having neglected to stop time at the glorious moment when the rich blood, unbeknownst to the owner himself, was bringing rich drunkenness.

"Just before the pinnacle when time must be cut short," Mishima adds, "is the pinnacle of physical beauty." He knows he has passed the first pinnacle and reached the second, he seems to be explaining in this last novel; and, unlike Honda, he has no intention of ignoring "the glorious moment." If this is true of his purpose in *The Decay of the Angel*, his hara-kiri simply stopped time for him: endless physical beauty would therefore be his "special prerogative."

This is a literary explanation in keeping with many of the ideas that had obsessed Mishima for most of his life, but it seems too simple when one remembers Mishima's delight in role playing—how he must have enjoyed explaining the "glorious moment" to posterity—and especially the events of that last day. We have seen how his plans changed, how Morita provided essential support, how the police and the army failed to intervene effectively—it is easy to imagine how that last day might have turned out differently, and Mishima would have missed his "glorious moment" and perhaps lived on like Honda (and yet he was such a determined man and rehearsed his death so many times that it has an inevitability about it). Even in *The Decay of the Angel*, there is an ironic undertone throughout. Honda's failure to stop time and his slow aging seem to bring certain compensations, as if the narrator is perhaps questioning his

302 The Life and Death of Yukio Mishima

earlier soliloquy about the glorious moment. Nothing is simple: is everything in doubt? At least in Mishima's last novel, one is wary of seizing on an obvious message: it may be merely another confession of a mask and not the true meaning of the real man, that complex, perceptive student of human nature, including his own. Perhaps even unknown to himself, at an unconscious level, his last novel may express some doubts of what he was about to do. Do we sense a growing sympathy, even envy, for Honda, who missed the glorious moment but went on living?

Many of Mishima's contemporaries did not accept a simple explanation for what had happened even months after the conclusion of *The Decay of the Angel* had been published. In the spring of 1971 the *Japan Quarterly* published an article by Junro Fukashiro entitled "Post-mortem" which summarized the popular theories about Mishima's motives: "The 'insanity theory,' which needs no further explanation; the 'aesthetic theory,' which holds that the beauty sought by Mishima in his literary pursuits could only be completed by his own ultimate dramatic death; the 'exhausted-talent theory,' which suggests that Mishima had written himself out in the course of almost thirty years of writing and had nothing left to look forward to but despair; the 'love-suicide theory,' which asserts that he was a homosexual who committed a shinju [double suicide for love] with [Morita] in pursuit of some ultimate eroticism; and, finally, the 'patriotism theory,' which postulates that Mishima sought to incite members of the Jieitai to carry out a coup d'état that would realize Mishima's personal ideal of Japan as a nation-state united under the Emperor."

2

Even if one accepts that Mishima in his own eyes had chosen the "glorious moment," one must relate it to his nar-

cissism and his homosexuality, two complex aspects of the
man. Homosexuality, I believe, was a key to his suicide. My
speculation is that he was having an affair with Masakatsu
Morita and that the two committed a lovers' suicide. The evidence is circumstantial: Mishima and Morita planned the
incident at Ichigaya together and then brought in the three
other Tatenokai. They decided that only they would commit
suicide and they communicated their decision to the others
afterward—at the meeting at Misty sauna club on November
3, 1970.

After the suicides, two people who had known Mishima
personally made statements to me, in response to general
questions, which supported the idea that it had been a
shinju. One of these was a senior police officer who had
access to the huge police dossier on the Mishima Incident.
A number of outsiders interested in the suicides sought his
help because he was known to have been close to Mishima
and because of his high rank. The day before I called on him
at his office in February 1971, he had had a phone call from
the conservative politician, Shintaro Ishihara, who questioned him about the relationship of Mishima and Morita.
The police officer was eager to talk about Mishima, provided I did not quote him by name, and I was impressed by
the humorous, ironical way he answered my questions. He
remarked that Mishima and Morita were probably lovers, although only the two dead men knew for certain and so we
could never be sure.

My other informant was a very different kind of person—a woman who had known Mishima intimately all
his adult life, an elegant and accomplished patroness of the
arts and the wife of one of the leading politicians in Japan. I
met her over lunch at a Western hotel in Tokyo in the early
spring of 1972, and my secretary was present to interpret, if
necessary, as all our conversation was in Japanese. She was
someone I knew only slightly, but she showed no lack of
trust and talked freely about Mishima. He had once proposed marriage to her and she had a voluminous correspondence, part of which she later showed me. "Mishima

was deeply in love with Morita," she claimed. In her view, Morita had had a considerable influence on Mishima; she believed that Mishima alone would not have committed suicide (and missed the "glorious moment"?). She saw Morita as a conventional, not very bright, right-wing student, and Mishima as the man he was—a brilliant, intelligent, charming writer with a streak of instability, a man whose ideal was a beautiful death. The interests of the two men had coincided. Morita was in fact the first to propose that the Tatenokai stage a coup d'état (the police confirmed this); he made the suggestion in the autumn of 1969 and Mishima then turned him down, only to endorse the idea a few months later. Thus the Mishima Incident had its genesis in the mind of Masakatsu Morita. It was adopted wholeheartedly by Mishima as it suited his ends perfectly once he knew that he was to finish *The Sea of Fertility* within a short period of time. In a sense, Morita stepped into a ready-made drama and unwittingly triggered off the mechanism which began it.

When I saw the two men together at Camp Fuji in 1969, they were obviously on close terms. Morita remarked that he could understand the ideal of the Emperor only through Mishima, who was mystically related to the Emperor. The Emperor was Morita's ideal and his worship presumably carried over to Mishima, too. This is crucial to an understanding of the relationship between the two men—if one follows Mishima's thinking about the Emperor. In his essay which accompanied the trilogy of works on the Ni Ni Roku Incident, Mishima stated that love was only possible under the aegis of the Emperor. *A* might love *B* and *B* might love *A*, but their relationship would only be meaningful if the Emperor existed; otherwise, it would be hollow. He compared the situation to a triangle, in which the apex was the Emperor and the two lower angles were the lovers.

Mishima's thinking on the subject of leadership also throws light on his relationship with Morita. He was rough and autocratic in his ways in the Tatenokai, but he was also ready to accept criticism. One of his favorite books, the *Hagakure*, the eighteenth-century record of samurai ethics—

Mishima once called it his favorite reading—explains the relationships between samurai warriors in terms of love; indeed, the samurai often were homosexual lovers. The *Hagakure* also states that subordinates, or followers, have the principal duty of "remonstrating" with their superiors or feudal lords if the latter stray from the path of righteousness. Mishima, so Morita thought, was not serious about the Tatenokai, and would not commit the private army to action. Morita, the faithful follower and passionate admirer, goaded Mishima into action.

Eros and "Blood" had a close connection in Mishima's literature, and it must surely have been his dream to achieve this ideal combination in reality. Although Mishima and Morita were both careful to destroy correspondence and diaries that might have told us for certain, the person with whom Mishima died, by whom he was killed, has to have been his lover.

3

The "insanity theory"? Some of the anecdotes and conversations I have described toward the end of his life show that Mishima was under considerable strain. I remember particularly that strange dinner at which he described Japan as being menaced by a "green snake." Many of the later photographs he posed for show him acting out his fantasies. Surely, for example, Mishima as St. Sebastian was crossing the pathological border, and in the famous photograph brandishing the giant sword with which he was to be killed, his expression seems demented. But Mishima was such an incredible actor and stage manager in life that one must still wonder to what extent even there he was play-acting.

The testimony of experts on Mishima's mental condition is not very helpful. The one psychologist who ever examined him, Dr. Kataguchi, who subjected him to Rorschach ink-blot tests in 1962—a long eight years before his death—came up with no clear opinion beyond the fact that Mishima was homosexual. After Mishima's death, however, he wrote an article describing Mishima as paranoid, psychopathic, and schizophrenic; this was not a great contribution to a deeper understanding of the man. I prefer a more common-sense approach based on what we have seen of his childhood. Throughout his life he attempted to compensate for his frailty by prodigious actions. He had a consuming desire to prove that he was *not* weak, and in his battle to do so, he sought to control everything around him. This must, over the years, have been a tremendous strain on him. And if those close to him, those who saw him regularly, missed the signs (his widow said afterward she thought something was going to happen, but perhaps the following year), outsiders and particularly his readers noticed. About a year before he died, an incident took place at Mishima's home which reflects this. Early one morning a young man took up a vigil outside the house (a standard technique in Japan for introducing oneself, and the longer the petitioner waits the more his sincerity is respected and the better chance he has of meeting the famous man). He waited for an entire day, and toward evening Mishima, whose family had seen the young man, relented and sent his maid to invite the young man in. Mishima greeted him with the remark: "I am a busy man and I will let you ask one question, no more. Right?" The visitor paused for a moment. "Sensei," he asked, "when are you going to kill yourself?"

One remembers the reflection of the aging Honda in *The Decay of the Angel:* "He knew now that a more comprehensive view of the world was to be had from physical depression than from intelligence . . . ." Was this a reflection of Mishima's own state of mind? Did his image of an ugly, materialistic Japan in this last novel mirror an unbalanced despair? As Edward Seidensticker, the translator of the novel, has written of Toru: "The hero is a young boy given over to glittering and utterly empty cerebration. It is obvious that Mishima hated the boy, who is withal a brilliant creature of fiction, and who reminds one of no one so much as Mishima himself." But to an adherent of Yomeigaku—the neo-Confucian philosophy which inspired Isao to commit hara-kiri in *Runaway Horses* and played a part in Mishima's own decision to die—it would not be enough to recognize the rot within himself in a fictional confession; he also had to take action to escape hollow cerebration, and it must be a real suicide, not a botched one like Toru's.

The importance of Yomeigaku to Mishima was underlined in a letter he wrote to one of his translators, Ivan Morris, just before his death, in which he asserted that he had been influenced by Yomeigaku and believed that "knowing without acting" was not sufficient knowledge and that the act itself did not require any effectiveness. It was not enough for Mishima, in my interpretation of his last letters to Morris (he wrote a similar one, also mailed after his death, to Donald Keene), to regret the vanishing of Japanese tradition by "mere verbal expression"; he could only truly "know" the situation in his country if he took action. As he believed that Japan was in a disastrous condition, only the most extreme response, suicide—an act of remonstration— would represent a "consummation of knowledge." And he had to kill himself in dramatic style, for drama was the keynote of the actions of the well-known nineteenth-century heroes of Japanese history who espoused Yomeigaku. What could be more dramatic than to hand over the end of his last novel and then commit hara-kiri virtually on television? As he wrote to Ivan Morris, he parted with *The Decay of the Angel* "on the very day of my action in order to realize my Bunburyodo."

No, the "insanity theory" is far too simple and convenient an explanation. It may be, as one of my friends commented, that the three principal factors were homosexuality, Yomeigaku, and Emperor worship, and that together they form a "gorgeous mosaic." He thinks that no one element was decisive, however. What mattered was the overall effect, for even in his work—particularly in his plays— Mishima had often been far more interested in form than in content. Like many an artist with suicidal tendencies, he saw his death as his final and most important work of art. "I want to make a poem of my life," he wrote at twenty-four. This was part of the strong Narcissus quality in him. His overriding aim was to die beautifully, and his life-long aesthetic of "Death and Night and Blood" dictated that swords and knives, not guns, be the weapons. Hara-kiri for him was a supreme sexual act—the "ultimate masturbation," as he told a visitor in the summer of 1970. By that time, believing that the supremely beautiful event was the violent death of a young man, he could not afford at forty-five to wait much longer.

But this too seems an oversimplification: the explanation for Mishima's death lies in his entire life. This whole book is my explanation.

4

It was certainly an event which had moved a vast number of people. It greatly affected the men of Mishima's own generation in Japan, not because they respected his arguments, as laid out in the gekibun or before that in *Eirei no Koe,* but because his action reminded them of the Emperor worship which they had espoused during the war, when all of them had expected to die for the Emperor. In wartime the highest virtue had been to sacrifice oneself on the battlefield for the Emperor; hence the prestige of the kamikaze pilots whom Mishima praised in *Eirei no Koe.* Mishima, for many, had revived the old ideal of the Emperor, and his death moved many of his contemporaries more deeply than any event since 1945. In their eyes, it was a measure of the sincerity of his imperialism.

A newspaper poll showed that about one third of students had a degree of understanding for Mishima, though they condemned his hara-kiri. The entire press commented unfavorably on it, and he was condemned not only by the opposition parties but by the conservatives as well. Scarcely anyone was prepared to say a favorable word for him in public. But although the vast majority of Japanese said they disapproved of what Mishima had done, there were a great many people who had a kind of sympathy for him, and this increased the more the shock of that grim event faded into the past.

Many people who were close to Mishima were critical of his suicide. Shortly afterward, Yasunari Kawabata arrived at the Ichigaya headquarters and was shown the corpses and was briefed by the police on the spot. Kawabata had very little to say to the press thereafter. "What a waste!" he remarked. He was the first person to call on Mrs. Mishima, and it would seem that both of them disapproved of the suicide. One indication of her attitude was her choice of the photograph which hung above the altar at the public funeral. She avoided pictures of her husband in Tatenokai uniform, selecting one of him wearing a dark t-shirt. She also took swift steps to bring the Tatenokai to an end. On February 28, 1971, a brief ceremony was held at a Shinto shrine in Tokyo, attended by Yoko Mishima, at which the Tatenokai was disbanded. This action implies that the Tatenokai was a personal organization of Mishima's, a suicide vehicle; it suggests that with Mishima dead, the private army had no reason to exist.

Yoko Mishima in fact revealed herself as a veritable samurai widow, showing far more strength of character than her husband sometimes had done. She had a great deal of work to do as the heir to most of Mishima's literary estate, and she dealt with the problems which faced her with extraordinary strength of mind. Before long, she was in a greater position of power in the publishing world than her husband had been. Practical and businesslike in her conduct of affairs, she made all the necessary arrangements for Mishima's estate; this was growing rapidly, as the sale of his books had greatly increased—the first year after his death, income on his estate was more than $250,000, mostly from sales in Japan.

Yoko, however, never spoke of her husband in public

after his death. Little pieces of information came from the family through friends. Mishima had wanted, it was learned, to give his children a treat in early 1970 and had proposed to Yoko that they take the children on their first overseas trip in the summer—to Disneyland. Yoko, saying that he should finish his long novel first, had turned him down. What she thought, and what she thinks, about her husband may never be known. Quite possibly she was the only person outside the Tatenokai group who sensed that he was planning something major, but he apparently gave her no direct warning and let her go off that morning to school with the children without any final goodbye.

She wished above all to protect her husband's reputation. She wanted him to be remembered as an international writer, not as a right-wing extremist. At her home she put up the large photograph that had been displayed at the funeral, and by it she placed a smaller one of Morita—Mishima, after all, had been responsible for his death.

Other members of the family also disapproved of Mishima's suicide. His father objected; his son had not even said goodbye to the family, he grumbled. Mishima's younger brother, Chiyuki, who was serving in the Prime Minister's office at the time of the suicide, and who had the task of dealing with the press at Mishima's home, also refrained from saying a word of approval of the suicide. The only member of the family who took a sympathetic attitude was his mother. Shizue was bitterly critical of the rest of the family, saying that they had never understood her son. Shizue accused her husband, Azusa, of being a philistine and said that Yukio would have never killed himself if he had had a better wife than Yoko. The disagreements in the Hiraoka family were publicized by Azusa, who wrote articles in the press describing the quarrels. He told how Shizue wept at the Buddhist altar in their home, on which she had placed a volume of Nietzsche for her son to read; Azusa, beside himself with irritation, would step out into the garden to smoke a cigarette and calm himself.

To disapprove of Mishima's suicide was one thing; to

prevent it getting under one's skin, another—so the case of Yasunari Kawabata demonstrated. The year following Mishima's death, he threw himself into a whirlwind of activities; he campaigned for the conservative candidate for the governorship of Tokyo, and he gave a press conference in which he said that he had been inspired to act by Mishima's example. Kawabata was in a depressed state of mind and told friends that he wished sometimes, when he went on a journey, that his plane would crash. He was haunted by the ghost of Mishima, he said; the specter would visit him when he was alone at his desk or trouble his dreams. Although the old writer had more than once expressed disapproval of suicide, in April 1972 he gassed himself in his apartment.

5

My own attitude toward Mishima's suicide is ambivalent. I was both deeply moved and repelled by it. He had been a friend of great charm, generosity, and wit; he had the gift of persuading people whom he met that they alone mattered to him; he was endowed with extraordinary energy and made those of us who had only a fraction of his vitality feel like pale worms. His outstanding asset was his intelligence. Almost alone among modern Japanese intellectuals, he was familiar with Western and classical Japanese culture. He also had an enormous sense of humor. An evening with him passed quickly as he told one anecdote after another about events and personalities in Japan. His most striking feature, in my own experience, was his ability to empathize with others, to understand what they were thinking and to respond to it. No one of my Japanese friends had one fraction of his uncanny ability to know what was going on in my mind. That he had put an end to his life seemed for many months afterward a totally inconceivable and unimaginable fact. When finally, after many attempts, I succeeded in writing a description of his suicide—which forms the first chapter of this book—I had a terrible nightmare. I dreamed that Mishima came to my home in Glastonbury in England and knocked on the door. When I saw him standing there, I struck him down with a mattock. I was in fact for a long time revolted by his suicide, his self-murder; I could see nothing beautiful in it. I loved him and I felt that I had been betrayed by his death (I had to master this feeling before I could be objective enough to start the research for this book). Many of those who knew him had similar reactions. His Japanese biographer, Takeo Okuno, has related how he had nightmares about Mishima for two or three hundred nights in a row! He was indeed an extraordinarily strong personality. How else could he have had such an impact on those who knew him—or read him?

One aspect of his charm was his self-knowledge and his ironic wit, and remembering this makes any simple interpretation of his actions suspect. In a conversation which he recorded with the older novelist Jun Ishikawa in the autumn of 1970, Mishima said—and his death was close at hand: "I come out on the stage determined to make the audience weep and instead they burst out laughing." He knew, in other words, how foolish—and how unbeautiful— his suicide would appear to the audience that beheld his last actions. What a farce his last speech was! There he was, derided by a large audience, up to the very last moment of his life. He appears to have known that this would happen, though he was disappointed by the *absolute* failure of his audience to respond.

How will Mishima be regarded by posterity?

He will be remembered, for one part, as a Fascist agitator. The manner of his death, and the literature on imperialism which he left behind him, leave no doubt of his Fascist tendencies. He resorted to violence in the name of the Emperor; he attempted to steer his country onto the path of militarism, demanding that the Emperor should once again be restored to a position of honor and that the Constitution be revised in order to sanctify the role of the Armed Forces in the state under the command of the Emperor, as in pre-World War II days. Alone among leading Japanese intellectuals of his generation, he endorsed the benighted system of Emperor worship which led Japan into a futile war, from which it emerged with millions of dead and a devastated homeland. The fact that he committed hara-kiri, the ultimate spiritual action in the Japanese tradition, commended him to the right-wing in Japan, which, though it remains weak, could play a greater role in the affairs of state in the latter 1970's. There is already a powerful element in the ruling conservative party, the group known as the Seirankai ("Blue Storm Association"), which favors imperialism, rearmament, and the colonization of Taiwan and Korea, and among whose members are to be found politicians who sympathized with Mishima's final action; one of them, Shintaro Ishihara, remarked after his death that Mishima had "died to defend what he loved."

I would prefer, however, that he be honored as a novelist rather than denigrated as a right-wing fanatic. He spent the greater part of his life writing plays and novels—his collected works were published in thirty-six volumes after his death—and was regarded, in fact, until the late 1960's, as a writer with vaguely leftist sympathies, as he never expressed reactionary opinions until the last five years of his life. During his youth he was invited to join the Communist Party, and in his late thirties he remained intensely suspect to the Uyoku, the fanatical right-wing in Tokyo. None of his novels suggests that he was in any way affiliated with the right wing in Japan—and he never had, in fact, any contacts whatever with the Uyoku, whom he regarded as gangsters. His reputation as a novelist has, meanwhile, never stood higher than at present in the West. *The Sea of Fertility* is regarded as the best of his numerous novels; it is a panoramic vision of Japan in the twentieth century and tells more of modern Japan than any other work in translation. The descriptions of Japan in the early Taisho period, the chronicle of Isao (the right-wing terrorist of the early 1930's), and the depressing account of modern Japan in *The Decay of the Angel* are brilliant evocations of a country that is little understood in the West.

Mishima probably wrote best, however, about himself. He may be compared to André Gide, whom he resembled in so many ways, as an individual and as a writer. Like Gide, Mishima was born into an upper-middle-class family in which the mother had the dominant role. The fathers of both men were weak, ineffective figures, and the mothers were principally responsible for their sons' upbringing (in Mishima's case, his formidable grandmother must be taken into account). Both men had strong narcissistic tendencies, both were homosexual, and both enjoyed the game of double identities, appearing under their own names in private life while adopting nom de plumes in their literary activities. The most important of Gide's works were his early autobiographical writings; and in my opinion Mishima's finest "novel" was his autobiographical *Confessions of a Mask*. Their limitations were that they found it hard, impossible perhaps, to put a distance between themselves and their work. Their strained childhoods—being brought up alone, apart from other children—drove them into little worlds of the imagination from which they never emerged. These worlds were fascinating places, subjected to intelligent scrutiny, but they were nonetheless limited.

One day someone will write a "psychobiography" of Yukio Mishima comparable to the classic work by Jean Delay, *La Jeunesse d'André Gide*. He will have access to family correspondence and will have the cool detachment that only the passage of time brings—we are still too close to the event. I thought at the start of my work on this book that I would be satisfied if I found in his life the hint of an explanation for his death. Now at the end I remember that last note he left on his desk: "Human life is limited, but I would like to live forever." This book then has been an attempt to describe how he will live—in my memory, at least.

Glossary

A Note on Pronunciation: Japanese is a syllabic language. All syllables are sounded and all are given approximately equal stress. In this edition we have not distinguished between short and long vowels. Kimitake Hiraoka, for example, is pronounced "Ki-mi-ta-ké Hi-ra-o-ka"; Shizue is pronounced "Shi-zu-é."

AKAGAMI The "red paper" which summoned men to serve in the Japanese Imperial Army during WW II. Equivalent to an (honorable) sentence of death in Japanese eyes.

ANPO The U.S.–Japan Security Treaty, the foundation of Japanese foreign policy after World War II. Came under fire from the left in 1960, when there were massive demonstrations in Tokyo.

BAISHAKU-NIN The "go-between" at a formal Japanese wedding, who has no practical function but to sit in on the wedding, and call on guests to make speeches. He receives a small payment for these services, an honorarium.

BAKAYARO The most insulting word in the Japanese language. Imprudently used, it may occasion murder. Rough equivalent in English: "mother-fucker"; but the word does not have as much force as "bakayaro."

BU The ethic of the sword, from which is derived Bushido, the creed of the samurai, or the Way of the Warrior.

BUNBURYODO The dual way of the literary and martial arts espoused by the proudest samurai in feudal times and by Mishima in modern times as a guide to his life.

BUNDAN The Japanese literary "establishment," far more inbred than comparable circles in London, New York, or Paris. Stifling, incestuous.

BUNGAKUZA The most prestigious theatrical group in Japan, with which Mishima worked for a decade before quarreling with them in 1964.

BUNGEI Literature. Bungei-bu means literature circle.

BUSHI A word equivalent to samurai, from the root "Bu."

CHUO KORON The leading intellectual magazine in Japan; publishers of Mishima's essay "Bunkaboeiron" ("On the Defense of Culture," 1968). Politically hyper-cautious after attempt by right-wing terrorists in 1961 to assassinate the president of the organization.

DANNASAMA Old-fashioned word for the head of a household, used ironically about himself by Mishima.

DEMOKURASHI "Democracy," used as an "amulet word" in postwar Japan.

FUNDOSHI Loincloth of traditional cut worn by Mishima at photographic model sessions and on the last day of his life.

GAIJIN Descriptive word meaning "foreigner"; also used in pejorative sense.

GAKUSHUIN The Peers School attended by Mishima between 1931 and 1944; still very much in operation, although the "aristocracy" disappeared under the American Occupation of 1945–52.

GEISHA A female entertainer, not a prostitute; must be skilled in conversation and the arts, not only love-making.

GEKIBUN A manifesto of the kind written by the rebel officers in the Ni Ni Roku Incident in 1936; their style was imitated by Mishima.

GENTEIBON A luxury edition. Mishima's were expensive and some were in good taste; the best of them is *Barakei* ("Torture by Roses").

HACHIMAKI A headband worn by the Japanese as a sign of militancy. Originally, just a headband.

HAORI A short jacket with short sleeves, worn with a kimono.

HARAGAKE A bellyband, favored by yakuza, as in the last scene of *Confessions of a Mask*. Haragake I wore on Mt. Fuji was a modified version of the traditional band.

HARA-KIRI Literally, "belly cut." The word is not used by the Japanese, to whom it sounds ugly; but Mishima liked to use it.

HOSSO The most intellectual of Japanese Buddhist sects; rare today. Only a few temples are Hosso.

JIEITAI The Armed Forces in Japan, known in English as the

Self-Defense Forces. Their constitutionality is in doubt, as Mishima stated.

JIKACHUDOKU Literally, "auto-intoxication." However, the precise nature of Mishima's childhood illness is unclear.

KABUKI Baroque, colorful theatrical form developed in the seventeenth and eighteenth centuries. Stylized; huge stage. The actors are men, and those who take female roles are known as onnagata.

KAISHAKU The second stage of the classical hara-kiri, the decapitation.

KAMIKAZE The "divine wind," literally; the suicide pilots of 1944–45. The expression is derived from twelfth-century history.

KAPPUKU The first stage of the classical hara-kiri, cutting the stomach.

KENDO Japanese fencing in medieval armor; Mishima's sport.

KOAN Buddhist riddle. Mishima enjoyed such Zen puzzles.

KOBUN The highly competitive examination for the Japanese civil service.

KOTO A thirteen-stringed musical instrument, laid on the ground, plucked.

MEISHI A visiting card, essential when meeting a stranger in Japan, filed for reference. Mishima refused to use one; could get away with it because he was famous.

MIKAN The Japanese tangerine, less sweet than European and Californian varieties.

MITAMASHIRO Small, sacred Shinto tablet carried by the leader of the Shinpuren Incident samurai.

MOHITSU Brush used for writing Japanese characters in black ink. Mishima planned to do this before his hara-kiri but lost interest.

NIGIRI-MESHI Rice balls, a humble dish.

NINGEN SENGEN The announcement made by the Emperor in a speech on New Year's Day 1946 in which he denied that he had any of the attributes of the Godhead. Infuriating to right-wingers.

NI NI ROKU INCIDENT The most spectacular of the coups of the 1930's, during which rebel soldiers and officers occupied the center of Tokyo for a week from February 26, 1936. Personally crushed by the Emperor. The second of Hirohito's offenses, in the eyes of right-wing nationalists.

NIPPON ROMAN-HA The Japanese romanticists, a small group of wartime intellectuals who believed in the "holy war" and whose central philosophical notion was "irony," an idea never well defined by Yojuro Yasuda, the leader of the group. Influential on the young Mishima.

NO The noblest of the Japanese theatrical forms, reserved for the Imperial Court in feudal times.

OBASAMA An archaic form of address—like "Okasama," the use of which by Mishima amused his contemporaries greatly.

OKURASHO The Ministry of Finance, the center of power in the Japanese bureaucracy.

OMIAI The formal meeting between a young couple not previously acquainted, which is the preliminary to an arranged marriage. Still common in Japan.

OMIKOSHI A portable Shinto shrine.

ONNAGATA In Kabuki drama, the male actors who take the female roles.

RONIN A masterless samurai; one who has lost his lord.

SAKÉ Rice wine.

SAMBON SUGI Marks on the blade of a sword of the type of Mishima's seventeenth-century samurai sword, made by Seki no Magoroku. They are small, and hard to see—a series of smoky, dark semicircles which interlock in a line parallel to the cutting edge of the sword. A connoisseur looks for them in such a sword.

SAMURAI A privileged warrior class who constituted about five percent of the population of feudal Japan. The expression has little application in modern Japan, outside such contexts as "samurai spirit."

SENSEI An honorific expression, used by Tatenokai members when speaking to or of Mishima. Very common in Japan: used by schoolchildren when speaking to their teachers, etc. "Respect" language is crucial in Japan.

SEPPUKU The Japanese term for hara-kiri, which has an element of awe of the ritual.

SHINJU A double suicide for love, popularized in the seventeenth century by the Kabuki theater. Homosexual shinju have been rare in history; Takamori Saigo, a nineteenth-century general and hero, attempted it, and succeeded only in drowning his lover.

SHINPUREN INCIDENT The incident of 1877 on which Mishima

modeled his own "Putsch": an attack by samurai on a modern barracks with swords; repelled with great loss of life. A mass suicide, with a pathological element.

SHUZAI Collecting information and making notes, a "journalistic" practice used by Mishima when preparing to write a novel; he went to the spot, notebook in hand.

SONNO JOI Resonant chauvinist slogan: "Revere the Emperor and Expel the Barbarians"—liked by Mishima in certain moods.

SUMI Black Chinese ink.

SUMO Wrestling by fat men plumped up on barrels of beer and mountains of rice.

TORII Entrance to a Shinto shrine. Shaped like the Greek letter π.

UYOKU The violent, extreme right in Japan. Minute in size and effective out of all proportion to its size; composed of hundreds of mutually hostile groups, clubs, study societies, some of which have comic names; e.g., the Japan Goblin Party. Linked to the ruling conservative party, and crucial to an understanding of Japan.

YAKUZA Gangsters; comparable to the Mafia. The yakuza control all entertainment centers in Japan.

YOMEIGAKU A neo-Confucian school of thought which came to Japan in the seventeenth century from China, where it played a radical part in the reaction against traditional Confucianism. Still more potent in Japan, in certain ways. Mishima's interest in this philosophy, the best-known tenet of which is: "To know and not to act is not yet to know," was probably dilettante; nonetheless, he acted on its principle.

YOROIDOSHI A straight dagger with a blade one foot long.

ZAIBATSU The vast industrial-commercial combines which dominated Japan before the war and do so once again, to the peril of the Japanese.

ZENGAKUREN All Japan Federation of Student Councils. The ultra-left members of the Zengakuren movement caused the student riots of 1967–9, the most violent disturbances in postwar Japan, in which fifteen thousand policemen and an unknown number of students were injured.

ZENKYOTO Student council (at a particular university). Mishima had an open debate in May 1969 with the Zenkyoto of Tokyo University.

Chronology

1925
January 14. Birth of Kimitake Hiraoka (Yukio Mishima), eldest son of Azusa and Shizue Hiraoka, in Tokyo. The boy is named by his grandfather Jotaro, at a ceremony one week later, after a friend of the latter, Baron Kimitake Furuichi. Taken from his mother by his tyrannical grandmother, Natsuko, on his twenty-ninth day. Brought up by his grandmother.

1928
Birth of Mitsuko, Mishima's sister.

1929
Mishima taken severely ill and his life despaired of. The illness is jikachudoku (auto-intoxication), and the boy is enfeebled by this recurrent sickness. He does not recover his health until adulthood.

1930
Birth of Chiyuki, Mishima's younger brother.

1931
Mishima starts at the Gakushuin (Peers School), where he is far from outstanding. The school is the choice of his grandfather Jotaro.

1937
Enters the middle school at the Gakushuin, at which he is successful academically. Leaves his grandparents, with whom he has been living, and is now under the care of his mother, Shizue. For two years he has been living with his grandparents in a different house from his parents'; a move enables his parents to claim

the boy from his jealous grandmother, who is ill and near the end of her life.

1938
Comes to the attention of older boys in the Gakushuin, especially members of the Bungei-bu, the literary club. Despite the differences in age, he is accepted by boys older than he as a companion and friend—on account of his literary gifts. He is a regular contributor to the school magazine, *Hojinkai Zasshi*, from the time of his arrival in the middle school.

1939   •
Prospers in his academic work and embarks on an ambitious novel, "Yakata" ("Mansion"), in which his idea of the "murder theater" is first developed. He does not finish "Yakata"; it is almost the only unfinished work of his life. Death of Natsuko on January 19.

1940
Introduced to Ryuko Kawaji, a well-known romantic poet, by his mother, and writes poems under his guidance. One of these, "Magagoto" ("Evil Things"), contains a hint of the character of all his writing. His favorite authors are Raymond Radiguet and Oscar Wilde.

1941
Shortly before the outbreak of World War II, completes his first long work, *Hanazakari no Mori* ("The Forest in Full Bloom"), which is published by the magazine *Bungei Bunka* through the introduction of a teacher at the Gakushuin, Fumio Shimizu, who takes a special interest in Mishima's work. Takes the nom de plume Yukio Mishima. His writing is highly praised by Zenmei Hasuda, a schoolteacher friend of Shimizu, who becomes an influence on Mishima.

1942
Enters the senior school at the Gakushuin, where he has a brilliant career. He publishes patriotic poems in the school magazine, and his taste for the Japanese classics develops. Under the influence of Hasuda and Shimizu, he takes an interest in the Nippon Roman-ha (Japanese Romanticists), a literary movement led by Yojuro Yasuda, an advocate of the "holy war."

1943
Excels at his books and tries in vain to have *Hanazakari no Mori* published in book form. Meets Yojuro Yasuda; his enthusiasm for

the Nippon Roman-ha is tempered by appreciation of the austere Japanese literary tradition of Ogai Mori.

1944
Graduates from the Gakushuin at the top of his class and receives an award, a silver watch, from the Emperor; the ceremony is held at the palace, to which he is accompanied by the school principal. In May he passes an army medical, but he is not drafted and starts his studies at Tokyo Imperial University in October. In the same month *Hanazakari no Mori* is published in Tokyo.

1945
Is working at an airplane factory when his draft call comes in February. He takes leave of his parents in Tokyo, who share his belief that they will not see him again and that he will die in the war. He fails his medical—an inexperienced army doctor makes a false diagnosis of incipient tuberculosis (assisted in the error by the sharp-witted Mishima, who gives misleading replies to the doctor's questions). Mishima returns to Tokyo. The war ends in August. Mitsuko dies of typhoid in October.

1946
Is reading law at Tokyo University; attempts to have his short stories published—the first step for an aspiring novelist in Japan. With the help of Yasunari Kawabata, he succeeds in getting a story published ("Tabako"); is disappointed by its reception and buckles down to his law studies.

1947
Obtains a position at the Okurasho (Ministry of Finance) in a competitive public examination, and enters the ministry at the end of the year, resolved to continue work on short stories and a novel, *Tozoku* ("Robbers").

1948
Succeeds in placing his work with literary magazines in Tokyo. In September he resigns from the Okurasho, believing that he will be able to support himself by writing. In November he starts *Confessions of a Mask,* an autobiographical novel in which he describes the homosexual and sadomasochistic fantasies of a youth of his generation.

1949
Confessions of a Mask is published in July and Yukio Mishima is hailed as a rising star in the literary firmament. A first play, *Kataku* ("Fire House"), is performed by a leading theatrical group.

1950
Mishima has a second major novel, *Thirst for Love*, published.
It is highly praised by the critics. He moves to a new home in
Midorigaoka, a fashionable suburb of Tokyo, with his parents.
Writes his first modern No play, *Kantan*.

1951
Completes *Forbidden Colors*, a controversial novel about homosexual society in Tokyo. In December goes on his first world trip,
setting out for America on board the *President Wilson*. Has had to
overcome many obstacles to obtain foreign exchange for his
travels and is acting as special foreign correspondent for *Asahi
Shimbun*, the leading daily newspaper. His father has helped him
to obtain the sponsorship of the *Asahi*.

1952
Travels to America, where he discusses translation of *Confessions
of a Mask* with his first translator, Meredith Weatherby. He visits
Brazil and Europe; the high point of the journey is Greece, which
feeds his "classical aspiration." Returns to Japan in good spirits.

1953
Completes a sequel to *Forbidden Colors*, which is less well
viewed by the critics, and resolves to write "classical" works.

1954
Publishes the best seller *The Sound of Waves*. Also writes a play,
Shiro Ari no Su ("The Nest of the White Ants"), which establishes
his reputation as a playwright. The rights to *The Sound of Waves*
are sold to Toho, the leading film production company in Japan.

1955
Takes up body building and persists with his training despite
much physical difficulty. His body-building activities attract public attention, which he welcomes. Pictures of him wielding
weights are published.

1956
Writes two of the greatest successes of his career: *The Temple of
the Golden Pavilion*, a novel; and *Rokumeikan*, a play. Establishes
a connection with the Bungakuza, the leading theatrical company
in Japan. *The Sound of Waves* and *Five Modern No Plays* are
published in America by Alfred A. Knopf; Mishima cultivates
good relations with his translators.

1957

Invited to America by Alfred A. Knopf and makes an address at Michigan University. Stays six months in America and spends an unhappy autumn in New York, where he waits in vain for performance of his No plays. He learns to speak English and sees every play running in New York, where he keeps up body building.

1958

Decides to get married, having been told that his mother has cancer (a false diagnosis). Has an omiai (a formal meeting between two people who are contemplating an arranged marriage) with Michiko Shoda, a tennis-playing beauty; their meetings are ended, probably at the behest of the Shoda family, and she becomes engaged to the Crown Prince. Mishima is married to Yoko Sugiyama, twenty-one, daughter of a well-known traditional Japanese painter. Decides to build a modern house for himself and his bride, at great expense; next door he constructs a home for his parents. *The Temple of the Golden Pavilion* and *Confessions of a Mask* are published in America.

1959

Mishima's "anti-Zen" house is completed in May 1959 and Yoko has their first child, Noriko, a girl, the following month. Mishima is working on an ambitious novel, *Kyoko no Ie* ("Kyoko's House"), which he completes in the autumn, and which is judged a failure by the critics. Takes up kendo, Japanese fencing.

1960

Writes *After the Banquet*, a witty novel of political life in Japan. He acts in his first movie, *Karakkaze Yaro* ("A Dry Fellow"), playing the part of a young yakuza, a gangster, and appearing naked with his co-star. The Anpo (U.S.–Japan Security Treaty) riots take place—a turning point in Mishima's life; the riots excite his imagination and stir him to write a short story, "Patriotism," in which he describes the hara-kiri of a young army officer at remarkable length.

1961

Mishima, who has been traveling overseas with Yoko, visiting New York, returns to Japan to find himself in trouble. A suit for damages has been brought against him on account of *After the Banquet*. Receives threatening phone calls from rightist thugs who threaten to burn down his home and kill him; they object to his praise of a short story, "Furyu-Mutan," which they regard as anti-imperialist. Mishima has a police bodyguard for two months. His son Ichiro is born.

1962
The pattern of Mishima's life in the first half of the 1960's becomes apparent. He concentrates on writing plays and does not tackle a major novel; *Utsukushii Hoshi* ("Beautiful Star") is an SF novel. "Within two or three years," Mishima states, "I must make a plan for life."

1963
Quarrel with the Bungakuza, the theatrical company with which Mishima has been associated for a decade. Mishima leaves the Bungakuza and charges the members with hypocrisy. Poses for the photo album *Torture by Roses*.

1964
The year of the Tokyo Olympics. Mishima reports on the events with gusto and writes about his kendo (fencing) experiences. He still has not found his "plan for life."

1965
Death of the older novelist Junichiro Tanizaki. Mishima mentioned as a candidate for the Nobel Prize in news-agency dispatches from Stockholm. Has embarked on the first volume of his tetralogy *The Sea of Fertility* and has begun an autobiographical essay *Sun and Steel*.

1966
Makes his only speech to the foreign press in Japan. He completes *Spring Snow* and starts *Runaway Horses*, the second volume of *The Sea of Fertility*. He approaches the Jieitai, the Self-Defense Forces, for permission to train at army bases. Mishima poses for the photo of himself as St. Sebastian.

1967
Trains at Jieitai bases. Has a meeting with students from Waseda University with a view to attracting them to join what is to be his private army, the Tatenokai. He fails; inaugurates the private army at a blood-oath ceremony in Tokyo. Pays a visit to India with Yoko, at the invitation of the government; travels to Benares, Ajanta, and Calcutta.

1968
Completes *Runaway Horses* and embarks on the third and most difficult volume of the tetralogy, *The Temple of Dawn*. He an-

nounces the formation of the Tatenokai. In October the Nobel Prize for Literature is awarded to Yasunari Kawabata; Mishima has been considered a strong contender for the prize, but his age is against him.

1969

Is in some doubt about the Tatenokai. He cannot find a role for his private army. Ignored in Japan. Following publication of *Eirei no Koe* ("The Voices of the Heroic Dead") in 1966, he has acquired a reputation for right-wing views and has lost popularity in the Bundan, the literary establishment. The creation of the Tatenokai is regarded as a foolish gesture by his friends and ignored by others. The Tatenokai members dispute among themselves.

1970

Early in the year Mishima resolves to die when he completes *The Sea of Fertility*. He is not sure by what method he shall die; he decides to use the Tatenokai as a vehicle for his death. After completing *The Temple of Dawn*, the third book in his tetralogy, he secretly organizes a small group within the Tatenokai and discusses with them the possibility of staging a coup d'état. The youths are naïve and do not understand Mishima's character. Masakatsu Morita, the student leader of the Tatenokai under Mishima, encourages Mishima to take action; his support strengthens Mishima's resolve. About June, Mishima decides to commit harakiri and fixes the basic plan for the suicide. Two months later he completes the last scene of *The Sea of Fertility*, which he holds for the publishers. On November 25, hands over the last installment of the book and commits suicide with Morita.

Acknowledgments
and Sources

Many people assisted me in the preparation of this work and I would like to mention the special aid and comfort given to me by Gilbert de Botton of Zurich. He encouraged me to start the book, advised me on the manuscript at all stages, found me a publisher, and also put me up when I had the misfortune to be thrown out of my Zurich apartment.

A number of eminent scholars helped me with the book. There is very little literature on Mishima in existence in the English language; and I was dependent on the leading scholars in the field when I began to do research. Professor Ivan Morris encouraged me to direct my studies toward Mishima's aesthetic, and by doing so saved me what might have been a long detour into his "politics." Professor Donald Keene advised me at various stages of this work and, like Ivan Morris, read a first draft in 1971; he was helpful on the subject of the authenticity of *Confessions of a Mask*, enabling me to determine which parts of that seminal work I might rely upon as autobiography and what segments I must ignore. I have also received invaluable assistance from the Japanese police and from the Jieitai. The former saved me much time by killing some of the wild rumors which circulated in Tokyo after Mishima's suicide; and the latter gave me access to the room in which that suicide took place.

In Japan the person who helped me most was Nobutoshi Hagiwara, the eminent historian and journalist; he has been a critic of this work, a first draft of which he read. I would also like to thank Junro Fukashiro of the *Asahi Shimbun,* who encouraged me to carry on with the book over a period of three years. I would also thank my staff in Tokyo, especially Michiko Shimizu, who carried out research for me; Kanji Takamasu joined me at a late hour in the research effort and translated difficult passages from Mishima's works, and also criticized the seven drafts through which the book passed; Michiko Murasugi studied Mishima's theater career on my behalf. Finally, I would like to thank Mrs. Yoko Mishima, who took an objective view of my project from the beginning and offered me advice on the dangers which faced one who chose to write about a Japanese novelist without being a master of the language.

In addition, I would like to thank my friends among the foreign correspondents in Tokyo, especially Bernard Krisher of *Newsweek*, who originally intended to do the book with me, and also Samuel Jameson of the *Los Angeles Times*, who telephoned me when he heard the news on the radio on November 25, 1970. One other person has followed this project from the beginning: Takao Tokuoka of the *Sunday Mainichi*, also a friend of Mishima's and probably the man who knows most about this work, bar myself.

My editor at Farrar, Straus and Giroux, Bill Weatherby, helped me a great deal in the final stages of the preparation of the manuscript. I would also like to thank Mr. Robert Giroux, who obtained permission from Mishima's publishers for me to quote from some of his works, and I am grateful for their generosity in this matter to Alfred A. Knopf, New Directions, and Kodansha International. I am particularly appreciative of Knopf's kindness in providing uncorrected proofs of the translation by Edward Seidensticker of *The Decay of the Angel*, so that I could quote certain key passages. Many other people assisted me with this book: especially Akiko Sugiyama, Paolo Carosone, and Jason Roussos. I would like to thank also *The* (London) *Times*, for permission to quote an article; Georges Borchardt, my agent in New York, and his assistant, Becky Kapell; the Swire Group and Phillips & Drew, for finance; and my father and two of my sisters, Susan and Charity, for guidance.

In addition, I would like to point out a source problem. The first chapter of this book contains plentiful dialogue. No one knows, however, exactly what the participants in the drama at Ichigaya on November 25, 1970, said to one another; to some extent, I had the choice of excluding dialogue from my account or inventing it. So far as was possible, I based my dialogue on a reading of official documents, especially papers furnished by the police (to the prosecution at the trial of the three Tatenokai youths who survived the day), notably the so-called *Boto Chinjutsu*. I also took note of the evidence given at the trial by the participants in the drama: General Kanetoshi Mashita; the three Tatenokai students; and senior Jieitai officers. In addition, I interviewed police and Jieitai personnel with access to confidential records of the affair. A second source problem may be mentioned: in writing up my diaries and notes for the prologue I was dependent, to some extent, on my trained memory; though I took extensive notes on my meetings with Yukio Mishima, there were gaps at some points. I made a very full record of my visit to Camp Fuji to participate in the abortive all-night exercise to which Yukio Mishima summoned me in March 1969. I utilized this in the preparation of my long account of that exercise. My principal sources for this book have been, however, the works of Yukio Mishima. On the whole I avoided conducting interviews. There is enough published material to occupy a rapid reader of Japanese for at least several years, and to provide for a host of books on Mishima (thirty-three have been published in Japanese already).

Finally, I would like to thank certain Japanese publishers for permission to quote from untranslated works by Mishima: Shinchosha Publishing Company, for *Niniroku Jiken to Watakushi* and "Isu"; Kodansha Publishing Company, for *Watakushi no Henreki Jidai;* the Tobu Department Store, for extracts from its catalogue to the Mishima Exhibition. For other works, I would like to thank the following: *Shokun* and *Bungei* magazines, for recollections of Mishima; *Asahi Shimbun,* for extracts from articles, interviews, and letters; *Mainichi Shimbun,* for extracts from articles and interviews; and *Pacific Community* for extracts from Edward Seidensticker's article on Mishima from their April 1971 issue. In certain cases, I have slightly *condensed* material from hitherto untranslated sources, without so indicating in the text.

Bibliography

This list of Yukio Mishima's books was prepared with the help of Donald Keene. A few of the titles could not be translated satisfactorily, and so I have left them untranslated. The bibliography includes the *Collected Works* being published by Shinchosha in thirty-six volumes and excludes all other collected-works editions. Mishima wrote many of his books for commercial reasons; he condered these to be worthless as literature and I do not discuss them in my book, although they appear in the bibliography.

1944	Hanazakari no Mori	*The Forest in Full Bloom*
1947	Misaki nite no Mongatari	*A Story at the Cape*
1948	Tozoku	*Robbers*
	Yoru no Shitaku	*Preparations for Night*
1949	Hoseki Baibai	*Traffic in Precious Stones*
	Kamen no Kokuhaku	*Confessions of a Mask* *
	Magun no Tsuka	*The Passage of Demons*
1950	Todai	*The Lighthouse*
	Kaibutsu	*Monster*
	Ai no Kawaki	*Thirst for Love* *
	Junpaku no Yoru	*The Pure White Night*
	Ao no Jidai	*The Blue Period*
1951	Seijo	*The Holy Virgin*
	Kari to Emono	*The Hunter and His Prey*
	Tonorie	*Riding Club*
	Kashiramoji	*Initials*
	Kinjiki (vol. 1)	*Forbidden Colors* *
	Natsuko no Boken	*Natsuko's Adventure*
1952	Aporo no Sakazuki	*The Cup of Apollo*
1953	Manatsu no Shi	*Death in Midsummer* *

* Published in English translation.

	Nipponsei	*Made in Japan*
	Yoru no Himawari	*Twilight Sunflower*
	Higyo (Kinjiki, vol. 2)	*Secret Medicine* *
	Aya no Tsuzumi	*The Damask Drum* *
1954	Migoto na Onna. Todai. Uma	*Wonderful Woman. The Lighthouse. Horse*
	Shiosai	*The Sound of Waves* *
	Koi no Miyako	*The Capital of Love*
	Kagi no Kakaru Heya	*The Room with a Locked Door*
	Wakodo yo Yomigaere	*Young Men Come Back to Life*
	Bungakuteki Jinseiron	*Literary Discussion of Life*
1955	Shizumeru Taki	*The Sunken Waterfall*
	Megami	*Goddess*
	Radige no Shi	*The Death of Radiguet*
	Shosetsuka no Kyuka	*A Novelist's Holiday*
1956	Shiroari no Su	*The Nest of the White Ants*
	Kofukugo Shuppan	*Departure of the SS Happiness*
	Kindai Nogakushu	*Five Modern No Plays* *
	Shi o Kaku Shonen	*The Boy Who Writes Poetry*
	Kame wa Usagi ni Oitsukuka	*Will the Tortoise Catch up to the Hare?*
	Kinkakuji	*The Temple of the Golden Pavilion* *
	Nagasugita Haru	*The Spring That Was Too Long*
1957	Rokumeikan	
	Bitoku no Yoromeki	*The Faltering of Virtue*
	Gendai Shosetsu wa Koten Tariuru ka	*Can a Modern Novel Be a Classic?*
1958	Shishi	*Lion*
	Hashizukushi	*The Seven Bridges* *
	Tabi no Ehon	*Travel Picture Book*
	Bara to Kaizoku	*The Rose and the Pirate*
	Nichiyobi	*Sunday*
1959	Fudotoku Kyoiku Koza	*Lectures on Immoral Education*

	Bunsho Dokuhon	*A Textbook of Style*
	Kyoko no Ie (vol. 1)	*Kyoko's House (vol. 1)*
	Kyoko no Ie (vol. 2)	*Kyoko's House (vol. 2)*
	Ratai to Isho	*Nakedness and Clothing*
1960	Zoku Fudotoku Kyoiku Koza	*Lectures on Immoral Education (continued)*
	Utage no Ato	*After the Banquet* *
	Ojosan	*The Young Lady*
1961	Star	*Star*
	Kemono no Tawamure	*The Sport of Beasts*
	Bi no Shugeki	*The Assault of Beauty*
1962	Utsukushii Hoshi	*A Beautiful Star*
1963	Ai no Shisso	*Love Runs Wild*
	Hayashi Fusao Ron	*On Fusao Hayashi*
	Gogo no Eiko	*The Sailor Who Fell from Grace with the Sea* *
	Ken	*Sword*
1964	Nikutai no Gakko	*A School for the Flesh*
	Yorokobi no Koto	*The Harp of Joy*
	Watakushi no Henreki Jidai	*My Age of Travels*
	Kinu to Meisatsu	*Silk and Insight*
	Daiichi no Sei—Dansei Kenkyu Koza	*The First Sex—Studies of Males*
1965	Ongaku	*Music*
	Ame no naka no Funsui	*The Fountain and the Rain*
	Me—Aru Geijutsu Danso	*Eye—Fragmentary Reflections on Art*
	Sado Koshaku Fujin	*Madame de Sade* *
1966	Han-Teijo Daigaku	*The Book of Anti-chaste Wisdom*
	Yukoku	*Patriotism* *
	Eirei no Koe	*The Voices of the Heroic Dead*
	Taiwa—Shin Nihonjin Ron	*Dialogue on the Japanese People*
1967	Areno yori	*From the Desolate Fields*
	Geijutsu no Kao	*The Face of Art*
	Hagakure Nyumon	*An Introduction to Hagakure*
	Yakaifuku	*Evening Dress*

	Suzakuke no Metsubo	*The Fall of the House of Suzaku*
1968	Fukuzatsu na Kare	*A Complicated Guy*
	Taidan—Ningen to Bungaku	*Dialogue on Man and Literature*
	Mishima Yukio Reta Kyoshitsu	*Yukio Mishima's Classroom in Letter Writing*
	Taiyo to Tetsu	*Sun and Steel* *
	Wagatomo Hittora	*My Friend Hitler*
	Inochi Urimasu	*I Will Sell You My Life*
	Haru no Yuki	*Spring Snow* *
1969	Honba	*Runaway Horses* *
	Bunka Boeiron	*On the Defense of Culture*
	Kurotokage	*Black Lizard*
	Mishima Yukio vs Todai Zenkyoto	*Yukio Mishima vs. Tokyo University Student Struggle Association*
	Raio no Terasu	*The Terrace of the Leper King*
	Wakaki Samurai no tame ni	*For Young Samurai*
	Chinsetsu Yumiharizuki	
1970	Akatsuki no Tera	*The Temple of Dawn* *
	Shobu no Kokoro	*The Heart of Martial Spirits*
	Kodogaku Nyumon	*On Action*
	Gensen no Kanjo	
	Sakkaron	*Essays on Authors*
	Tennin Gosui	*The Decay of the Angel* *
	Ranryoo	
1973–5	Mishima Yukio Zenshu	*Collected Works* (36 *vol.*)

Mishima's Plan for Death

Mishima's Bunburyodo, or dual way of Art and Action, required that he progress along the road to death while committing himself simultaneously to literature and to soldierly action, as one may see from a summary of the activities of the last five years of his life.

	LITERATURE	ACTION
Autumn 1966	Completed *Spring Snow*	Applied to train in the Jieitai
Summer 1968	Finished *Runaway Horses*	Founded the Tatenokai
Spring 1970	*The Temple of Dawn* completed	Formed an action group within the Tatenokai to stage a coup d'état
November 25, 1970	Handed over the last installment of *The Decay of the Angel*, thus completing *The Sea of Fertility*	Committed hara-kiri with Masakatsu Morita

Index

339